ORDER AND CHANCE

The Pattern of Diderot's Thought

ORDER AND CHANCE

The Pattern of Diderot's Thought

GEOFFREY BREMNER

UNIVERSITY COLLEGE OF WALES
ABERYSTWYTH

CAMBRIDGE UNIVERSITY PRESS
CAMBRIDGE
LONDON   NEW YORK   NEW ROCHELLE
MELBOURNE   SYDNEY

Published by the Press Syndicate of the University of Cambridge
The Pitt Building, Trumpington Street, Cambridge CB2 1RP
32 East 57th Street, New York, NY 10022, USA
296 Beaconsfield Parade, Middle Park, Melbourne 3206, Australia

First published 1983

Printed in Great Britain by
Redwood Burn Limited
Trowbridge, Wiltshire

Library of Congress catalogue card number: 82–23597

British Library Cataloguing in Publication Data
Bremner, Geoffrey
Order and chance
1. Diderot, Denis – Criticism and interpretation
I. Title
843'.5   PQ1979.A76

ISBN 0 521 25008 0

RB

CONTENTS

Contents

FOREWORD

This study began as a Ph.D. thesis at the University of Reading, and my first debt of thanks is to Dr Christopher Thacker, who by his careful supervision and tactful advice saved me from many aberrations and errors of judgment, and by his wide knowledge of less conventional aspects of eighteenth-century culture led me to some interesting insights and generally enriched my understanding of the period. I am also grateful to Professor Colin Smith for his wise and perceptive comments on the thought of the period. As for my debt to previous writers on Diderot and the eighteenth century, the bibliography must stand as a supplement to this foreword. All the works listed have helped me in some way, and I am uneasily aware that, with more perception and concentration on my part, many of them could have helped me more.

I should also like to acknowledge the help given by the Gregynog Fund of University College, Aberystwyth, towards the cost of preparing this book for publication.

My greatest expression of gratitude – and this is not to devalue anything I have said in the first paragraph – must go to Dr Will Moore of St John's College, Oxford. To his memory this book is dedicated. First as my tutor, then as someone who took a continuing and sympathetic interest in my activities, he seemed almost incapable of making a comment or judgment which did not provide a stimulus for further thought and a guide towards new understanding. His whole approach to the history of literature and ideas has shaped mine. I hope there is not too much in these pages that he would have wished to disown.

THE TRANSLATIONS

For the English versions of passages from *Le Neveu de Rameau* and *Le Rêve de d'Alembert* I have used the translation by Leonard Tancock.* It is no criticism of Tancock's work to say that this has occasionally presented difficulties. A translator aims, among other things, at elegance and naturalness, and this often affects his decisions about the rendering of a phrase which presents problems. In some cases I have found that my comments on certain problematical passages have demanded a more literal translation; this I have made, often at the expense of the easy flow of Tancock's prose. Certain key words have also presented difficulties, including the all-important 'sensibilité', and this I have sometimes felt obliged to translate 'sensibility', at other times 'sensitivity'. The only other translation I have used is Peter France's selection of the letters to Sophie Volland.† In all other cases the translation is my own.

* Diderot, *Rameau's Nephew, D'Alembert's Dream*, translated with introductions by Leonard Tancock. Penguin, 1966.
† *Diderot's Letters to Sophie Volland*, translated by Peter France, Oxford University Press, 1972.

INTRODUCTION

This study is based on the conviction that beyond any particular categories such as politics, aesthetics or ethics, there is a pattern in Diderot's thought. The pattern is defined by the shape in which reality presented itself to him and the characteristic nature of his response. It is partly peculiar to Diderot himself and partly conditioned by the thought-structures of his time, partly the product of his conscious thinking, partly moulded by the unquestioned assumptions of the period in which he lived. My starting point, order, needs some justification, since it has already been much discussed, notably by Lester G. Crocker in *Diderot's Chaotic Order*.

Order is not simply one amongst the multitudinous aspects of Diderot's thought which offer promising fields for study; it is a fundamental concern of the whole period. The preoccupation with order was directly associated with the growing conviction that any guarantee of order and purpose which might be found in the universe was no longer to be discerned in the will of God but in the workings of the universe itself. To seek order was to look for meaning in life. Caught between a teaching based on spiritual values which seemed to deny the true nature of life and a reality governed by contingency which seemed to deprive it of value and dignity, men sought a point of equilibrium which would preserve the human mind both from the tyranny of theology and from the servitude of chance.

The problem of order in this particular sense is not one which concerns man at any stage in his history: this order is not simply an ideal to be contrasted with the imperfection which characterizes our everyday lives. The specific problem which troubled the minds of the *Ancien Régime* was the conflict between an order which, it was felt, should have an objective existence, a permanent validity, and a reality which seemed to have no status, no validity. Yet at the same time there existed a conviction that this reality was despite everything more real, more relevant to the human condition than the ideal

1

to which it was inferior. A deep-rooted attitude such as this is rich in tensions and contradictions, and they are responsible for many of our problems in interpreting the literature and thought of the time, as well as for much of its greatness. Diderot's works are probably one of the best hunting-grounds, for the problems and the greatness, and this is why he needs to be studied in this context.

In his article 'Diderot et le problème de l'expressivité' (p. 296), Roland Mortier observes, 'Diderot has too often been explained in terms of the historical situation or a literary and philosophical context: it would be better to explain him in terms of himself.'[1] It is my contention in this study that we cannot explain Diderot 'in terms of himself'[2] without reference to a context which is both historical, literary and philosophical, because this is the context which made Diderot what he was. What I am suggesting here – and 'suggesting' is not a euphemism for 'stating', since in at least some areas my approach is exploratory and my conclusions tentative – is that Diderot's patterns of thinking, and hence his concept of order, are rooted in a conceptual structure which is much less modern than is usually accepted. I believe that he, with the rest of his age, was unable to escape from a dualist way of thinking of which, in one sense, he was unaware; unaware not because he failed to think the matter through, but because it would not – could not, given the epistemological limits of eighteenth-century thought – have occurred to him to see the world in any other way.

This will not be an attempt at a synthetic view of Diderot's work, despite the fairly wide range of works discussed, but an examination of certain important attitudes and assumptions which form an essential basis for a total understanding of the man as a whole. The fact that many aspects of his thought are neglected does not therefore mean that they are being denied or discounted. Because it will be suggested that Diderot's concept of order is static, I do not for a moment wish to deny that much of his thinking is dynamic. Because I think that this concept of order is present, virtually unchanged, throughout his life, I am not by any means implying that his conscious ideas did not change during the course of it. Because the order I am trying to define appears idealist in nature, I am not saying that Diderot did not evolve a consciously materialist philosophy.

In more specific terms, this study will not be concerned with the development of Diderot's thought, and very little with the chronology of his works, because the particular pattern of thought I am discussing remains more or less unchanged. It will make very little mention of some of Diderot's important works like the *Supplément au voyage de Bougainville, La Religieuse* and his contributions to Raynal's *Histoire des Deux Indes*, because they do not at this level add anything of significance to what is revealed by his other works, nor do they suggest any difference in the general pattern. It will take little account of the way in which Diderot was influenced by recent or contemporary thinkers, because its aim is to identify a set of attitudes which is deeply rooted in the society of the *Ancien Régime*, not the consciously evolved ideas which Diderot adapted from such thinkers.

Any attempt to assess how far an original thinker is a product of his age and how far his contribution goes beyond it is beset with all kinds of difficulties. We are all to a certain extent imprisoned within certain ways of thinking, certain conceptual structures which define our way of perceiving the world about us and solving the problems it poses. On the other hand some people at times conceive ideas which mark them out from their fellows and which may often be qualified as advanced, forward-looking, even ahead of their time. Traditional criticism has often made it its business to establish exactly what a writer owes to his age and what is personal to him, in an effort to define his originality. This almost quantitative approach, and the underlying assumption that there is some dividing line between the two, seem to me to involve a misunderstanding of the problem.

Let us assume the existence of a civilization which believes that the universe is governed alternately by a strict god, then a lenient god. Each rules for six-month periods, coinciding respectively with a dry season and a rainy season. It is unlikely that in the writings of such a civilization we should find many statements telling us that the world is in fact so governed. Moreover, statements which might seem to be giving this information would probably be ritualistic or celebratory in intention. On the other hand we should be very likely to find statements which derived from the assumption, itself taken for granted, that a totally different form of behaviour was appropriate in one half of the year from the other. We can imagine that the notion of two contrasting and successive types of behaviour would affect other concepts, particularly that of time. We can also suppose that ideas of behaviour would be governed by the opposing poles of freedom and restraint rather than sin and virtue as we know them. It is quite possible that these attitudes would also inform thinking about the seasons, the availability of certain foods or the type of dress appropriate to each season, all of which would take on an ethical colouring. It might be that water, associated with the lenient,

3

rainy season would automatically be linked with freedom or licence in people's imaginations, while thirst would have connotations of restraint, and perhaps punishment: offenders against the law might therefore be subjected to long periods without water.

But if these basic attitudes and their imaginative associations were universally taken for granted, never called into question, this does not necessarily mean that such homogeneity would operate at every level of thought. For example there might be considerable doubt about the relationship between the rulers of states and the gods: should a ruler imitate the attitude of the reigning god, transmitting his leniency or his strictness, or should he try to compensate, being strict under the lenient god, and vice-versa? should rulers alternate in the same way that gods do? should the implementation of the gods' will be vested solely in the ruler, or in a council of priests? and so on. Perhaps from time to time a great statesman or thinker would emerge to propose brilliant new solutions to problems, but without calling into question the basic truths about the gods and their function.

So far we have a picture of a civilization in which there is a large measure of consensus and also a fair degree of controversy and change, but all rooted in the same fundamental beliefs about the nature of the universe. Let us now suppose that, thanks to the building of larger boats, conceived perhaps as a means of coping with the widespread floods in the rainy season, a few adventurous people navigate further afield and discover other civilizations whose dry and rainy seasons are of unequal length, or which perhaps have other climates altogether. As these discoveries slowly take their effect on people's minds, a variety of theories might be put forward: perhaps the two gods behave differently towards different communities; perhaps each climatically different area has its own gods. More daring thinkers might suggest that the gods behave in a quite arbitrary way, ignoring the human beings with whose fate they were believed to be concerned; and even more outrageous spirits might go so far as to suggest that there were no gods at all, or that if there were, one might just as well ignore their existence.

We would now be in a period when controversy raged not only over traditional matters, but also between tradition and innovation, and the study of such a period, based only on its writings, would be correspondingly more difficult and complex. But the complexity would not end there, for it is very unlikely that even the most inno-vatory thinkers would have shaken off the habits of thought, the deeper assumptions which had governed their civilization for hundreds of years. They might propose different forms of government, religious worship or education, but they would probably continue to think in the old ethical terms of restraint and freedom rather than in categories of good and evil more appropriate to the newly discovered order. Even the atheists would probably be slow to lose the idea that different seasons were somehow associated with the way one is supposed to behave. Certain associations would probably linger on, like that between water and freedom, or thirst and punishment. There would in fact be a lengthy period of transition during which the more advanced thinkers of this civilization tried, without properly realizing it, to apply old patterns of thinking to new ideas which contradicted them. This society in transition, like any society undergoing a fundamental re-evaluation of its beliefs, would not only be the scene of disputes between consciously held ideas representing tradition and innovation, but also of unresolved tensions between unquestioned assumptions about reality and ideas which presuppose a totally different conception of it.

Now the distinction between unconscious assumptions and consciously formulated ideas is a perfectly familiar one in some areas of study. It is fundamental to anthropological studies and, via structuralism, it has now assumed an important role in the study of literature and thought. Moreover it was recognized long ago by A. O. Lovejoy in his study of the Great Chain of Being in Western thought, and perhaps the great value of his work will lie not so much in his tracing of the evolution of this idea as in his recognition of the unconscious contradictions contained within it. But despite all this, literary scholars and historians of ideas have generally been slow to acknowledge the force of unconscious assumptions in the writers and thinkers they have studied.

One problem is that, where modern Western thought is concerned, we are probably not far enough away in time, or space, to identify those areas where the attitudes of the past are truly different from or own. Superficial resemblances between ideas expressed by thinkers of the past and our own can easily lead us to see in them a deceptive modernity. Another point is that we are generally reluctant to admit that thought in its higher forms may contain contradictions, especially contradictions of which the thinker may be partially or totally unaware. This difficulty may itself stem from a very traditional habit of thought, the habit which associates the irrational and contradictory with the passions, and reason and logic with the mind. Certainly we are prepared, just as our predecessors back in the seventeenth century were, to admit that thought may in general be influenced by unconscious, irrational factors, but we still tend to baulk at the idea that the great minds of the past, the finest flowering of European civilization, were not altogether in control of what they thought and wrote. Such an idea is, in short, an offence to reason.

And yet at every stage in the history of modern Western culture it would seem essential to recognize these processes, and eighteenth-century France is as good an example as any. On the most superficial level one can see new political and social ideas trying to impose themselves within the traditional structure of the *Ancien Régime*. On a deeper level a longstanding pattern of thought, providential, dualist, idealist, is being challenged by a whole range of new ideas which, in their more extreme manifestations, present a totally conflicting picture of the universe. It would not seem surprising therefore if our difficulties in discerning coherence and unity in the works of the Enlightenment did not always lie in ourselves, but in the sheer impossibility, for thinkers of this period, of adapting their inherited attitudes to the new ideas they were advancing.

In fact the persistence of traditional patterns of thought has not by any means gone unnoticed in studies of the Enlightenment;† but there is an understandable reluctance to make categorical statements about such matters, especially where literature is concerned. We are heirs to a tradition, widely challenged but still powerful, which says that interpretation, seen as a partly subjective matter, is permissible where works of the imagination are concerned, but that a more objective approach is called for in the study of thought. The study of attitudes, assumptions, mentalities, is felt to lie somewhere in between these two areas: it cannot be regarded as clearcut, like thought, nor as a subject of interpretation, like a work of art. Certainly it is perfectly reasonable to expect that pronouncements about the more elusive attitudes of a period should be supported by some kind of evidence, but really satisfactory evidence can probably only come from an ambitious computerized undertaking, together with a refinement of research techniques. In the meantime we must rely on acquiring as much knowledge as possible with a view to developing a 'feel' for the period.

Further critical uncertainty arises where individual writers are concerned from a reluctance to admit that, because of contradic-

† As, for example, in Carl Becker, *The Heavenly City of the Eighteenth-Century Philosophers;* Henry Vyverberg, *Historical Pessimism in the French Enlightenment*; and Lester Crocker, *An Age of Crisis*. See also the works mentioned in the note on p. 13 below.

tions in a writer's thought, his individual works may be flawed. The quest for unity is widely considered to be a prime duty for students of thought and literature, and in one sense this is only right and proper, since thinkers and writers themselves aspire to unity in their works. On the other hand it might be said that we do writers a considerable disservice by setting up unity as one of our criteria, and then concluding that they – or we – have failed when unity does not seem to be present. We should surely measure the achievement of an author not simply by his ability to solve problems but by his power to recognize them. Coherence is not a virtue in itself: the meanest mind can be coherent if it tackles an area as mean as itself. When we assess great minds some kind of balance must be struck between the complexity of the problems they recognize and the power and breadth of their conceptual and aesthetic response to them. It may even be that greatness in thinkers and artists lies precisely in their power to envisage, on an unexpected level, tensions of which they are only obscurely conscious in the world around them.

As long as the study of literature or thought consisted in picking out the great minds and studying them as examples of greatness, then the inconsistencies just discussed did not obtrude, since they were judged by their differentness, both in the degree to which they stood out above the common attitudes of their time and in the extent to which they differed from other writers. Certainly account could be taken of the age in which they wrote, but only insofar as they succeeded in expressing and resolving its problems. It is when we regard a writer not just as one who expresses himself but also as one who expresses his age and is an expression of it that we become involved with two conflicting sets of criteria. The more we emphasize the hidden influence of the thought-patterns of the age, the more the individual achievement is likely to be submerged. There comes a point in fact where the question why Diderot should have had conflicting ideas on politics or natural history is a problem of the same order as why his ideas should have conflicted with those of Rousseau or Buffon.

A way out of this critical problem is of course to opt firmly for one of the possible approaches, and this tendency is most marked in French scholarship in which we can find at one extreme a rigid adherence to textual examination of specific works and at the other a concentration on the overall thought structures of a period. One method tends to bring literary history into the province of linguistics, the other moves it into the history of ideas. Both methods have yielded new and interesting insights, representing as they do the logical extremes of tendencies which appear to some degree in all modern literary scholarship; for this has increasingly emphasized both the importance of the internal structure of the text and that of the underlying thought-structures of the age, together with the relevance of minor writers in revealing it. To this extent we are all structuralists of a sort. But for all their intellectual rigour the more consciously structuralist approaches still leave us with the fact of Diderot, the fact of the eighteenth century and the existence of a highly complex relationship between the two, and no doubt we shall continue to study Diderot in the context of the eighteenth century. We know that his work is fixed within the pattern of his age, but we also know that he makes more inspiring reading than Batteux on aesthetics, Mercier de la Rivière on economics or Adanson on natural history, not to speak of his colossal achievement in other fields. It seems then that in the case of any writer who stands out from among his contemporaries, and who to that extent is untypical, one must, if one is to remain within the confines of literary history, steer a middle course, attempting to define his originality without losing sight of what he owes to his age.

By Diderot's age we traditionally understand the eighteenth century, or rather, in the case of France, that part of the century which history, Procrustes-like, has truncated at one end by allowing Louis XIV to live until 1715 and at the other by sending the Revolution in 1789. My contention in this study is not that we should give the eighteenth century back its twenty-six years, but that to talk of Diderot's age in any meaningful sense is to talk of a period running at least from the middle of the seventeenth century to the end of the eighteenth. When we are talking about patterns of thinking, underlying attitudes, the boundaries between centuries become obstacles, and where the subject of this study, order, is concerned, many of Diderot's basic attitudes had taken shape at the time of the Fronde.

Because literature is a few works which survive, because these survivals are the works which have tended to characterize a period for us, the seventeenth century has a very different look about it from the eighteenth. The peaks which dominate the seventeenth-century skyline are largely poetic, rhetorical and dramatic works, all, with some notable exceptions, couched in traditional forms, while the eighteenth century is overshadowed by prose works, many of them outside the traditional hierarchy of literary genres; and so we get the impression that the first period is one of formality, of aesthetic values, while the second is more experimental, more concerned with moral issues. It would be stupid to deny that there is truth in this impression, and equally so to suggest that this is the only factor which has led to our making a distinction between the two periods, but it is also true that these surviving monuments do help to conceal a similarity and a very real continuity between the two centuries. Another factor which tends to put our views out of perspective is the attitude of the eighteenth century itself, which so often condemned the seventeenth for views which seemed opposed to its own, whereas seen from a distance, the oppositions turn out to be superficial. A notable example is the widespread eighteenth-century criticism of Descartes.

Certainly it can be said that at any period, in any society, there is a pattern of thinking which transcends particular areas of thought, and which can be discerned in its social and political attitudes, its aesthetics, its philosophy and its sciences, to take the fields with which Diderot was most concerned. It is not a question of one area of thought influencing another, in the sense that one, say philosophy, occupies a special position in the hierarchy; philosophy is just as much an expression, a product of the temper of the age, as any other kind of thought. To allot a privileged function to one realm of experience, to cast it in the role of cause, seems at least premature in the present stage of research, and perhaps totally mistaken, in view of the complexity of human society and the constant interaction of all its facets. One of the most productive attempts in modern scholarship to locate a cause for developments in general attitudes has been that made by scholars of marxist or related convictions, who find it in economic forces, the class struggle, the changing function of money. Certainly such factors seem more concrete, exerting as they do a vital influence on the lives of all those whose attitudes they are claimed to form. Furthermore we have here something which actually happened: people's lives were physically altered by these developments. But here again, while it is certainly true to say that economic factors exert a powerful, tangible influence, this does not necessarily imply a difference in kind. After all, thoughts and beliefs are also phenomena, they also happen; they are merely more difficult to circumscribe, to define by scientific method.

The purpose of this study of order and chance will be to examine one feature which appears to characterize the main areas of Diderot's thought without suggesting that any one aspect of it is more influential, more decisive than another; to try to identify some of the ways in which this aspect of his thought was shaped by the assumptions and attitudes of his time, and to assess how far even the

more extreme expressions of his thought are a product and development of tensions already present in the thought-structures which he
inherited. It will therefore be less concerned with ways in which he
was influenced by other eighteenth-century thinkers than with
general assumptions which in varying degrees shaped the thinking
of all of them; less concerned with the circumstances of his social
position or the events of his life than with concepts which, I think,
transcended such considerations. To take an example, much has
been made of Diderot's class origins and the extent to which he
identified himself with his particular section of the bourgeoisie, and
a valuable study could no doubt be made of the development of
bourgeois class-consciousness leading up to Diderot's own position,
but it seems more important here to examine a concept such as order
in a more general, though not necessarily more abstract way. For the
bourgeois preoccupation with order on a social and political level is
only an aspect of a more universal concern with order at every level
of thought. As such, it is a concept which was gradually shifting
from its traditional centre in God towards its new centre in man, a
path which, during the eighteenth-century period of its transition,
took it through a certain concept of nature.

It might seem from some of the remarks I have so far made that a
study such as this would result in identifying the common ground
between Diderot and his contemporaries, and that this purpose
would be better served by a general survey of common assumptions
during the period. This is not the intention. My purpose is to
identify the originality of Diderot's achievement in a certain area,
and my claim is that this cannot be done without recognizing how
inextricably that achievement is bound up with the heritage
imposed on him by his age. From this approach I hope there will
emerge a picture of a body of thought and an imagination which are
perhaps less modern than some have claimed but which constitute a
brilliantly perceptive response to the challenge of his time.

ORDER AND THE ANCIEN RÉGIME

To twentieth-century eyes the *Ancien Régime* can still seem an attractive age in which to have lived. Its music, its art and much of its literature have a quality of elegance, calm, security and even serenity, features we regard as notably absent from our own world. We now know, and modern scholarship constantly reminds us, that this appearance is deceptive. Diderot and his contemporaries, and their predecessors in the seventeenth century, would have been amazed to hear their age described as one of calm and serenity and would probably have seen much to envy in our own from that point of view. Asked to describe their own world they would readily have used words like insecurity, instability, corruption and degeneration; but at the same time they would have pointed with pride, especially in the eighteenth century, to their progress in the arts and sciences. To us this seems paradoxical because we regard our own artistic and scientific achievements as *expressions* of our age in a sense which a citizen of the *Ancien Régime* would have found difficult to understand.

For us, the arts are a direct expression of the confusions, anguish and aspirations of our society, and the sciences are an expression of its needs and its achievements. Both are an integral part of our civilization, and we could say to the future historian, perhaps not with pride, but at least with some degree of conviction: 'This is what we were like.' If the people of the *Ancien Régime* hoped for the approval of posterity for their intellectual achievements, it was not because they saw them as a total expression of themselves, but as monuments to what there was of greatness in them, not as a clue to what it was like in their time, but as a body of achievements which was worthy to survive it. Moreover – and this is the distinctive feature of the period – they did not see their cultural triumphs as surviving the passage of time in the sense that all great art is timeless, but as achievements carried out in opposition to the imperfections of their own age, as triumphs of form over disorder.

11

In the period with which we are dealing the world was acquiring in men's perception the nature it now has, as something too vast and too diverse for the mind to grasp. But their minds had not yet acquired the concepts which enable us to accept that world as something existing in its own right; for them the knowledge which came from scientific discovery represented in some ways a threat to rationality and dignity, an offence to reason. The whole world-order had once lain within the compass of the human mind; it had had form, hierarchy, and a meaning beyond itself. Now this was no longer so: the structure of knowledge could no longer be embraced by the human mind, any more than could the cosmos, or the earth itself. This was not because there was too much knowledge, but because knowledge was no longer contained within a finite system. Neither nature nor human society could any longer be seen as working out a higher purpose; a world which had once been thought to have degenerated from its first perfection through original sin was now seen as simply degenerate. But the habits of mind appropriate to the world imbued with form and meaning survived its disappearance.

In order to believe in an absolute standard of truth one must logically believe in a world complete within itself, whose unity is guaranteed either by the existence of a God involved in all its workings, or by its own rational, self-contained structure. Of the first kind was the traditional world of Christianity; of the second, that assumed by a philosopher such as Leibnitz. The essential difference between the two systems is that one assumes a universe in which the will of God is manifest, while the other assumes a *Deus absconditus*, a God who has withdrawn from the world, so that the task of discovering meaning and purpose is left to man. The second situation increasingly characterizes the thought and attitudes of the *Ancien Régime*, and the responses to it range from attempts to prove that a concerned God does after all exist to the conviction that God is totally absent, if not non-existent, and that the world in which we live is completely unrelated to human needs and aspirations. At one extreme we might place the *Pensées* of Pascal, at the other the world of Voltaire's *Candide*. But underlying all these responses are certain common features, some of which suggest that the search for understanding always took the form of an attempt to re-establish the conditions of the traditional world. This was not simply because such conditions were felt to be desirable, but because it probably did not occur to the thinkers of the time to see things in any other way: again and again we find thinkers denying the existence of absolute truth, denying the separate existence of the 'two substances', thought and extension, but at the same time behaving as though these concepts are still operative.†

One reason for this is that the real world, as revealed by science and as experienced in everyday life, seemed to call into question the validity of traditional assumptions about the meaning and purpose of life. The natural reaction to it was therefore one of resistance: it was not a phenomenon to be accepted but a problem to be overcome; attempts to understand it were a preliminary to controlling it. Like literature and art, the other fields of mental activity, science, philosophy, ethics, and so on, were often conceived as a means of restoring order and purpose to a world which guaranteed neither, of imposing form on what was without form, confining the rebellious substance of the world within the ordered boundaries set by thought.

Thus one of the main preoccupations of the period is the idea of control, in the first place the self-control which the individual needs in order to cope with his own experience, and this is linked with the whole problem of the relationship of the individual to society and the world about him. The necessity for some kind of mental control, for intellectual lucidity, arising out of the awareness of a world which constantly threatens to elude rational judgment and dissolve into the formless realm of the contingent and arbitrary, is usually centred, in the more familiar literature of the seventeenth century, on the ruler, the monarch, and this fact obscures its more general application. We think of Corneille's Auguste, 'master of myself as I am of the universe',[1] or at the other extreme, of Phèdre asking how she can govern her people if she cannot govern herself. But this theme is only the expression in serious theatre of the more general preoccupation with the way the individual perceives and acts upon the world about him.

This is a theme which recurs constantly throughout the period. In the seventeenth century Cardinal de Retz (and other memoir-writers of the Fronde period), La Rochefoucauld, Pascal and lesser moralists like Saint-Réal are all concerned in various ways with the problem of an elusive reality and of the means by which the individual can establish some kind of fixed, or at least stable relationship with it. One of the conditions for such a relationship is

† This phenomenon has been noted in the case of Condillac by Isabel Knight, *The Geometric Spirit*; of d'Holbach by Annie Becq and Michel Delon, *Aspects du discours matérialiste*, pp. 7–72; and of d'Alembert by M. Paty, 'La position de d'Alembert par rapport au matérialisme'.

the ability not to be totally involved in the constant flux of reality, whether it be war, political intrigue or one's day-to-day dealings with one's fellow-men; it is the power to retain mental control, to preserve a detachment both from the affairs of the world about one and from one's own emotional reactions. In his memoirs Retz claims in retrospect that he often achieved this detachment which prevented his emotions from interfering with his political ambitions, and more often than not he is thinking not so much about a straightforward conflict between personal inclinations and public affairs as of the way in which fear or laziness or habit can cloud the judgment. The prime reaction to avoid is 'étonnement', astonishment, a generator of fear and indecision, and a product of too deep an involvement with one's immediate environment.

Pascal, with very different ambitions from the power-seeking cardinal, is also seeking emotional detachment from the instability of the surrounding world, even though this detachment finds a new centre in God rather than the self. But while Pascal sees man's failure to find certainty and stability as inevitable, since he is doomed to occupy an indeterminate point between two infinites, the prevailing pattern of thinking is more optimistic. Implicit in much of its expression is the assumption that the world within which the perception operates, or can be made to operate, is somehow manageable; concealed beneath the spectacle of change is an order, accessible to reason and quantifiable through logical or scientific thought. But this thought can only function effectively in emotional detachment, 'dans le silence des passions'. To be operative, it must be released from the grip of extension.

If one of the main purposes of eighteenth-century philosophy is to reverse the fall of man, to find in nature support for the conviction that man can in fact redress his condition, then this process surely began in the seventeenth. One of the peculiar features of the process was that it was seen then, and to a large extent in the eighteenth century, not as a total reorientation of thought, not as a sudden vision of a universe in which man, from being an integral part of an essentially imperfect creation, now assumed full responsibility for his own destiny, but as a marking out of limited areas where such responsibility was possible, a kind of colonization of areas in which reason could hold sway, and from which those two intractable realms of experience, the things of the spirit on the one hand and the workings of chance on the other, could be excluded. Thus Descartes delimited the area of *res extensa*, the physical world in which the causes of all activity could be reduced to a limited number of rationally accessible concepts. And it is no coincidence that this physical universe should be a *plenum*, where there is no space for the operations of chance, where no element can move without affecting its surroundings. However much Descartes was criticized later in the period, whatever advances Newtonian theory made as a scientific explanation of the physical universe, his fundamental conception of reality survived, as I shall try to show, in much of French thought throughout the eighteenth century, presumably because it corresponded more closely than that of Newton to men's awareness of the world about them.

One notable example in the eighteenth century of the attempt to create finite systems, areas which can be encompassed by the reason, is the enthusiasm for constructing Utopias,† enclosed regions where rational control is threatened neither by change nor by the unstructured accumulation of disparate things, and people, which characterize the real world. Whether we regard Voltaire's Eldorado in *Candide* as a proper Utopia or not, this land whose continuance depends on its isolation from the outside world is a striking case of the tendency to think in terms of finite, spatial schemes. Moreover, it represents one of the dominant themes of the story, for, as many commentators have noted, the 'gardens' at the beginning and end are not there for nothing.

Voltaire seems to be answering the question: 'Under what conditions is one most likely to be able to lead a rational existence, free from interference?' That the answer lies in another enclosed space seems to be a matter of convention, for the real answer is that one must have nothing which arouses the envy of others: the 'garden' is after all a 'métairie', not the personal property of Candide and his companions, and Candide's own relative security is due not to where he is, but to having no wealth, and a wife too ugly and unpleasant to interest anyone else. In the same way, the fool's paradise from which the hero is expelled at the beginning of the story is really an example of how a mistaken belief in absolute standards can arise out of ignorance. These three 'gardens' which define the architecture of *Candide* seem to be a matter of conceptual convenience, of the need to set out an idea in such a way that it can be seen and embraced by the mind's eye.

To return to the seventeenth century, an example in moral

---

† The literature on this subject and the present state of research have been covered by Raymond Trousson in his *Voyages aux pays de Nulle Part* and his 'Rapport de synthèse' of the discussions at the Fifth International Congress on the Enlightenment at Pisa (1979).

thought of a similar approach to that of Descartes can be found in the attempts of the moralists to develop a science of human behaviour. La Rochefoucauld, by delving beneath the 'paraître', the appearance of things, by stripping man so to speak of his secondary qualities, as Descartes had done for matter, reveals him as motivated by one force, that of self-interest. This vision surely has its parallel in drama in the plays of Racine, where the demands of *vraisemblance*, the 'rules', create a circumscribed area in which human beings can be examined in their most basic form, driven into action and reaction by a limited number of passions. Both La Rochefoucauld and Racine seem to present us with a pessimistic view of man, but this is only so in the same way as science is pessimistic, in that it concerns itself essentially with that area of our experience which is governed by cause and effect. As with scientific method in the physical world, this picture of man governed by a limited number of forces is at the same time a means of control. A contemporary of Racine, and a moralist in the style of La Rochefoucauld, Saint-Réal, saw the possibility in his *De l'Usage de l'Histoire* of 1671 of enumerating and classifying man's activity: 'men's actions are made up of nothing more than a certain limited number of circumstances and motives';[2] his aim was to 'accurately define their actions, identify the heading under which they should be classified'.[3] For him, history is the scientific study of man in action: 'Thus, knowing history is knowing about men, who provide its substance; it is judging these men sensibly: studying history is studying the motives, opinions and passions of men in order to see whence they spring, whither they twist and turn, in fact all the ways in which they can deceive our minds, and take our hearts by surprise.'[4]

This desire to see things mapped out before one, to achieve that distance which produces good judgment and avoids 'étonnement', is surely the same in Saint-Réal's history of man as it will be nearly eighty years later in Buffon's history of nature. It is unnecessary to point out that Buffon also attempted to classify the phenomena of the world about him, but it is worth noting that, like the moralists, he regarded this world as potentially hostile and that his purpose was to create a relationship which would neutralize the fear which is our immediate reaction to it. If we are to understand eighteenth-century science and its approach to knowledge in general, it is essential to recognize under what circumstances it developed out of seventeenth-century attitudes.

Because an eighteenth-century thinker inclined towards a study of the facts and was, like Buffon, Diderot and the materialists, antimetaphysical in his approach to knowledge, this did not mean that he understood scientific objectivity in the sense it has acquired in modern times, still less that he tended to adopt a phenomenological or existential attitude, though some thinkers such as Diderot may seem to have been hovering on the brink. The scientific attitude of the eighteenth century grew up in opposition to authority, a concept full of emotive connotations, in general denoting the traditional ways of thought of the established powers, the Church, the Monarchy, the Sorbonne. These bodies were seen as representing a philosophy which had lost touch with real people and real problems: associated with authority are such notions as tyranny, pedantry and rhetoric. This distrust of authority is of course a feature of seventeenth-century attitudes as well as those of the eighteenth, and in the seventeenth century a tradition of opposition to authority (authority, that is, as a concept rather than an institution) arose in the less formalistic works of moralists or memoir-writers, who gave pride of place to the man of action and the man of judgment. Such a man might be a soldier, a statesman, a member of a political faction, a place-seeker at court or an ambitious bourgeois. Ideally he is in touch with reality, assesses the true facts of a situation and acts accordingly, instead of trying to fit the situation to a set of preconceived ideas. In a broader sense judgment was all the more necessary because the period was not only aware of the burden of authority, but also of insecurity, an insecurity brought about by the irrelevance of authority itself, by the practical inability of government to ensure the rule of law or personal safety, and on the level of ideas by the expansion and disorientation of the known universe brought about by the accelerated pace of discovery in science and geography. As the old, stable-seeming world gave way, both on a social and a cosmic level, to the world of movement, the official thinking of Church and state seemed to remain stationary, to be concerned with other things, and the task of adaptation was left to the individual.

This opposition between authority and reality has a long tradition, and so has the conception of man set in a shifting, potentially hostile world. We find it in Montaigne, it is very much in evidence in the memoirs of those who took part in the Fronde, and as the authority of Louis XIV declines towards the end of the seventeenth century, we find that the man of action and the moralist, in their attempt to come to terms with this world, have been joined by the thinker and the philosopher. It is in this context that eighteenth-century thinkers must be understood, as men whose attitudes

17

originate in a philosophy of individual action, and for whom thought is a form of action, and a form of action directed specifically against the twin obstacles of authority and insecurity, and based on an effort to understand the true nature of reality. Thus Buffon early on in his *Histoire Naturelle*, writes: 'there is a kind of strength of spirit and courage of mind in being able, without being over-whelmed, to embrace Nature in the numberless multitude of her creations, and in feeling capable of understanding them and com-paring them'.[5] Like the man of action in a potentially hostile world, the man of science must confront nature 'sans s'étonner', without being overwhelmed. Diderot, concerned in *De l'Interprétation de la Nature* with the proper attitude to the world around us, sees the avoidance of 'étonnement' as linked precisely with the scientific approach, with the realization of nature's simplicity: 'We are often taken aback because we suppose the existence of several marvels where there is only one; because we imagine that there are in nature as many separate acts as there are phenomena, whereas she has perhaps only ever performed a single act.'[6]

That the discovery of order is primarily dependent on developing a mental attitude can be seen in a whole range of eighteenth-century writers. Beneath the various approaches to the problem, a largely unavowed and perhaps unconscious assumption seems to be present, which is that the prime agent in the process is man. This is not of course to be understood in the obvious sense that only man can be aware of order, but that order is simply a *potential* in nature, concealed beneath the apparent chaos of its workings, perhaps not everywhere present, but available to a sufficient degree to make possible a rational relationship between man and nature. The law of cause and effect was not enough to guarantee the accessibility of nature.† The eighteenth-century mind demanded that it should be capable of acting as though directed by a rational purpose, even if some thinkers at least denied that there was a rational creator behind it.

Thus, in the field of natural history, both Buffon and Maupertuis recognize in nature the means of creating superior kinds of animals, but regard it as man's task actually to do it, by systematic breeding. Nature can only produce such results by chance, and even then there will be no guarantee of their continuance. 'Nature contains the re-sources for all these varieties; but it is chance or art which bring them into being', says Maupertuis in the *Vénus physique* (p. 134).[7] In *La Nouvelle Héloïse* we find M. de Wolmar and Julie transform-

† This point is made by Lester Crocker, *An Age of Crisis*, p. 8.

ing the chance products of nature into art when they found a colony of wild birds by choosing a suitable site and supplying them with food and nesting materials (*La Nouvelle Héloïse*, Part IV, Letter 11). Such an enterprise demands first of all the readiness to build upon nature's methods and then the patience to follow them at nature's rhythm. M. de Wolmar points out that they would not have been able to establish the colony if there had not already been some birds present in the wood; and he attributes their final success to time and patience.

The purpose of Wolmar, as of Buffon and Maupertuis, is to achieve control over the world about them, albeit the kind of control which never does violence to the nature of that world. A more extreme, and less acceptable example of this process can be found in *Les Liaisons dangereuses* of Laclos, where both Valmont and Mme de Merteuil achieve control over other human beings. Both have acquired this power through experience and an emotional detachment (a quality of Wolmar too) which enables them to understand the mental and affective processes of the people about them. The supreme example is of course Valmont's seduction, and destruction, of Mme de Tourvel. Their ultimate failure is due not to a fault in their methods but to their own weaknesses.

The fictional worlds of Rousseau and Laclos may seem a long way from the theoretical writings of the *philosophes*, but the underlying preoccupations are the same. Wolmar and Valmont have achieved their success by developing attitudes which reveal similar concerns to those put forward in the works of Condillac, d'Holbach, d'Alembert or La Mettrie. It has been noticed, and I shall return to this point later, that eighteenth-century theoretical writings tend to lack a solid content, in the sense that they are primarily concerned with epistemology and method rather than with specific precepts, whether moral, political or anything else. The assumption seems to be that once we know *how* to seek knowledge, then the knowledge we find will automatically be right, and good. Certainly Wolmar's success is based on knowledge and method, and his experiment with the bird colony is only one example of the system he adopts throughout his estate, and this includes his servants. It is only with Julie and Saint-Preux, that is with people of equal standing with himself, that, as in *Les Liaisons dangereuses*, the system breaks down; but that is another story.

When we read Condillac's *Traité des Sensations*, d'Holbach's *Système de la Nature*, d'Alembert's *Discours préliminaire de l'Encyclopédie*, or La Mettrie's *L'Homme-machine*, we find that they all contain advice as to how we should see things. Indeed one often gets the impression that no proper distinction is made between the picture they draw of what man is like and the ideal they set up of how we should behave. It is as if the clear boundary we now see between descriptive and normative thinking was not visible to the eighteenth-century mind; the statue-man of Condillac and the man-machine of La Mettrie are at the same time scientific descriptions and ideals of behaviour. They are in fact heuristic devices, and to say this is not to diminish their status, given the importance the period attached to finding the right path to knowledge. In addition, all these works in varying degrees offer encouragement to their readers: they are invitations to take up the courageous attitude of which we have seen Buffon speaking in his *Histoire naturelle*.

Underlying all this is a conception of experience which has little to do with logic and is responsible for many of the irreducible problems in the thought of the time, as well as for our difficulties in understanding it. For although change and movement were acknowledged, accepted, made the subject of serious and systematic examinations as properties of the natural world, they were at the same time considered to be somehow 'wrong', they were not seen as being simply 'there'. A corollary of the differences between seventeenth- and eighteenth-century science and that of our own time is that for the earlier thinkers a state of affairs in nature could not be considered neutrally. For all the importance they allotted to facts, their facts were not our facts, to be accepted simply because they were so, their whole existence bound up in their simple presence. The phenomena which make up man's experience of the external world were in a sense either 'good' or 'bad'. This is perhaps most obvious in their attitudes towards nature, for as we know, there was in eighteenth-century thought both a 'good' and a 'bad' nature. This is not the place to discuss the highly complex relationship between the two, nor its variations from one thinker to another, but it is important to remember that the parallel existence of good and bad natures has its counterpart in attitudes to society; and here again these attitudes are very much in evidence in the seventeenth century.

Society at that time seems to have been envisaged as a kind of *plenum* in which each member occupied a space, or rather – and here the parallel with Descartes is more striking – was represented by and coincided with the space he occupied, just as in Cartesian physics space is the area occupied by matter. The whole attitude is closely linked with a conception of society based on land-ownership, the tendency for an individual to identify closely with the land he possessed and to regard it as an extension of his personality and an expression of his stature. Indeed, had it not been for this deep-rooted conviction that there is in each society a space allotted to each member, it would not have been possible for ambition, the desire to expand one's own space, to have been so generally condemned. The 'fureur de se distinguer', the mania for self-distinction, was seen as one of the chief disruptive forces in society precisely because an improvement in one man's status could only be achieved at the expense of another's; an expansion of one man's space meant the contraction of another's, an upsetting of the proper balance between the elements of society.

Equally condemned, because it seemed to give official sanction to ambition, was the system of venality of office. Throughout the seventeenth and eighteenth centuries this system was one of the main targets of criticism as a symbol of social corruption – and occasioned a notable outburst by Diderot himself in his *Satire contre le Luxe* – for it combined the worst aspect of social mobility, the chance for a bourgeois to acquire noble rank, with the degradation of money, which, from being a guarantor of fixed values, became an agent of instability and imbalance.

Money could be the means whereby ambition gave visible expression to inflated stature in the form of grandiose buildings, gardens, monuments and, through artistic patronage, in inflated forms of expression. Social criticism in these two centuries is based on a more or less conscious awareness that values, as expressed in money, words or any form of art, have come adrift from the reality they should represent. Nature, it was felt, intended that human beings should occupy certain places in relation to each other, but the scheme of things has become distorted by the activities of those same human beings and by the forms in which those activities are represented. There is an awareness of the deceptive appearance of things, a preoccupation with 'être' and 'paraître', reality and appearance. In a society which should, it is felt, be stable and immediately accessible to the understanding, men seem to have become detached from the hierarchy to which they rightly belong, money has lost its fixed values, words no longer have a stable relationship with the reality they are supposed to represent.

One of the best satires on this state of affairs is Lesage's *Turcaret*. Its central figure is a man who has made a spectacular rise from the level of society to which he 'belongs'. He began life as a lackey, and now, as a successful financier, he seeks to convert his wealth into

rank by indiscriminately acquiring the appurtenances of the aristocrat: houses, furniture, a titled mistress, a poet, taste, and so on. The
gulf between appearance and reality is the most obvious feature of
the satire, but more important than this is the fact that all the chief
characters in the play subscribe to this fantasy. In different ways
they find their own advantage in bolstering Turcaret's view of
himself as a genuine aristocrat. A whole social structure is thus pre-
cariously built on a lie, and some of the best comedy in the play
comes from the occasions when the characters fight to preserve this
structure from the intrusion of truth, which repeatedly threatens to
destroy it.

This play appeared in 1709, but the picture it paints corresponds
to people's general impression of society at any time during the last
three reigns of the Ancien Régime. Lesage offers no solution. There
is not even one sincere character who might redeem this depressing
picture, because his intention is to show how the success of such a
system (and Turcaret's own success is of course directly owed to the
system of venality of office) demands that everyone should subscribe to it, and encourages them to do so. The world of *Turcaret* is
one in which money and language have become a means of enforc-
ing a false appearance, thus dominating and devaluing the
traditional standards: social rank, the arts, human relationships,
which they should simply represent. Movement, in the form of
social mobility, has caused social appearances to come adrift from
the essential realities of society, just as in the natural world the blind
movement of matter conceals the proper functioning of nature.

The result of all this in terms of the individual thinker is that his
effort to achieve some kind of positive relationship with reality is
made up of an attempt to stabilize his approach to the world of
movement coupled with the conviction that movement is disruptive
and 'wrong'. Thus, underlying much thinking, there seems to be the
paradox that, say, a complete understanding of the world of matter
in movement would produce a picture of total stability, or that a
total understanding of the forces acting in society would bring about
a system of government which eliminated all forms of change.

Such systems, whether scientific or political, ethical or aesthetic,
tend to be conceived in spatial terms, but are required to account for
a reality in movement, bound up in the passage of time. Created in
opposition to a reality whose constant vicissitudes obscure the 'true'
nature of things, they inevitably engender a truth of a different order
from that of directly observed reality; they thus unconsciously per-
petuate the duality of the two substances. Moreover it is not only a

philosophical dualism which is perpetuated but a religious one, in the sense that change, the world of matter in movement, is seen as a force which conceals and distorts the original nature of things in the same way that original sin distorts the true nature of man. This paradox arises directly from the way in which perception and action were conceived, and the process can be seen at work in the development of attitudes towards nature.

It might seem wrong to talk of a general attitude to nature covering both centuries, since we are more accustomed to see a contrast between the two periods in the sense that seventeenth-century man 'tames' nature, while his successor in the eighteenth century prefers it natural. But this interpretation, insofar as it is true, does not entirely represent an about-face in man's relationship with the natural world. The seventeenth-century noble or would-be noble who laid out a formal garden planned it as an extension of himself, as, literally, an expansion of his own space in society. It was formal, geometrical, because as such it could be dominated by the reason. It was not a denial of nature, but a reshaping of it in terms of reason as it was then conceived. But formality and geometry are not essential features: the process by which the age moved forward in its attempt to subject the external world to its mind and will was characterized by an increasing recognition of the nature of that world.

The modern mind tends to equate the conquest of nature with its transformation, with the reclamation of idle land, the damming of rivers, the taming of wild animals, emphasizing the final product at the expense of the understanding of nature which must precede it. The seventeenth and eighteenth centuries were certainly concerned too with the exploitation of nature, and perhaps Buffon is the most notable example of one for whom nature only acquires real significance when man has imposed order upon it;† but there is at this time a totally unmodern conception of the relationship between the mind and the external world. It can perhaps be described as one based on parallels rather than contrasts. More will be said of this later; the point at issue here is that nature was in a sense subject to the same range of laws as man. For example it, like man, like society, could be the subject of value judgments; it could be right or wrong. D'Alembert in the *Discours Préliminaire de l'Encyclopédie* compares the eccentricities of nature with the abuses of reason:

---

† The seventh and culminating period in Buffon's *Époques de la Nature* is entitled 'Lorsque la puissance de l'homme a secondé celle de la Nature' ('When the power of man has come to the aid of Nature') (*Oeuvres philosophiques*, p. 187).

23

'Nature has its lapses and reason its abuses. We have related monsters to nature's lapses; and it is to reason's abuses that all those sciences and arts must be related which reveal only the greed, wickedness and superstition of man, and which dishonour him.'[8] The judgment here seems to be a moral one, but is just one example of the general tendency to see the workings of nature and all aspects of external reality as behaving along the same lines as the mind of man. The corollary is that, insofar as man can do something about himself, he can do something about nature.

Because such a parallel is felt to exist, perception is not a passive process by which external phenomena are merely noted; it is a form of action, in which the object perceived is annexed by the reason and integrates itself into the order of nature. In the *Système figuré des connaissances humaines*, the scheme which provides a basis for the knowledge exposed in the *Encyclopédie*, natural history is divided into two parts: 'Uniformity of Nature'[9] and 'Lapses of Nature'.[10] To make a distinction of this kind, to establish an area in which nature is 'uniform', is to mark out the limits within which nature is accessible to reason, and this is the same kind of appropriation as takes place when – to return to the subject of gardens – a man marks out an area within which nature has become subject to his will. In this sense the formal garden differs from the landscape garden only to the extent that the new fashion represents a more complete annexation of nature in its reality, a step forward in the conquest of those regions formerly considered to lie outside the province of the rational mind. Order has been established in an area previously thought to be beyond its reach.

It might be objected that to mark out the limits of the reasonable world is also to acknowledge an area beyond these limits which cannot be charted, and that these vagaries of man or nature therefore belong not to a 'full' world, a *plenum*, but essentially to an area which has no boundaries and resists all definition. A partial answer is that for some thinkers at least – and Diderot is one – the possibility was felt to exist that the limits of reason could ultimately be pushed outwards to embrace all the phenomena of the universe; but a more fundamental explanation lies again in the relationship of perception and action. Because the two processes are of the same order, because they involve an appropriation, a re-ordering, a recreation even, of the experience perceived, the reality thus annexed, the area made relevant to man, is only that area which has been brought under domination and re-expressed in terms accessible to reason; and this is necessarily a full world, one which can have no gaps, no obstacles to the steady processes of reason. The assertion that nature makes no leaps is not therefore contradicted by the existence of monsters or other phenomena which do not form a continuous chain within 'the uniformity of nature', for the world which is understood, that is, the world which obeys the laws of nature, is defined as that which has possibility for the rational mind. It exists side by side with that which cannot be generated by rational thought but only by the imagination, by the workings of fantasy; and these two opposites exist together in the same way as the *vraisemblable*, the probable, exists with the *invraisemblable*, the improbable, socially acceptable behaviour with the anti-social, or reason with fantasy.

Throughout the period these two aspects of nature, two aspects of the mental process, together define the general pattern of thought. The relationship between the two is fixed not in terms of fact and fiction as we know them, but in terms of validity; for the kind of distinction we now make between fact and fiction, and also between moral and aesthetic judgments, was subordinate to the question of whether a phenomenon or idea could exist in a viable relationship with others. The type of man who came in for general condemnation, whether in the field of art or science or politics, was the one whose view of things threatened to impose a system which did not accord with the supposed nature of reality. The tyrant whose system of government did actual violence to the proper relationships between his subjects and the man of speculation whose theories were out of touch with the true relationships between things were distrusted and feared for the same reason, because of the discrepancy between the individual worlds they created and the demands of what was felt to be the real one. We tend to think of the seventeenth century in particular as favouring the man of action at the expense of the thinker, and this is true in a sense; but it is not so because one acts while the other just thinks. It is because the unreal world which the thinker or the artist can create by the force of his imagination is just as much a product of action, and of exactly the same order as that of the despot who denies the true nature of a society in the interests of his own glory, or the individual who upsets its equilibrium in the pursuit of his personal ambitions. The fact that thought and action, so far from being incompatible, are activities of the same order, becomes clearer when we see them merged in the *philosophes*, and perhaps most of all in the *Encyclopédie*. Here thought and action combine in an enterprise designed to change people's attitudes, to fix the nature of their experience in a stable form; it is an attempt to set out the total quantity of real experience in order to stabilize the quality of that experience.

Seen in this light, thought and action become simple aspects of a relationship with reality based on experience, and the ideal relationship is one which occupies a precise point midway between the total detachment from it of pure speculation, or the uncontrolled use of the imagination, and the total involvement in it of the man who is at the mercy of his passions, his immediate needs and immediate surroundings. Control consists in achieving the right mental and emotional distance from the external world, and in the same way, the perfect world, born of control, is that in which the individual elements are held in a perfect balance, at a perfect distance from one another, so that the forces which constantly threaten to break out in disorder are held in check by the equal pressure of other forces. It is a system of perfect equilibrium, and one born of the true nature of things, not of an arbitrary force imposed from without.

It is at this point that the pursuit of order defeats itself. This perfection, this attempt to achieve total control by the containment, or else the banishment, of those forces which belong to the world of chance was only possible in a state of immobility, where the perceiving mind and the objects perceived observed an exact equilibrium, in a total denial of movement and action. It seems as though, in the attitudes of the period, any form of action going beyond the act of perception itself, that is to say, involving movement, belonged to the world of matter and change. Human action, motivated by the passions, could only be conceived of as upsetting equilibrium, as inimical to the processes by which truth was perceived. It is within these epistemological limits and in terms of this paradox that some of Diderot's finest works were produced. He evolved a philosophy which contained both a characteristic interpretation of the nature of order and control and a positive role for the play of chance in natural and human affairs. The ensuing chapters will examine the important ways in which these concepts of order and chance coexisted in the different areas of his thought, sometimes as warring principles, but in his best works as complementary ones.

I
PERCEPTION AND ACTION

1

PERCEPTION

Universal Sensibility

'Once I have seen inert matter change into something sensitive, nothing else need surprise me...',[1] says d'Alembert from the depths of his dream, thus unwittingly providing the key to unlock the mystery of life, and the means by which man can cease to be a victim of his environment and become its master. There is no doubt that the concept of universal sensibility was one which dominated Diderot's thinking about the universe and man's role in it. Despite the fact that it forms the basis of so much of the argument in the *Rêve de d'Alembert*, he knew that its universal presence in matter could not be proved. It was a theory, but one in which he desperately needed to believe and in which he had immense faith. 'One day they will succeed in demonstrating that sensibility or touch is a sense common to all things. There are already phenomena which suggest it. Then matter in general will have five or six essential properties, live or inert force, length, breadth, depth, impenetrability and sensibility.'[2]

Seen in the most general terms, the sensibility of matter was the concept which enabled Diderot to account for our awareness of being separate from the world about us, of consciousness in fact, without forcing him to postulate a separate principle for it. To say that much of Diderot's writing centres on the paradox that man is of the world yet separate from it is only to say that he shares the dominant preoccupations of his age. To say that he denied the necessity of a specific principle to explain this separateness is to group him with those thinkers who denied the theory of the two substances. We only get close to defining the individual quality of his thought when we understand that he saw in sensibility the phenomenon which both unites us with external reality and separates us from it.

If the great purpose of eighteenth-century thought was to find an answer to man's fear of being swept away in the chaos of which he was increasingly convinced of being a part, then one of the great aspects of Diderot's genius was to see that the means of dominating it might lie in the very stuff of which that chaos was made. 'The wise man is simply a combination of insane molecules.'[3] This statement, in the section of the *Éléments de Physiologie* entitled 'Les Passions', has the brevity and depth of significance of a maxim of La Rochefoucauld, and perhaps represents a way of looking at the human condition which La Rochefoucauld would have shared. As a creative truth it not only provides answers but also gives rise to a number of problems and paradoxes which will be discussed in the course of this study. What I shall try to show in this first part is that Diderot's theory of life and his solution to the problems it presents are dualist in form. More precisely, his monist interpretation of the workings of nature, based on the universal presence of sensibility in matter, is not simply an interpretation but also a form of resistance to its implications. The theory and the resistance which it incorporates together form a dualist structure, which reflects the theory of the two substances it sets out to replace.

Any study which tries to describe an individual thinker's achievement in the context of contemporary attitudes involves at least four considerations: his personal thought; the innovative thinking of others which contributed to it; the traditional thinking which it opposed; and the pattern of unconscious assumptions which underlies it. Thus Diderot's theory of universal sensibility is distinctive in its conception of sensibility as a means whereby matter both partakes of the nature of blind creation and offers the means to achieve control over it. It owes much to the ideas of other progressive thinkers, most specifically to the research done on the nervous system by Bordeu. It is conceived in opposition to the Cartesian theory of the two substances and more generally to the religious concept of a transcendental power directly influencing the workings of nature. Finally, it is bound up with traditional patterns of thought in that it is conceived as a dualist system: the mechanism by which sensibility achieves control over the initially disordered substance in which it originates results in an organism of a different order, what is effectively another substance. The discussion in this section will mainly be concerned with the first and last categories. I have set these points out briefly at the beginning for the sake of clarity, since some of the discussion which follows is complex and threatens to submerge the main lines of the argument.

The self and the outside world

The question of the relationship of the self with reality has a special importance when we are concerned with the eighteenth century. Cassirer has pointed out that eighteenth-century thinkers and their thought cannot be separated and studied independently, and this is surely so not just because any thinker's works cannot be detached from him and looked at in isolation if one is studying the history of ideas, but because many eighteenth-century thinkers consciously set out to establish a relationship between themselves and the world around them. This is perhaps clearest in Diderot's approach to science, clearest to us, that is, because we are accustomed to regard scientific study as something essentially objective, and its products as independent truths. One might say that the eighteenth century is as responsible as any period for the fact that we now see science in this way, but it must be remembered that many eighteenth-century thinkers, Diderot among them, insisted that science should be relevant to human needs, and this in a way which we should now consider quite 'unscientific'. When Diderot, in *De l'Interprétation de la Nature*,[4] stresses utility as a guideline in scientific research, he is not, as a modern might imagine, favouring applied science at the expense of pure science, even if the effect may sometimes be similar. He is claiming that scientific knowledge should be connected to man in an active, two-way relationship which would today be regarded as thoroughly subjective and invalid.

When, in the *Rêve de d'Alembert*,[5] Diderot opposes the theory of preformation, he does so on the grounds that it is contrary to 'experience and reason'.[6] Reasonable enough, perhaps. But what is this 'experience'? It is that which 'would search in vain for such germs in the egg and in most animals under a certain age'.[7] And the 'reason'? That which teaches us 'that in nature there is a limit to the divisibility of matter (even though there is none in our theoretical reasoning), which resists the idea of there being a fully formed elephant inside an atom, and within that another fully formed elephant, and so on ad infinitum'.[8] Diderot is making a plea not for a more scientific attitude in the modern sense of the word, but for a return to common sense, to the 'experience' which is our everyday reaction to life, an area of accessible, perceptible facts, the area within which we normally function. And the 'reason', at least in this passage, is effectively the same; it is the faculty which enables us to establish a relationship with the real world, and is here contrasted with 'theoretical reasoning',[9] which seems to be equated with the speculative intellect.

Common sense is what should make it possible for d'Alembert to see the futility of the 'two substances',[10] and the reasons for admitting the sensibility of matter: 'you will come to feel that by refusing to entertain a simple hypothesis which explains everything – sensibility, a property common to all matter, or a result of the organization of matter – you are flying in the face of common sense and plunging into a chasm of mysteries, contradictions and absurdities'.[11] One might imagine that Diderot was merely bringing in common sense to give support to his arguments, but there is no doubt that he thinks of it as something more clearly defined, as a notion which can claim a positive status in scientific enquiry. The point has been made by Gillispie ('*The Encyclopédie* and the Jacobin philosophy of science') who, like Vartanian (*Diderot and Descartes*), sees a strong Cartesian element in Diderot's thinking. 'To the Cartesians', he says, 'nature was the seat of rationality, and Newton's laws appeared intellectually trivial. To the Romantics, nature was the seat of virtue and Newton's laws were morally unedifying. The work of Diderot's generation, therefore, had to be to preserve the continuity of man and nature by opening its personality to reality rather than its intellect. For if nature *is* congruent with man, if science is the correspondence, it has to be a continuum, a whole, a "tout" as d'Alembert is made to see in his dream' (p. 258). And, commenting on Diderot's stress on utility, he remarks that he 'restores the mind, in a sense, to a finite cosmos, by wrapping science tight around humanity' (p. 262).

But to say that Diderot's approach is positive, or that it attempts to bring knowledge into the world of reality, is not to define it. If 'the useful circumscribes everything',[12] where exactly do the boundaries of the useful lie? We find that any hints of a more precise definition are expressed in terms not so much of usefulness as such, as of ways in which we can establish a relationship with nature. In Section VII of *De l'Interprétation de la Nature*,[13] the problem is expressed through an image, that of a chain, held firm at one end by observation and at the other by experience, or experiment, and weighted along its length by 'experiments'[14] or 'arguments',[15] or a combination of the two. For 'as long as things are in our intellect alone, they are our opinions; they are ideas, which may be true or false, granted or contradicted'.[16] They have no objective validity, and are therefore not 'useful';[17] they lack the 'consistance', the consistency or solidity, which can only come from their being linked with the external world, otherwise the chain, or 'thread'[18] as he later calls it, would become the plaything of the slightest movement of the air'.[19] The use of a metaphor here, with its opposition between stability and susceptibility to the slightest influence, suggests that Diderot is not concerned with a precise scientific method but with an attitude of mind. He is trying, as he is in the *Encyclopédie*, to change our ways of thinking and seeing, and this is borne out by his use of other images in the next two sections. In VIII,[20] notions without any foundation in nature are compared to those northern forests whose trees are without proper roots, susceptible, like his unattached chain, to the movements of the air. In IX,[21] the quest for truth is likened to the activity of bees, constantly shuttling to and fro between the flowers and the hive; in this way the constant movement of scientific enquiry between reflection and sense impressions is defined as a physical relationship with nature. Once again, the use of imagery and analogy suggests a mental approach, not a rigidly defined set of rules. Even though he says, in this same section, that 'the laws governing the investigation of truth are severe',[22] the severity seems to lie in a kind of self-discipline, a controlled relationship, recognizable more by the extremes it must avoid than for what it must aim at.

There is another illuminating point in this *Thought*.[23] In describing this to-and-fro movement from the senses to reflection and back Diderot uses the expression: 'ceaselessly returning to one's self and leaving it'.[24] The implication here that using the senses involves 'leaving (one's self)'[25] might not be worth insisting on were it not for the fact that it links up with other statements which suggest that Diderot sees the self, and perhaps even the body, not as a fixed entity, but as capable of expansion and contraction, according to the extent to which it is aware of the outside world. The implication that the self coincides with the objects of its perception is taken up by Bordeu in the *Rêve de d'Alembert*.[26] Our nerve-centre, the seat of our judgment, 'gives almost infinite space to the individual, or else reduces him almost to a point';[27] and to his own question: 'What really sets a limit to your true extension, I mean the real area of your sensations?'[28] he at first offers no answer, simply insisting on the self's possibilities of concentration or expansion. Julie de l'Espinasse knows that she sometimes 'exists as a single point';[29] the properties of the material world cease to exist: 'the universe is reduced to nothing for me, and I am nothing to the universe'.[30] Bordeu completes the picture by adding that there are in fact 'two infinites' (to use the Pascalian term) for the self, the 'sensibilité': 'once the true limit of your physical sensitivity has been passed,

33

whether by retreating and so to speak condensing yourself, or by extending outwards, there is no knowing where it might lead'.[31] A similar notion of sensibility occupying a space, and a variable one, comes up in the *Lettre sur les Aveugles*,[32] in Diderot's reflections on those who are born blind: 'although sensation is indivisible in itself, it occupies, if one may use the term, an extended space, to which a person born blind has the power, through thought, of adding or subtracting, by enlarging or diminishing the part concerned'.[33] One can see the importance Diderot's efforts to project himself into the perceptual world of the blind may have had in the development of his ideas about the self occupying the area of its immediate awareness: 'he will even have a solid as large as the terrestrial globe, if he imagines the end of his finger to be as large as the globe and occupied by sensation in its length, breadth and depth'.[34]

When we are dealing, however, with Diderot's attitude to knowledge, then the possibilities of change in our awareness, the poles of sensibility, become undesirable extremes. His studies of medical thought which are so evident in the *Rêve* and the *Éléments de Physiologie* have developed, or confirmed, a conviction that the line between the normal and the pathological in our relationship with the external world is a very uncertain one, if indeed it exists at all. As far as physical awareness of our own bodies is concerned, the 'right' state is clearly that in which it coincides with the real space which we occupy, but even here Bordeu cannot be too specific, for various pathological states are possible in which the subjects believe their bodies to be bigger or smaller than they actually are. As Julie concludes: 'so in physical as well as moral things we tend to think ourselves bigger than we really are?'[35] and later, speaking of La Condamine,[36] who was able to feel in his extremities: 'he exists beyond the limits of his sensory impressions'.[37]

As so often, Diderot's approach is exploratory rather than affirmative here, and it would be unwise to pursue his statements too far, in the hope of discovering a coherent theory of perception based on physiology. What is of positive interest about these images of movement amongst natural phenomena and of changing dimensions of awareness is that they imply a oneness with the external world mediated by sensibility. On this level Diderot's scientific thinking is consciously opposed to tradition, for one of the main objections to traditional science was not so much that it was not objective as that it was detached and impersonal. The most popular object of criticism, medicine, came under fire because its theories took no account of the reality of the patients themselves; it was, so to speak, a form of thought which had no direct relationship with the substance it was supposed to influence. It is true that eighteenth-century science appears to aim at objectivity when it demands that researchers look at the facts, and it certainly proposes that we should arrive at these facts by observation and experiment, but the purpose is not primarily to achieve the separation between the observer and the observed which we now associate with scientific objectivity, the elimination of the will which enables things to be seen 'as they are'. What Diderot and his contemporaries sought was a kind of involvement with reality, an intimate link between thought and matter which is closer to intuition than to objectivity.

But this is only the beginning of the problem, for the sensibility which can bring about our involvement with nature is itself part of that nature and threatens to produce not a deeper understanding but total identification to the point where our judgment ceases to operate. If Diderot's main purpose in the *Interprétation de la Nature* was to establish the basis of a genuine relationship with nature, his aim in the *Rêve de d'Alembert* is to go a step further and define the mechanism whereby we can exploit the advantages of sensibility and avoid its dangers. What he arrives at is a relationship characterized by physical separation from nature but perceptual continuity with it. It is a highly original solution, but also one which betrays Diderot's inability to escape from a dualist way of thinking.

A spatial order

Of equal importance with Diderot's attempt to find a physical, or physiological basis for our perception of reality is the fact that he conceives of the problem in spatial terms. Just as our awareness of ourselves lies at a point somewhere between complete abstraction, where the self becomes 'un point', and total expansion, when the self seems to occupy the whole universe, so, when we perceive the outside world, we must achieve the ideal position between total absorption in external phenomena and total absorption in thought. And just as this position, with regard to the body, is where our conception of it coincides with its actual dimensions, so the ideal relationship with the phenomena of the external world would be one where we perceive them exactly where they are, or – the real point – exactly as they are. Bordeu's use of words like 'tension' and 'étendue', 'extent', in his account of physical self-awareness is very significant. 'In their natural undisturbed state, the threads in the bundle have a certain tension, a tone, a normal energy which governs the real or imaginary extent of the body.'[38] Here Diderot is talking about the limits of the body again, but the idea is extended beyond it in the image of the spider's web, expressing our continuity with something which is, and yet is not, ourselves. Julie wonders[39] why she is not able to know everything which goes on in her own body, or in the outside world, and she is told that this would be possible if there were continuity, not just contiguity, throughout the universe.[40]

This statement raises certain problems which will be dealt with later, but the point of immediate relevance is Bordeu's next statement: 'through your oneness with all the beings in nature you would know everything that is happening, and thanks to your memory you would know everything that has been happening'.[41] Now the continuity of which Bordeu speaks here is a physical one, the continuity which makes of each creature a unified organism, and not a mass of adjacent molecules, and this continuity, if pushed to the limits of creation, would presumably mean that Julie became the universe, or, as Bordeu says, God.[42] But on a perceptual level it is precisely continuity which makes the real world accessible to reason. This is one of the dominant themes of *De l'Interprétation de la Nature*, and it seems hardly necessary to quote the various statements which hammer this point home. Perception is thus a form of action by which we almost appropriate to ourselves an area of reality which is in itself independent of us.

Understanding, then, implies a coincidence of the mind with the phenomena it perceives, and between the mind and reality stand our sense impressions which both by their inherent limitations and the vagaries of our organism threaten to distort that assessment of reality which only they can mediate. As far as the variations in our own bodily condition are concerned, ordered perception occurs when the right tension prevails in the 'threads',[43] the right balance between the forces exerted by the 'centre of the network'[44] on the one hand and the senses concerned on the other. As for the limitations of our various senses, the physical continuity which our bodies lack with the rest of the universe can only be compensated for by *successive* observation of phenomena. It is because sight and hearing only operate effectively at certain distances, because touch involves contact, and so on, that we need, like the bees in Diderot's analogy, to move among the phenomena of the external world in order to know them, and that the relationships between them are only accessible through the relationships which we set up with them ourselves. The nature of experience has to be fixed spatially by our own efforts to establish the right distance, the right tension, between ourselves and what we experience.

It is worth mentioning in this context that, at least as far as the intellectual heirs of Locke are concerned, the emphasis is not on a visual universe, but one of dimensions and proportions. Roger Kempf (*Diderot et le Roman*, p. 81) takes up Langen's point that eighteenth-century rationalism is a 'Kultur des Auges', a visual culture. It is only this in the sense – very important it is true – that eighteenth-century thinkers are often preoccupied with the possibility of *simultaneous* representation of reality, which is most easily associated with vision, with a picture. The essential, as it were inalienable nature of reality lies beyond the individual senses in a world of relationship where things have their appropriate positions, properties and spaces in relation to the whole. In the establishment of this reality all the senses have a role to play, and the preoccupation of thinkers like Diderot and Condillac* with them all stems partly from a need to establish the area of validity of each one. Just as in the external world each constituent part stands in a state of potential rivalry with the others and order can only result from an equilibrium between these forces, so the senses, in Diderot's thought, constantly threaten to encroach on each other, so that the removal of one results in the others trying to take over its function. It is significant that the *Additions à la Lettre sur les Aveugles* should be mainly concerned, in a section interestingly entitled 'Phénomènes', with examples of sight being compensated for by other senses: the artist who judged roundness by touch, rather than by eye; the blind man who recognized colour by touch;[45] Mademoiselle de Salignac, who could tell how tall a person was by the direction from which the voice came,[46] or the dimensions of a room by 'the space circumscribed by the sound of his feet or the resonance of his voice'.[47]

Diderot's purpose here, in opposition to the perhaps natural opinion that sight is the king of the senses, is to rehabilitate the others: 'the eye is not as useful to our needs, nor as essential to our happiness as one might be tempted to believe'.[48] Not that the eye is by any means denied its superiority: in the *Lettre* itself, Diderot even suggests that touch may be less necessary than other philosophers thought for distinguishing the limits and distances of objects.[49] The important point is that Diderot refuses to allot a precise role to each sense. Their function is defined not *a priori* but by their relationship with one another. Diderot seems to find the subject of relationship

* Especially of course in Condillac's statue-man in the *Traité des Sensations*.

much more interesting than the discovery of the exact area in which each sense is unique and irreplaceable. As in so many other aspects of his thought, he is less concerned with the essential core of each phenomenon, than with the shifting, uncertain area where they impinge upon each other. Moreover, to return to the *Rêve de d'Alembert*, the *sensorium commune*, the 'centre of the network',[50] lies beyond individual sense impressions: the network 'has at its centre no sense that is its own: it cannot see, hear or feel pain. It comes into being and receives nourishment; it emanates from a soft, insensitive, inert substance, which acts as a cushion on which it is enthroned, hears cases, considers its judgment and pronounces verdicts.'[51] Just as the diaphragm, the seat of emotional reaction, is ideally controlled by the centre which knows no emotions, so the senses are answerable to an authority which has no involvement with any one of them.

Thus the impressions which come to us through the senses do not acquire real meaning until they are processed by the judgment, and then only when that judgment has the right degree of authority over the senses. To put it in the words of David Funt (*Diderot and the Esthetics of the Enlightenment*): 'A perception is a piece of experience which has been made stable, and which opens the world to us, rather than the fleeting sensation which in its raw, untransformed state is useless' (p. 40). As Funt points out (pp. 41–9), this does not, cannot mean that Diderot has opted for the total dominance of the mind over the senses or the passions. The whole tendency of eighteenth-century thought was after all to find some kind of viable relationship between thought and the world which was accessible through the senses, to find some means of accepting the one without displacing the other. The emphasis on the importance of the real world, on the primacy of facts, and the parallel rejection of the 'systematic', and, by Diderot, of the mathematical, is a plea for the rehabilitation of the external world in its own right. This is a general problem, and one which exercised the minds of both seventeenth- and eighteenth-century thinkers. What distinguishes Diderot from the others is the particular way in which he tries to retain a grip on this external reality, but without destroying its autonomy, tries in fact to establish control without tyranny. It is therefore of the greatest importance to define as clearly as possible what Diderot understood by this central authority, this 'centre of the network' which seems to have provided him with the key to so many problems.

Control: a dualistic structure

The argument whether the 'sens interne', the inner sense, is in fact the scholastic *sensorium commune*, and whether either or both are the same as the 'centre of the network', falls into place if we trace it back to the idea of control which runs through the thought of the whole period. The general dichotomy of reason and judgment on the one hand and the passions and the senses on the other does not disappear with the sensationalism of Locke. Acceptance of such a theory does not constitute a reversal in ways of thinking about perception but a necessary stage in a process by which reality is reassessed and brought within the domain of reason. The underlying idea that the senses and passions are potential sources of error is still there. As Diderot remarks in his additional notes to the *Éléments de Physiologie*: 'Are not the passions so many coloured lenses over our eyes which distort the objects we see?'[52] The need remains for a means of fixing the truth beneath the appearances.

Diderot certainly equates the *sensorium commune* with 'the centre of the network' in the *Éléments de Physiologie*,[53] where he describes how unequal degrees of fatigue in separate organs produce a 'disjointed succession of images, sounds, tastes and sensations at the centre of the network or *sensorium commune*'.[54] The 'inner sense'[55] is mentioned in the *Lettre sur les Aveugles*,[56] where he sees its existence as best proved by the heightened ability of those born blind 'to feel or recall the sensation of bodies even when they are absent and no longer acting on their senses'.[57] The last phrase in particular suggests the absence of immediate effects of sensation which has been noted in connection with 'the centre of the network'. It is simply that the emphasis is different. The comment on the 'inner sense' is concerned with its power to preserve the quality of an experience, while the 'centre of the network' is usually thought of as a kind of filter, eliminating as it were the secondary qualities of the sensations we receive, allowing us to perceive reality at one remove, divested of its immediate and deceitful impact. The essential function of both is to give us not immediate reality but a true representation of it.

It seems that Diderot in his letters on the blind and the deaf and dumb already assumed the existence of some central principle able to combine and process the impressions emanating from the separate senses. The exact function and nature of this principle is not altogether clear, and David Funt indicates this when he disagrees with other interpreters on whether Diderot has in fact got the scholastic *sensorium commune* in mind.[58] He seems to be thinking mainly in terms of geometry, of the possibility of abstracting a common element from the data of each sense. In the *Lettre sur les Sourds et Muets*,[59] where he imagines the consequences of each of the five senses leading an independent existence, he observes that the one level upon which they could all communicate would be that of geometry. The idea is not developed as far as one might wish, but we can compare this possibility of the senses meeting on a level beyond sensation, in a pure awareness of spatial relationships, with the seat of judgment in the *Rêve* mentioned above. Another important aspect of Diderot's fantasy about the five senses, which comes up in the *Lettre à Mademoiselle* ***[60] is that, existing together in a society, they would inevitably be at war with each other. The implication is that only their subordination to a higher organism is capable of making their coexistence in the body harmonious.

Diderot, then, is forced to rely for his perception of an unstable world on a set of senses which partake of the same instability. The self-control which we must seek within ourselves is of the same order as the control which is necessary to our relationship with the outside world. In its basic form this is a truth which was realized a hundred or more years before by those thinkers who claimed that a sovereign must first govern himself if he is to be able to govern his people. What Diderot has done is both to clarify and complicate the problem by providing a physiological basis for this awareness, and in particular by introducing the hypothesis of universal sensibility. This, while accounting for our separateness from the rest of creation, by making of us a self-conscious organism, has at the same time produced a state of potential continuity with that creation. Although Diderot was as anxious as anyone in his age to establish a fixed boundary between ourselves and the outside world without which human dignity and even self-preservation were jeopardized, the whole tendency of his thought is to recognize a situation in which that boundary is hard to define and subject to constant fluctuation.

So we have here two key problems, which will come nearest to being solved in the *Rêve de d'Alembert*, the need for equilibrium amongst the potential forces of disorder in the self: the senses, the passions and sensibility; and the nature of the control which alone can ensure this equilibrium. This is an aspect of the preoccupation with unity and diversity which is so often mentioned in connection with eighteenth-century thought, and in particular that of Diderot, and it is, I think, the dominant one. But dominant preoccupations tend to be dominant because they present special difficulties, and the difficulties here, for Diderot, for his contemporaries (and for that matter for his modern commentators), lie in their inability to free themselves from a dualistic conception of reality.

The first person to object to this interpretation might of course be Diderot himself, since much of his scientific and philosophical writing is concerned with attacking the Cartesian doctrine of the two substances, thought and extension, and replacing them with one. Moreover, with the *Rêve de d'Alembert* before us we can hardly deny him a considerable degree of success. What he failed to do – and this is only possible to see with hindsight – was to replace the conceptual structure which the theory of the two substances embodied. The human organism which Diderot is able to develop from his theory of sensibility remains very much a Cartesian structure. The 'soft, insensitive, inert substance'[61] which neither sees, hears nor suffers on the one hand, and the sensual world outside it, existing essentially in space on the other, are still thought and extension, despite their common origin in one substance. But it is very unlikely that Diderot would have considered his theory to be only a partial solution, at least in this respect, because it would simply not have occurred to him that there was any other way of looking at the problem. For him, as for his contemporaries and his predecessors in the seventeenth century, truth and reality were distinct entities, existing in opposition, and paralleled by such equally opposed concepts as the ideal and the real, mind and matter. Moreover, it was an unquestioned assumption that truth, the ideal representation of reality, was absolute, unchanging and timeless, while the everyday world which obscured it from our perception was relative, in constant movement, and caught up in the passage of time. Ordered perception, as opposed to mere sensation, was thus an operation carried out in opposition to time and movement; it was an effort to create a timeless representation, and therefore a spatial one, of a reality distorted by change.

Since the eighteenth century the Western mind has ceased to assume a distinction between truth and reality; the world around us is no longer an imperfect representation of itself, a subject of value-judgments; it simply *is*, and contains its value within itself. It is because we have lost this distinction that the thought of the eighteenth century has become so alien to us, but we should not forget, even when it seems to resemble our own, that it *is* alien. The thinkers of the period, especially the materialists, often seem to be expressing very modern ideas, and some of them have, after all, provided the

41

foundations of our own thought, but I think it is a mistake to imagine that when Diderot in the *Rêve* or *Le Neveu de Rameau* or *Jacques le Fataliste* shows such acute awareness of 'modern' concepts, he is not also thinking them within a context which is not modern at all. The fact that, as we are now able to see, Diderot was trying to integrate new ideas into a traditional pattern of thought which was alien to them, creates certain inconsistencies, as I shall try to show in the next section; but his obscure awareness of the problem, the intuitive awareness of an artist, perhaps, also created some of the finest aspects of his fictional work, and this I shall deal with in later chapters.

2

ACTION

Action and reaction: an unresolved problem

Diderot's response to the problem of the right human relationship with a disordered world can be found most clearly in the *Rêve* and to a lesser extent in the *Paradoxe sur le Comédien*. It is sometimes assumed to be one of the few coherent aspects of a notoriously intractable body of thought, but, as I have suggested, there is at the centre of it an unresolved problem, and one which lies at the root of much of his thinking.

One of the most disturbing aspects of the picture of the world offered by materialism, and the *Rêve*, is that of a universe in which everything, including man, is *in fluxu*, and it seems hardly in keeping with the expressed hope of the *philosophes* that they could cast out fear by increasing the stock of human knowledge. It is not altogether surprising then that one of the chief points of interest in the *Rêve* is Diderot's conception of the ideal man, the type best fitted to cope with such a situation. Some of the confusion over the interpretation of this concept of the great man (in the cases where confusion has in fact been seen to exist) arises to a certain extent out of the two uses of the word 'sensibility', in its general sense of proneness to emotional reactions, and in its more limited scientific sense of a property of some or all matter; but a deeper confusion arises out of the persistence in Diderot's mind of traditional attitudes and, most important of all, the fact that the concept itself is an attempt to deal with an unresolvable paradox.

This factor is evident not so much in his account of the balance or imbalance of different elements in the human personality[62] as in his description of the 'great man'.[63]

The great man who has unfortunately been born with this kind of disposition will constantly strive to suppress it, dominate it, master its impulses and maintain the hegemony of the centre of the network. Then he will keep his self-possession amid the greatest dangers and judge coolly but sanely.

43

He will omit nothing which might fit in with his aim or serve his ends. He will be difficult to take by surprise.[64]

Such a man may achieve greatness as a king, a minister, a politician, an artist, an actor, a philosopher, a poet, a musician, or a doctor. 'He will be master of himself and everything round him';[65] and he will be 'freed from all the tyrannies of this world'.[66]

The stress here is on self-possession, judgment, the ability not to be thrown off balance by the unexpected; self-control will lead to control over his environment, and resistance to tyranny. All this – with the notable exception of the various professional men listed, artists, musicians, doctors and so on – might easily have come from the pen of a seventeenth-century writer. These qualities are exactly those which could lead the noble to glory; it is just that they have been generalized, but now, as then, these qualities originated in the same need for people to be emotionally detached from the vagaries and unpredictability of the surrounding world, to be in control of their own reactions in order not to be engulfed by a succession of discrete and potentially hostile circumstances. Diderot was not alone in having such a personality as his ideal. Buffon, for example, in his *Histoire Naturelle* speaks of the wise man as the only type of man worthy of consideration:

he is master of events as he is master of himself; content with his lot, he desires only to be as he has always been, to live as he has always lived; sufficient to himself, he has but small need of others, and cannot be a burden to them. Continually engaged in using the faculties of his mind, he perfects his understanding, cultivates his mind, acquires new knowledge and satisfies himself at every moment without remorse, without disgust; he takes pleasure in the universe as he takes pleasure in his own being.[67]

This passage is worth quoting at length because, developing the idea further than does Diderot in an Epicurean direction, it portrays an ideal which, in its God-like self-sufficiency and superiority to time and change, represents the opposite principle to that of a world of matter in movement and at the same time points up the paradox towards which Diderot's own thought is moving.

The idea of the great man undergoes a much fuller treatment in the *Paradoxe sur le Comédien*; it is indeed one of the chief elements in Diderot's thought, but it is not one which can be directly induced from what is generally regarded as his materialism. This is worth insisting upon, because the concept which is so fully worked out in the *Paradoxe* does seem to link logically with what we find in the *Rêve*. The illogicality lies in the *Rêve* itself. The concept of the great man in the *Rêve* is, as we know, partly based on the physiological theories which Diderot learned from Bordeu. When Bordeu and Mademoiselle de l'Espinasse are discussing the 'general manifestations'[68] of the personality, reason, judgment, imagination, madness, and so on,[69] and Mademoiselle de l'Espinasse associates these – 'wonderfully well',[70] as Bordeu says – with the 'original or habitually acquired relationship between the centre of the network and its ramifications',[71] Bordeu enlarges on the idea:

If the principle or trunk is too vigorous in relation to the branches, we find poets, artists, people of imagination, cowards, fanatics, madmen. If it is too weak we get what we call louts or wild beasts. If the whole system is flaccid, soft, devoid of energy, then idiots. On the other hand, if it is energetic, well balanced and in good order, the outcome is the great thinkers, philosophers, sages.[72]

Now Bordeu's 'principle' or 'trunk' and his 'branches'[73] are clearly a metaphor for the 'centre of the network'[74] and its 'ramifications', so that the dominance in the system of the 'centre of the network' produces people who are in fact dominated by their imagination. These are the people whose ideas tend to run away with them and lose touch with the reality represented by the 'ramifications'. The parallel is clear with the traditional notion that thought without the sanction of experience loses touch with reality and produces at best art and at worst wild fantasies, but it is important to note that the only specific reference to real action in Bordeu's remarks is to the uncontrolled movements of the 'louts'[75] and the 'wild beasts'.[76]

If we look at a statement by Bordeu a little later[77] and immediately before the description of the 'great man', we find:

But what is a sensitive being? One who is a prey to the vagaries of his diaphragm. If a touching word strikes his ear or a strange sight his eye, then at once he is thrown into an inner tumult, every thread in the network is stimulated, a shudder runs through him, he is overcome with horror, his tears begin to flow, he is choked with sobs, his voice fails him, and in fact the centre of the network doesn't know what is happening to it; all calm, reason, judgment ... have fled.[78]

Here then is a somewhat similar result brought about by the dominance of the diaphragm over the 'centre of the network', which suggests a serious confusion in Diderot's mind about the relative functions of the two centres. The chief difference, and an important one, between the two passages, is that the first deals with the outward effects of thought and action, while the second is concerned with reaction, with felt emotion.

As we have already seen, the great man is the one in whom the 'centre of the network' controls the movements of the diaphragm, who 'will constantly strive to ... master its impulses ["its" referring here to the tendency towards sensibility, to the diaphragm in fact], and to maintain the hegemony of the centre of the network'.[79] The nearest we get to a great man in Bordeu's analogy with the trunk and the branches is in the last sentence: 'the great thinkers, philosophers, sages',[80] but here the stress is on the thinker rather than the man of action, and the preceding sentence: 'if the whole system is energetic, well balanced and in good order'[81] avoids explaining exactly what relationship between trunk and branches would produce such a man.

Now in a passage from the *Paradoxe sur le Comédien* which is often linked with the *Rêve*, and where Diderot develops the distinction made in the *Rêve* between those who are on the stage and those who observe the spectacle, we find this:

Great poets, great actors, and perhaps in general all the great imitators of nature, whatever they may be, if they are gifted with a fine imagination, sound judgment, subtle technique and reliable taste are the least sensitive of beings.[82]

Here imagination, sometimes associated with sensibility, and judgment, seem to be granted equal status in the make-up of the artist; and this does not seem to be a question of the one dominating the other, as with the great man of the *Rêve*, since these artists are also 'the least sensitive of beings'. Another passage in the *Paradoxe* puts the great imitator of nature squarely on the same level as social and political leaders:

The man of sensibility is too much a prey to his diaphragm to be a great king, a great politician, a great magistrate, a just man, a profound observer and therefore a sublime imitator of nature unless he is capable of forgetting himself, abstracting himself from himself and using a powerful imagination to create, and a retentive memory to keep his attention fixed on the phantoms which serve as his models; but in such cases it is no longer he himself who acts, it is the mind of another controlling him.[83]

This is a fascinating picture of the detachment, alienation even, which must be achieved by the great artist, and by implication the great man of action. It is paralleled in another passage earlier in the work: 'The man of sensibility obeys the impulses of nature and conveys nothing but the cry from his heart; as soon as he moderates or forces this cry, he is no longer himself, but an actor playing a part.'[84]

In both these passages greatness is achieved not by having a lack of sensibility to start with, but by having a powerful sensibility. Diderot's use of the word 'imagination' seems to be closely related to sensibility in that it is the power to involve onself, to project oneself into some real or imagined figure in the outside world. In either case the product of the sensibility or imagination is dominated, or more exactly placed at one remove from oneself, and this applies to the great man in the *Rêve* as much as it does to the various examples of superior beings in the *Paradoxe*, for the paradox in this work is surely not so much concerned with the fact that great actors lack sensibility, as with the fact that great men have the qualities of an actor.

And so despite Diderot's assertion – and one which he would never have denied – that 'sensibility always implies a weakness in the system',[85] it seems essential for such sensibility to be present, not just that presumed quality of matter which enables an organism to come into being, but the powerful tendency to emotional involvement which, left to itself, is a source of disorder. For what kind of men are they who have, so to speak, the control without the sensibility? There are the type, says Diderot, who are 'too concerned with watching, identifying and imitating to be deeply affected within themselves. I see them forever with a pad on their knees and a pencil in their hand.'[86] Once again we are back with the thinker, the objective observer, the cold man who remains unmoved by what goes on around him. He never loses his head, unlike the man dominated by his sensibility, who 'will never be a great king, a great minister, a great captain, a great lawyer or a great doctor'.[87] But on the other hand he will never achieve anything great.

Diderot offers evidence then that the man of pure sensibility will never be great; that the man without sensibility will be a good observer and possess good judgment; but we are never positively told what the exact relationship is between sensibility and control in the true man of action. Certainly Diderot is thinking here in terms of that equilibrium beween the phenomena of the personality which is central to his thinking, that exact distance between involvement and detachment which makes for perfect order. But perfect order and equilibrium are by definition opposed to action and movement, and even the idea put forward by Diderot that the successful man of action is in fact playing a part, acting out his life as it were by proxy, is an interesting and significant notion, but goes nowhere towards explaining the problem of action, successful or otherwise, in an ordered world.

Part of the explanation for this difficulty is that in seventeenth- and eighteenth-century psychology the energy necessary for action can only come from the passions. In his writings at the period of the

Rêve and the *Paradoxe*, references to the passions are, perhaps understandably, rare, except as a factor to which man reacts, as something potentially disruptive through their effect on the diaphragm. In an earlier work, the *Pensées Philosophiques* (1746), we find a very traditional reference to the passions as the only source of great actions:

only the passions, and the great passions at that, can raise the soul to great things. Without them there is no sublimity either in manners or in works of art; the arts revert to infancy and virtue becomes mean-spirited.[88]

and a little further on: 'Unusual men are debased by trying to moderate their passions. The greatness and vigour of nature is destroyed by constraint.'[89] This could suggest that Diderot's opinions had changed considerably by the time he wrote the *Rêve* and the *Paradoxe*, and this is the opinion of Robert Mauzi (*L'Idée du Bonheur*, p. 445). But it seems more likely to be a question of a difference of emphasis, a separate line of thought which leads Diderot to neglect, consciously or unconsciously, another belief equally firmly held.

The passions were certainly as important a feature of thought about the middle of the century as they always had been. Lester Crocker shows this in his chapter on the subject in *An Age of Crisis* (ch. 9, 'Reason and the Passions') and Richard Fargher, in *Life and Letters in the Eighteenth Century* (pp. 84–5) points out that this belief in the driving force of the passions was closely linked with the glorification of human energy in action. This was certainly a preoccupation of Diderot's and one which comes out particularly in his aesthetic writings. Fargher quotes a passage from Helvétius which suggests that a powerful passion can make for more effective judgment than simple common sense: 'In fact it is the strong passions which, providing more illumination than simple good sense, are alone able to teach us the distinction between the extraordinary and the impossible; sensible people nearly always confuse them because, not being inspired by strong passions, they are never anything but mediocrities.'[90] This might easily have come from the pen of Cardinal de Retz, and is an excellent description of another aspect of the man of action, his energy and dynamism, as well as his recognition of the outer limits of possible action. It would be pointless here to examine the precise differences between the views of Helvétius and Diderot on the function of the passions. Probably Helvétius was primarily concerned in this extract with passion as a form of motivation, as was Diderot in the *Pensées Philosophiques*, but in his later writings Diderot is much more preoccupied with the problem of motivation without emotional involvement, another perennial problem, and one to which the *Paradoxe* claims to propose a solution.

In fact the solution is only a partial one. The traditional idea of a man who can dominate himself and the world around him is essentially based on detachment, on an absence of emotional involvement. Now Diderot gives us an account of how a person can dominate the centre of emotional reaction, the diaphragm, by the exercise of the 'centre of the network', but the difficulty arises when we consider that these emotional reactions are of the same order as the passions. There is no provision in Diderot's psychology for a distinction between emotional action and reaction. In a statement already quoted Diderot describes the passions as factors which distort our true picture of reality. Here he is speaking of reaction, of the influence of the diaphragm on the senses. But the passions are also active forces, and it seems that in the general thought of the period they are associated, or seen as analogous to, the forces which create movement in the material world.

In fact there is nothing very surprising about this. The opposition between truth and reality, characterized respectively by stability and movement, which I have already discussed, forms part of a religious conception of the universe dominated by the idea of the Fall. In modern thinking the Fall is primarily associated with humanity, and if we were to use the vocabulary available to Diderot we would no doubt say that human perfection has been lost through the activity of the passions. They are the agents which both lead us into evil and prevent us from seeing the good; they distort our actions in the world and our reactions to the world. What is harder for the modern mind to grasp is that the Fall was once seen as affecting the whole of the material world, and although we do not find in Diderot, as we do in many seventeenth-century writers, the idea that the world is drawing to its end, we certainly find the assumption that the universe exists now in a degenerate form, and that it is matter in movement which creates chaos and obscures the truth of nature from our eyes. Movement, whether arising from the nature of man or from the nature of matter, is thus disruptive, and it follows that, in an obscure but profound sense, it is felt to be somehow wrong, an expression of evil. To this point I shall return later, but it is something which needs especially to be borne in mind when we are considering a writer such as Diderot, so much of whose conscious effort was devoted to recognizing and expressing change and movement as a valid feature of our experience.

The nature of matter

Diderot's dominant conception of the nature of matter is defined by his belief in heterogeneity: this is what accounts for the apparently chaotic movement which characterizes the world about us. In this connection there are two comments in his *Principes philosophiques sur la Matière et le Mouvement*. Insisting, in the face of potential critics, on the fact that movement is a property of matter, he says:

If, in a given body, they do not imagine any more inclination to rest than to movement, then they must regard matter as homogeneous; in other words they are discounting all the qualities which are essential to it; they are considering it to be unchangeable at the almost indivisible moment when they contemplate it, they are arguing from the relative state of rest of one aggregate to another aggregate.[91]

And again:

The molecule, endowed with a quality proper to its nature, is in itself an active force. It acts on another molecule which in its turn acts on it. All these paralogisms originate in the false assumption of homogeneous matter.[92]

These statements are complemented by one of his comments on Hemsterhuis:

I believe that the form in which matter presently exists is necessary and determined, as are all the diverse forms which it will successively assume to all eternity. But this process of change, this development, which is a perpetual flux, is a necessary thing. It is a consequence of its essential nature and of its heterogeneity. And I see nothing contradictory about this assumption.

If it is essentially heterogeneous, it is essentially in a process of change.[93]

The last sentence, as the editor of the text points out, seems to have been added as an afterthought, but it represents one of the basic tenets of Diderot's beliefs about the universe, and gives rise to one of the most imaginative passages in D'Alembert's dream.

Everything changes and passes away, only the whole remains. The world is ceaselessly beginning and ending; at every moment it is at its beginning and its end. There has never been any other world, and never will be.

In this vast ocean of matter not a single molecule resembles any other, not a single molecule remains for a moment just like itself: Rerum novus nascitur ordo, that is its unvarying device...[94]

Diderot's basic objection to his critics is that by not recognizing movement as an essential property of matter they must be limiting themselves to observing the universe at a single point in time; failing to recognize the fact of change, they are extreme victims of the 'fallacy of the ephemeral'.[95]

Diderot's thought may represent an advance on that of some of his contemporaries in that he incorporates time and change into his picture of the universe, but how does man cope in practice with the constant change brought about by movement in matter, and passions in men? The problem is that sensibility can indeed provide the means to hold together this 'coordination of infinitely active molecules',[96] this 'chain of tiny forces which everything conspires to separate',[97] to hold up the constant process of disintegration which Diderot sees as an essential feature of the universe, but it is nevertheless – or, one might say, necessarily – a phenomenon of a similar order to the heterogeneous matter in movement which it has the possibility of controlling. This is not merely because, by enabling these molecules and organs to work together it can produce even more frightening effects than would these elements acting in isolation, but because in Diderot's thought sensibility belongs in the same category, follows the same pattern of activity. This is made clear early on in the *Rêve*[98] where Diderot explains to d'Alembert how sensibility moves from its inert state to one of activity through the analogy of the 'inert force' becoming a 'live force'[99] by the removal of an obstacle: 'for what do you do when you eat? You remove the obstacles which were resisting the active sensibility of the food.'[100] Vernière quotes a parallel passage in Diderot's letter to Duclos of 1765:

Sensibility is a universal property of matter, an inert property in insentient matter, as is movement in heavy bodies arrested by an obstacle, and a property which is made active in the same bodies when they are assimilated by a living animal substance.[101]

Obviously the obstacle to active sensibility is not exactly of the same kind as the one which opposes movement in matter. Sensibility comes out of its inert state by contact with other molecules which are already in an active state, and the scientific details of the process are beyond Diderot to explain, in particular why it should happen in some cases of contact and not in others. One can only say that the explanation belongs in the realm of chemistry and not physics, and it should be remembered that chemistry, especially biochemistry, was Diderot's favoured science. In fact the process is much easier to understand on a moral level, when sensibility is taken in its more general sense, as productive of extreme emotional reaction, where the personality is as it were assimilated into some person or event which arouses its previously dormant passions. On this level sensibility is one of the essential features of the world of change and unreliability, like movement itself. The raising of the obstacle leads – or can lead – to the annihilation of order, of that clear distinction between phenomena and, in particular, organisms, which sensibility should ideally create.

And yet this vision of universal sensibility is nevertheless a brilliant one in that it attempts to show how order can be created out of this chaos by a property and process which partakes of the same qualities as that chaos itself. Diderot is one of the eighteenth-century thinkers who tried hardest to incorporate the notion of change into our perception of the world, and while no one could deny that he of all thinkers is conscious of the fact of change, diversity, heterogeneity and so on, one wonders whether his thinking has gone beyond the simple recognition of the predominant status of change, whether in other words he offers a solution to the problems of ordered activity in a world of potential chaos. Certainly the *Encyclopédie* comes to mind as a practical step towards the establishment of order, but although it was obviously conceived with the intention that its readers would go on to act upon its principles, it is in itself, like the judgment of the 'great man', merely an ordered *representation* of the world about us. Just as the great mind, the genius, is characterized by an ability to see the 'rapports', the hidden links between apparently disparate phenomena, to create a perceptual continuity where only contiguity is immediately apparent, so the system of cross-references in the *Encyclopédie* acts as a form of sensibility, creating organic form amongst a mass of arbitrarily (alphabetically) disposed elements.

But what happens when the student of the *Encyclopédie* tries to put these ideas into practice? What is the mechanism by which the man whose way of thinking has, in accordance with the *Encyclopédie*'s purpose, been changed, actually tries to reshape society in terms of this changed perspective? Since such a man must initiate some kind of change, his passions must come into play, and at first sight it might seem that this presents no problem. It was a generally held belief that the passions were not bad in themselves; they represented a force which could work either for good or evil, and Diderot certainly regarded a 'fine action' as something which would bring him more satisfaction than any other accomplishment. But when we look at what he has to say about the passions, the picture is rather different. The *Pensées Philosophiques* admittedly support the view that the passions are in themselves morally indifferent, but already there is a suggestion of Diderot's future preoccupations when he says that the passions must be in harmony if their action is to be acceptable: 'Once establish a balanced harmony between them, and there need be no fear of disorder'.[102] The underlying assumption is that the passions, like matter, like the separate organs of the body, are potentially autonomous and tyrannical, always threatening to create disequilibrium. The idea of harmony is taken up much more fully, and given a different emphasis in the *Éléments de Physiologie*,[103] where Diderot distinguishes between 'the healthy animal'[104] or 'the calm animal',[105] which does not know its own strength, and the immense power which comes to the same creature under the influence of passion or sickness (the juxtaposition of the two states speaks for itself). 'For in a disordered state, all the forces of the machine conspire together, whereas in the healthy or calm state they act separately: there is only the activity of the arms, or the legs, or the thighs or the hips.'[106] In the healthy state the individual organs are not so much autonomous as separately controlled by the central organ – although the question still remains how that movement is motivated unless by the passions – whereas in disorder, all the parts join forces, not in harmony, but in a form of despotism in which one function wrests the power from the centre and carries all the others along with it. The picture Diderot seems to have is of an organism in which ideally all the component parts have a limited autonomy, limited to the exact point where this autonomy, this individual, particular function does not infringe on the functions of the others. In this state their essential heterogeneity presents no threat to order. But as soon as one function expands beyond these limits it takes over the functions of the others, creating out of them a homogeneous force which generates disorder by its multiplied power.

Of the examples Diderot gives,[107] there is one where Buffon is imagined tearng away the panelling from the walls of his burning house and carrying it into the courtyard, and another of a miser carrying his safe, again from a burning house, into the garden. In both cases we have to do with people acting under exceptionally strong motivation, a motivation which can only derive from the passions. Diderot makes it quite clear in the *Éléments de Physiologie* that the will is subordinate to the passions: 'It is said that desire is born of the will; but the contrary is true; it is from desire that the will is born. Desire is the offspring of physical organization.'[108] The same phenomenon which Diderot evokes in the case of Buffon and the miser is referred to in the section dealing with the passions:[109] 'Nothing reveals so well the conspiracy of the organs as what happens in passionate states such as love, anger or admiration.'[110] In such states the organs are subject to extreme, abnormal tension: 'In attacks of violent passion the parts of the body draw closer, become shorter and hard as stone. However brief the duration of this state, it is followed by a period of immense lassitude.'[111]

Again Diderot is speaking of passions which are violent, but presumably a milder motivation would only represent a difference of degree. Diderot never suggests that there is a critical point beyond which passion becomes pathological, and such an idea would be contrary to his way of thinking in terms of gradation and continuity. What this passage reveals is that Diderot thinks of the individual passions not only as potentially autonomous and disruptive, not only, like individuals in society, or molecules in matter, as tending to exert forces against each other, but also as having the power, given by sensibility, to combine, again like people or molecules, to produce a force greater than the sum of the individual parts. When the passions are only considered in terms of the diaphragm, as our means of reacting to external stimuli, they are simply sources of confusion, bad judgment and extreme emotionalism; but considered as active forces, they are able to assume partial or total control of the body. The whole system is reorientated away from its proper centre towards the obsession of the moment. 'Conspiracy of the organs' is in fact an appropriate and revealing term, since Diderot almost certainly has a parallel in mind with times when the power in the state is shifted from the sovereign to a conspirator who for a time channels the energies of the state in another direction. The two kinds of sickness which Diderot describes in the *Éléments de Physologie* are exactly analogous to war and internal dissension in the state.

There are two kinds of sickness. One is produced by an extraneous cause which brings disorder with it, the other by too vigorous an organ which upsets the functioning of the machine, like a citizen who is too powerful in a democracy.[112]

But conspiracy, madness, the obsessive desire to preserve oneself or one's valued possessions, however 'natural' some of them may be, are all forms of disorder, all tending, as I have suggested, towards the pathological. If, as Diderot says, 'good reasoning, good judgment presupposes a good state of health, or an absence of uneasiness or pain, self-interest or passion',[113] then it seems that any degree of passion, or more to the point, any degree of action, leads to a diminution of judgment. The only state in which judgment can operate effectively is one of total detachment, total immobility. The ordered mind on which judgment depends can only perceive the change and movement of the external world as a series of discrete states of immobility, each at an infinitesimal distance from the next.

This is not to deny the distinction, so important to Diderot, between mere sensation, the momentary awareness of immediate phenomena, and perception, the integration of those phenomena into a spatio-temporal order based on the 'chain'[114] made possible by memory.[115] This feature of consciousness has been emphasized in various contexts by many Diderot scholars, and perhaps most suggestively by Ian W. Alexander in his article 'Philosophy of Organism and Philosophy of Consciousness in Diderot's Speculative Thought', who concludes that 'the activity of consciousness is essentially one of concentration within the space-time unit of reflection, the creation of a sort of *totum simul*' (p. 17), and that 'self-consciousness is the experience of the self as cause, as wholly responsible for the world which it has remade "for itself", which it has mastered and comprehended' (p. 19). In fact this condition of total awareness in which change is absorbed into extension is the ultimate illustration of the fact that Diderot's conception of consciousness excludes movement, just as it excludes the possibility of an ordered self being an active participant in the world it perceives.

It would seem then that however much Diderot was committed to reform, to positive, beneficent action, he was unable to evolve a philosophy to encompass it. To look at the problem from a different angle, the world of movement was seen both as the 'real' world and as a threat to any kind of value, in particular to any kind of human dignity. Thinkers such as Diderot therefore, whose attitudes were formed in the tradition of a meaningful, providential world, felt the need not only to understand the nature of this mechanical universe but also to resist it, to 'save' it. Diderot perhaps provided the most brilliant solution to the problem in positing a force, sensibility, which would both explain and 'save' this universe. But the very assumptions which motivated him also made it impossible for him to account for any mechanism which might actually improve it. As far as I can see, there is no evidence in his philosophical works that he was aware of this paradox. The problem needs further discussion, but it seems that it is only faced, and rather differently resolved, as we shall see later, in the two great fictional dialogues. Suffice it to say for the moment that there are really two paradoxes here: one is that he had developed an apparently materialist philosophy which could nevertheless make it possible to give value to phenomena; the other that value can only be given under conditions which preclude activity.

The dual role of sensibility

This section began by stressing the importance to Diderot of the idea of universal sensibility; it continued with a discussion of the nature of ordered perception in a world of constant change and of the relationship between this and the various elements which affect such perception. These notions have been linked with the apparent paradox that ordered perception and right judgment are incompatible with action, with movement. It is now appropriate to try to define the relationship Diderot saw between sensibility and the other elements which make up the personality and the world of matter in general. Sensibility seems to have been for him not only a potential source of disorder but also a means of salvation – salvation, that is, on a purely secular level. This is perhaps most clearly brought out in the *Entretien entre d'Alembert et Diderot*. In a world whose raw material consists of isolated, blindly motivated phenomena, only sensibility can create order unless we are to assume that such order is introduced from outside by a power of a totally alien nature.

Although, then, it is sensibility which gives us consciousness, our awareness of being separate from the reality about us, it is also essentially a principle of continuity or organization: that which gives us the promise of power and autonomy which was traditionally associated implicitly, if not explicitly, with religion. The difference, as far as Diderot is concerned, is that the special status once conferred by possession of a soul must now be provided from the same substance, originating in the material world, which potentially denies us that status. Throughout the *Rêve* and the *Éléments de Physiologie* we see sensibility defined as the quality which, once brought out of its inertia, brings to life and links up the molecules which compose the organs and the organs which compose the total organism. In fact there is no other principle in Diderot's world which accounts for continuity – continuity, that is, and not contiguity, for it is necessary here to emphasize the distinction. When Diderot says in the *Interprétation de la Nature* that no philosophy is possible if 'phenomena are not linked to one another',[116] he is talking about the simple linking of cause and effect, a situation brought about by contiguity, by the fact that changes occur through forces acting and reacting upon one another. The continuity brought into being by sensibility is clearly distinguished from it in the conversation already referred to in the *Rêve*[117] where Bordeu tells Julie that if there were continuity throughout the universe she would be God.

This is a very different matter from the total contiguity of all the elements which make up the world: this is the Cartesian *plenum*, in which, as it happens, Diderot also believed. As Bordeu says: 'between Saturn and you there are only contiguous bodies, and not continuity, as there would need to be'.[118] The fact that Julie would be God if there were continuity between her and the rest of the universe may well imply, as Vernière suggests,[119] that Diderot accepts 'at least as a logical hypothesis'[120] the doctrine of immanence, but the emphasis is really on the immense potential she would have to create change, whether ordered or disordered. She would be like the spider at the centre of the web, but of a web which extended to the limits of creation, or – magnified to cosmic proportions – like the case mentioned in the *Éléments de Physiologie*: 'What should we make of the looms in the mill at Lyon if the weaver and the reeling-girl formed one living whole with the weft, the chain and the simple? It would be an animal like the spider, who thinks, wills, eats, reproduces itself and weaves its web.'[121] And he goes on: 'Without sensibility and the law of continuity in the animal organism, without these two qualities the animal cannot be *one*.'[122] A little further on he compares this unity with a soul: 'The animal is a unified whole, and it is perhaps this unity which, with the aid of memory, constitutes the soul, the self, and consciousness.'[123]

Sensibility, continuity, then, is a means of salvation because it brings power, the ability to coordinate and direct a number of forces in a given direction, but the mere fact of sensibility is not enough in itself, because the same continuity which can create order is equally a power for disorder. We have seen the ravaging effects described by Diderot of the 'conspiracy of the organs', of the extreme tension experienced during 'attacks of violent passion'.[124] There are similar ideas in Diderot's commentary on Hemsterhuis where he takes this unenlightened thinker to task for his belief in the two substances.

The calm animal is unaware of its strength. But if an attack of fever, a fit of passion, a powerful interest, a movement of pride, the fear of losing honour, life or fortune, a real or hysterical terror should cause tension in its nerves, accelerate the movement of its fluids, contract the vessels which contain them, and if above all, intention, will or spirit are not involved, you will be horrified by the effects it will produce.

In that state it is reduced to a creature of sensation alone.[125]

Here again is an example of the extreme tension of all the organs of the body conspiring together to produce disastrous effects. Unity may, as Diderot suggests in the *Éléments de Physiologie*, constitute some kind of equivalent of a soul, but it apparently also has the ability to by-pass it, to render it impotent. The point should be made that in his commentary on Hemsterhuis's work Diderot uses terms like 'intention, will or spirit'[126] because he wants to refute Hemsterhuis's theories about their role, but the important statement in this passage is the last one, where a being who is under the dominance of a strong passion is defined as 'sensation alone'.[127] The sensibility which alone can create a soul has the power to act independently of it. The apparent contradiction mentioned earlier in connection with the *Rêve* is of the same order: 'louts, wild beasts'[128] in one of Bordeu's classifications[129] are also creatures in whom the 'centre of the network' has lost its power to command the other organs of the body, and are therefore, presumably, 'sensation alone'.[130] On the other hand Bordeu's 'sensitive being'[131] is essentially a highly emotional personality, easily moved to fear, horror, tears. Both types have in common the fact that the control-centre becomes inoperative, that their sensibility is acting without constraint. The difference is that in the case of the brutes, of men inspired by powerful passions, of Buffon braving the flames to save the furnishings of his house, the continuity created by sensibility is purely internal: the whole body becomes a single, homogeneous unit, obeying as it were the physical laws of movement and reduced to a purely mechanical phenomenon. The sensibility which ideally can make us into superior beings, capable of reflection and judgment, has here produced an example of that blind force which characterizes the activity of the insentient world. When, on the other hand, Bordeu talks of a 'sensitive being', he is speaking of a passive emotional reaction, and in this case the continuity does not act as a unifying force within the personality, but as a principle which connects it with the outside world, as a powerful sympathy which, once established, obscures the boundaries between the self and the phenomena which act upon it.

It might be objected that Bordeu is speaking in this case of 'sensibility' taken in its more general and widely accepted sense of susceptibility to emotion in both aesthetic and moral experiences, and in a sense he is. 'This quality, so greatly prized, which leads to nothing great',[132] he calls it at one point, but there is no doubt at all that he does not distinguish it from the universal sensibility upon which he and Diderot base their physiological account of human personality. Without this identity of meaning, the *Rêve*, the *Paradoxe* and the *Éléments de Physiologie* would lose much of their point. In any case, it is not this aspect of sensibility which creates the problem. Bordeu claims[133] that he is quite capable of enjoyment and admiration without the emotional disturbance which accompanies it in sensitive creatures like Julie, and this critical enjoyment is achieved by the proper exercise of the 'centre of the network', by the ability to experience the emotional impact at one remove, by the filtering process characteristic of the nerve-centre. But when it comes to action, then only two possibilities are open: either a person becomes a blind force, an unreflecting component of the world of matter in movement, or else he adopts the solution of the great actor, playing out a role in which he is personally uninvolved, with that total emotional detachment which alone can ensure the proper functioning of the judgment, but which denies any value to the act performed.

The mind

One of the characteristics of Diderot's thought is that he is torn between the idea of man as being distinguished from all other creatures by the special qualities of his brain, and his awareness that the brain is in fact a very weak and uncertain element in the total personality. On the one hand he tells us that 'the characteristic nature of man is to be found in his brain, not his physical organization',[134] that 'his perfectibility is born of the weakness of the other senses, none of which predominates over the organ of reason';[135] on the other he insists: 'The brain is just an organ like any other. It is in fact only a secondary organ which would never come into action without the intervention of the other organs. It is subject to all the vices of the other organs',[136] and that 'there is a very marked sympathy between the diaphragm and the brain'.[137] Indeed, the conditions under which the brain can succeed in assuming its dominant role are extremely rare. 'In perfect health, when there is no predominant sensation making one aware of a particular part of the body, a state which every man has sometimes experienced, man exists only at a point in the brain: he is all where his thought is.'[138] But despite the infrequency of this condition Diderot comes back to it quite often. We have already noted Julie's state[139] in which 'I seem to exist as a single point; I almost cease to be material and am conscious only of thought. I have lost the sense of position, motion, body, distance and space. The universe is reduced to nothing and I am nothing to the universe.'[140] Another similar state is described in the article 'Délicieux' in the *Encyclopédie*. As in the *Éléments de Physiologie* a state of 'perfect health'[141] is a precondition; the system must not be disturbed by any worries or powerful emotions and the result is a state finely balanced between sleeping and waking, with no sense of past, present or future.

If one's thought could define this situation of pure feeling, in which all the faculties of body and mind are alive without being active, and attach to this delightful quietism the idea of immutability, one would have formed the idea of the greatest and purest happiness that man can imagine.[142]

To return to the *Rêve*, Bordeu throws a rather different light on the matter when he quotes various examples of the unusual control of mind over matter.

For example, if the centre of the network absorbs all the strength of a person into itself, if the whole system works so to speak from the inside outwards, as I believe happens to a man lost in deep meditation, a visionary who sees the heavens open, a savage singing amid the flames, or in cases of ecstasy or insanity, whether self-induced or involuntary ... the creature becomes impervious to feeling, it exists only at one point.[143]

Bordeu is obviously speaking of phenomena which are not just unusual, but unnatural, and although Diderot was obviously full of fascination and admiration for such examples of mental concentration, he is equally certain that they do not represent man's normal state; they are not examples of order, but of cases where, as Bordeu says, 'the principle or the trunk is too vigorous in relation to the branches',[144] and represent the opposite pole to that in which men act purely instinctively. To exist 'in a single point'[145] can therefore be seen as a source of the purest happiness or else as an abnormal, almost pathological state. A cynic might ask where the contradiction lies, and although Diderot cannot be classed as a cynic, the objection is in a sense reasonable. Once again, the apparent contradiction comes from a difference of emphasis. In some cases Diderot regards existence 'in a single point' as a subjective ideal, and as an instrument of perception; on other cases the notion uppermost in his mind is an objective, 'scientific' one, where the brain is considered as just one of a number of organs – in this case playing an exceptionally powerful role – and he is thinking in terms not of perception but of action.

The paradox of action

Diderot claims that man's natural state is one of activity.

Nothing is more contrary to nature than habitual meditation, or the state of being a scholar. Man is born for action. His health depends on movement. The true movement of the system consists not in constant motion away from the extremities to the centre of the network, but from the centre to the extremities of the threads... Natural man is intended for little thought, but much action. Science on the other hand is much given to thought and little to activity.[146]

The expression 'man is born for action' suggests the confidence and vigour of the eighteenth-century reformer, an awareness of belonging to a movement which has man as its centre, and yet Diderot's thought perhaps expresses better than that of any of his contemporaries the problem of a philosophy which feels the need to be anthropocentric but is forced by its epistemological basis to be egocentric. Moreover the ego at the centre, the 'centre of the network', can only be clearly conceived as an entity existing beyond the senses and passions, in independence of the very functions which not only make us active beings but are the sole basis for that centre's existence.

For Diderot as a physiologist, as a scientist, action can only be, as we have seen, a form of disorder: indicative of disorder in that it implies a weakening of judgment in the 'centre of the network'; creative of disorder in that it produces an imbalance in the surrounding world; and a product of disorder in that it seeks to redress some kind of dissatisfaction or discomfort in the organism. The lowest form of sensibility which Diderot recognizes, in Section LI of the *Interprétation de la Nature,* is defined as always seeking a position of rest and comfort 'which it would seek from a mechanical sense of discomfort, as animals sometimes move in their sleep ... until they find the position most conducive to rest'.[147] The point is taken up again in the *Éléments de Physiologie* in connection with the power of nature to effect cures.

Nature. What is this agent? It is the actual efforts made by the sick organ, or the whole machine... Nature performs at all times in the sick person what the discomfort of the machine carries out during sleep; it moves spontaneously, twisting about until it has found the most comfortable position...[148]

And if it should be objected that Diderot is only talking of sickness here, it should be remembered that perfect health is an almost inconceivable state in Diderot's world:

there is not on the whole surface of the earth a single man who is perfectly formed, perfectly healthy. The human species is simply a mass of individuals who are to a greater or lesser degree deformed or sick;[149]

and to complete the picture, he goes on:

I say this of man, but there is not a single animal, a single plant, a single mineral of which I cannot say the same... Anyone who wanted to make of all that the masterpiece of an infinitely wise and all-powerful being would be totally devoid of common sense.[150]

Once again we return to the point that the universe is essentially a state of disorder: the individual elements within it aspire towards a state of rest, but their very diversity, their heterogeneity, the extent of their deviation from the norm, makes any actual form of order impossible, except under momentary conditions produced by chance. It is the natural tendency of every man, indeed of every element of the universe, to seek something different, to have a different conception of the order which would satisfy them. This is the universe which God, if we could imagine one, has given us, and it is interesting to note that just as Diderot's perfect man, or perfect antidote to this situation, is echoed by the passage already quoted from Buffon, so Buffon presents us with a similarly chaotic picture of creation:

It does not appear that the Creator's hand has opened to give life to a certain fixed number of species; but that all at once it has emptied out a world of beings both related and unrelated, an infinite number of harmonious and dissonant combinations and a perpetual chain of destructions and renewals.[151]

With a picture like this of the universe, and it is a picture shared by many others in his age, probably in fact an underlying concept which shaped the thought of the whole period, one in which God has presented us with a meaningless universe and left us to cope as best we can, there are two reactions which seem to predominate. One is an effort to rise above it all, to withdraw into ourselves 'as it were into a single point',[152] to be perfect beings beyond time, space and change, to become ourselves the God who has deserted us. The other is a more practical one, based on an attempt to find within the universe some kind of shape or pattern, a system based on proportions and relationships, some concept which will enable us to find order in a world in which proportions constantly change between the infinitely great and the infinitely small, to set a proper distance between ourselves and a world in which things threaten either to engulf us or to escape us, and in which we ourselves are permanently subject to distortion through our passions, our senses and even the dimensions of our own bodies.

The first of these responses is an ideal, a dream of Augustinian repose which is perhaps briefly attainable by some, but offers no answer to the world's problems. The second, practical though it is, remains impossible in the terms in which Diderot conceives the nature of the universe, impossible at least as a system which might lead to meaningful action. Perhaps Diderot saw a link between these two kinds of response, at least at the end of his life, when in the *Essai sur les Règnes de Claude et de Néron*,[153] he reaffirmed his faith in scientific method, in the careful observation which may finally enable us to fill in 'the gap which separates phenomena'.[154] He goes on:

If we were to possess the whole sum of phenomena, there would be only one cause or hypothesis remaining. Then we should perhaps know whether movement is essential to matter, and whether matter is created or not; created or not, whether its diversity is not more of an offence to reason than its simplicity: for it is perhaps only by reason of our ignorance that its unity or homogeneity appears so difficult to reconcile with the variety of phenomena.[155]

In this strange and rather moving passage in which Diderot recognizes that the properties of the universe which he has so purposefully insisted upon may ultimately be invalidated by the very type of research he favoured, we see the ultimate paradox of Diderot's view of the universe. Total knowledge of this kind, it seems, would bring total power, the omniscience and omnipotence of God, and yet such knowledge is only attainable in a state of total detachment, total uninvolvement, a state in which we are unmoved by what we see around us. The idea was already with him a quarter of a century before, when he wrote in *De l'Interprétation de la Nature*:

We are often taken aback because we suppose the existence of several marvels where there is only one; because we imagine that there are in nature as many single acts as there are phenomena, whereas she perhaps only ever performed a single act.[156]

It is a grandiose notion, and yet a frightening one in that it would enable us to see the complete determinism which governs the universe, and, on another level, would enable the possessor of such knowledge to make it all a part of himself. But in Diderot's thought such knowledge would be without power, because of the particular role of the 'centre of the network'. The organ, although brought into being by the fact of sensibility, and dependent on it for its existence, has as its proper function to invalidate it. When the system is under the dominance of the centre, the factors of disorder in all our contact with the external world are filtered out. The stimuli are registered, as we have seen, in a kind of geometrical form, in an accurate but innocuous representation of themselves. The sensibility which brought them into our consciousness is neutralized, and the continuity which characterizes any meaningful perception of reality is deprived, so to speak, of its active life; it remains purely conceptual. There is no 'surprise',[157] because true perception is only possible 'in the silence of the passions',[158] so that when d'Alembert says: 'Once I have seen inert matter change into something sensitive, nothing else need surprise me...',[159] the emphasis is not so much on the existence of sensibility in matter as on the fact that d'Alembert has seen it, has understood it. To perceive something, to annex it with one's reason, is indeed a form of action and may, in Diderot's philosophy, be regarded as marking the limits of ordered action. As soon as the sensibility comes back into play under the influence of passions, sickness and so on, we are back in a world of localized and disordered action in which phenomena are isolated and merely contiguous.

Although Diderot cherishes the ideal of a man who would achieve perfect action through perfect detachment from himself as a 'sensitive being',[160] such an ideal is impossible of realization. The total power which might come from perfect knowledge, and the salvation deriving from it, are destined to remain purely conceptual, perpetually 'en puissance'.

At the start of this long discussion of the role of sensibility in Diderot's thought I pointed out that Diderot did not seem fully convinced that sensibility did in fact inform all matter. But perhaps this is not important. For him the concept of sensibility is primarily a way of looking at things. He was in search of a principle which would link the two worlds of thought and matter, a principle which combined the essential features of both, and in the notion of universal sensibility he found it. It is not an explanation which stands up to scientific examination so much as a device, a conceptual sanction for a monist universe. 'Its appeal is frankly in its convenience', says Crocker (*Diderot's Chaotic Order*, p. 28). But it must not be forgotten that Diderot's theory of sensibility could only take the form it did because he still saw the world in dualist terms, so that sensibility, far from eliminating dualism, as was Diderot's intention, simply reestablished it on a monist basis.

From a scientific point of view this no doubt constitutes a weakness; from every other point of view I think it is a strength. All thinkers and artists are part of their age, all of them see the reality about them in a way which to a later age will seem limited and to some extent alien. Even the genius cannot escape these limitations. In every age there are certain ideas which simply cannot be thought, and in the eighteenth century the notions of an absolute truth on the one hand and of an inherently imperfect reality on the other precluded the development both of evolutionary concepts and of scientific objectivity as we know them. But if a genius cannot escape the epistemological limits of his age, he can obscurely sense the tensions and contradictions which they impose, seeing as the paradox of life itself what a later age may identify as a partial blindness in the observer. In his response to these tensions the genius creates ideas which will lay the foundation for the thought of his successors, ideas which, from their point of view, would appear modern, but which, for all that, belong inescapably to the age which engendered them.

In the next two parts of this study I shall examine various aspects of Diderot's theoretical and fictional writings as the response of one eighteenth-century thinker to the problem of his age. I shall try to show how the theory produced a necessarily limited but generally coherent and certainly brilliant solution to specific problems, and how the best fictional works, from an intuitive recognition of those limitations, produced a distinctive kind of artistic achievement.

II
SYSTEMS OF ORDER

3

THE CONCEPT OF 'FULLNESS'

In the introduction to this study the point was made that in the thought of the seventeenth and eighteenth centuries there was a tendency to mark out circumscribed areas in which the reason could operate effectively. The tendency was seen both as a means of examining particular areas of experience and, on a practical level, of delimiting areas in which rational activity was possible. A link was indicated between this tendency and the concept of a *plenum*, an area of fullness, where the operation of reason was not disturbed by inexplicable gaps in the system. It is now time to examine this notion more thoroughly, since it is essential to the understanding not only of Diderot but of the whole background of thought, especially French thought, which pervades his approach to problems.

I say especially French thought, because this particular aspect of Cartesianism, the 'plein', seems to have had a hold on French thought which it never had across the channel. On this level at least, Newton's ideas found it much harder to make any headway against earlier scientific theories than they did for example in his own country. As Voltaire puts it at the beginning of the fourteenth *Lettre Philosophique*: 'A Frenchman arriving in London finds things very different, in philosophy as in everything else. He has left behind a full world; he finds an empty one'.[1] It should be added straightaway that the belief in a physical *plenum* was far from being universal in France; in fact the subject was hotly disputed; but underlying the purely scientific notion of the *plenum* there seems to have existed in much of French thought an attitude which, on a deeper level, abhorred a vacuum. It is an attitude which corresponds more to a pattern of thinking than to any clearly defined theory, and it is in this pattern of thought that Cartesianism seems to have been a powerful force in eighteenth-century France, despite widespread opposition to Descartes on various specific points in his philosophy, such as, of course, the two substances, and indeed the *plenum* itself, insofar as it concerns matter and extension.

69

It should be stressed that in this study the word 'Cartesian' is used as a familiar term to identify a certain philosophical attitude, a conceptual structure. It is not intended to imply that Diderot was necessarily influenced by Descartes in arriving at his conclusions. Enough has, I hope, already been said to show that I am trying to identify assumptions which pervade the unconscious thinking of a whole period and culture, and which, in this case, no doubt led Descartes to think in the way he did as much as they do Diderot. This being said, a convincing argument for the continuity of thought between Descartes and Diderot has been made by Aram Vartanian (*Diderot and Descartes*), and one valuable point he makes is that the *physical* world of Descartes is self-contained, not in the sense of being finite – which it is not – but in the sense that, once set in motion, it is independent of divine intervention – a claim which cannot be made for the cosmological system of Newton. For Descartes, matter and extension are identical. The system is associated with concepts like impulsion, resistance, impact, rather than with attraction. Diderot does not deny attraction, but it does not form an essential part of his philosophy. His uneasiness on the subject is conveyed in the *Observation* at the end of the *Interprétation de la Nature*,[2] and also in the *Éléments de Physiologie*,[3] when he lists the properties of matter which he thinks will eventually be scientifically established (including sensibility), and adds: 'I should have added attraction if it were not perhaps a consequence of movement and force.'[4] Much more important for him, as for Descartes, is the fact that matter automatically expands into any space available for it; everything in the universe touches something else. Diderot, we know, attaches immense importance to contiguity; and he talks of matter being held in check, of expanding, or exploding when obstacles are removed, as in his conversation with d'Alembert in the *Rêve*:

Take away the obstacle resisting that particular movement of the motionless body and it will move. If by a sudden rarefaction you take away the air surrounding the trunk of that huge oak, the water it contains will suddenly expand and blow it into a hundred thousand splinters. And I say the same thing about your own body.[5]

One of the key things about movement for Diderot is the distinction between potential and active energy. Moreover he believes, like Descartes, and unlike Newton, that the quantity of energy in the universe is constant (*Principes Philosophiques sur la matière et le mouvement*)[6]. We have seen that this idea of potential and actual movement leads him into that of 'inert sensibility'[7] and 'active sensibility',[8] enabling him to effect the identification of thought and extension and making a single system of the whole creation. On a deeper level Diderot's attitude seems to be that in any system, any whole – the universe, the world of sentient nature, society, man – the individual elements – molecules, creatures, members of society, individual organs – are constantly acting upon one another, are competitive, potentially hostile even, and although Diderot in the *Principes*[9] differs from the Cartesians on the question whether movement is or is not a property of matter, the key point is that these elements are in contact. It is not merely that 'the molecule, endowed with a quality proper to its nature, is of itself an active force',[10] which is anti-Cartesian, but that 'it acts on another molecule which in its turn acts on it'.[11]

All the same, the *Principes* are primarily intended to prove the non-Cartesian point that movement is inherent in matter, and although there is the same emphasis in it as we find in the *Rêve* and the *Éléments de Physiologie* on the way in which the elements are in a constant state of movement, jostling each other about, the main concern is with change, transformation, fermentation. But Diderot's ideas on contiguity and the essential 'fullness' of systems are more readily found in his thoughts on politics and scientific method. When he is talking about societies Diderot stresses the fact that their members are potentially hostile, trying to usurp each other's rights, to encroach as it were on the space which each member rightfully occupies. His view, as expressed in the Letter to Landois[12] and in the *Encyclopédie* article 'Modification', that men in society are not free but modifiable by example, punishment and so on, in other words by external pressures, seems to suppose a state of fullness, one in which there is no room for free individual movement, in fact; it is clear in both of these documents how the concept of fullness is linked with determinism, with the action upon us of causes external to ourselves. Diderot writes in his letter to Landois:

It is just as impossible to imagine a being acting without motive as one of the arms of a scale without the action of a weight, and the motive is always outside us, extraneous, linked to us by some nature or cause which is not ourselves ... There is only one kind of cause, properly speaking, the physical cause.[13]

And in the article 'Modification', having stated that 'man, whether free or not, is modifiable',[14] he goes on: 'there is no cause which does not have its effect; there is no effect which does not modify the thing on which the cause acts. There is not an atom in nature which is not subject to the influence of an infinite number of diverse causes'.

As so often with Diderot, the notion of a nexus of cause and effect is associated with diversity, complexity; and so it is in the *Rêve*, when d'Alembert in his dream takes up the same theme: 'all nature is in a perpetual state of flux ... there is nothing clearly defined in nature',[16] he says, but he is led on from this, via the concept of heterogeneity – 'Is there in nature any one atom exactly similar to another?'[17] – to the point that 'everything is bound up with everything else'[18] and that 'there cannot be a gap in the chain',[19] finally making this most extreme affirmation of the oneness of nature: 'there is but one great individual and that is the whole'.[20] Diderot seems to envisage the fullness of nature from two angles: one is that nature is a complete entity, a system in a physical sense; the other is that in a system of rigorous cause and effect there can be no gaps, no 'gap in the chain'.[21] Both ways of looking at the problem are logically linked, of course; it is really a question of emphasis. When Diderot the visionary is talking, then the stress is on nature as a whole, as a great mass in constant fermentation. When Diderot the scientist speaks, then we are made more aware of the logic of it all, of 'this general chain, which philosophy supposes to be continuous';[22] of the task of the philosopher: 'amongst the known phenomena which we relate to one of these causes, how many intermediate phenomena must be found to provide the links, fill the gaps and prove identity?'[23] Now such remarks as these suggest that for Diderot, and in general for the partisans of monist determinism, the *plenum* is not so much a matter of physics as a conceptual necessity, and nowhere is this more clearly expressed than in the *Essai sur les Règnes de Claude et de Néron*, when he speaks of the importance of observation:

It is by this means, and this means alone, that the gap which separates phenomena will gradually be filled by interposed phenomena; that a continuous chain of them will emerge, and they will explain each other by touching each other, and most of those which appear to us so different will take on the same identity.[24]

The recurrence of the word 'chain' throughout Diderot's comments on the natural world inevitably suggests an association with the great chain of being, 'la chaîne des êtres', that idea which, as A. O. Lovejoy made clear in his brilliant series of lectures (*The Great Chain of Being*), haunted Western thought in various forms from antiquity onwards. It haunted Diderot too, and yet although some idea of a hierarchy persists, the emphasis, in the speech just quoted from d'Alembert in the *Rêve*, that is, for Diderot the vision-ary, is on continuity; and in the *Éléments de Physiologie*, for Diderot the scientist, on contiguity. He has a special section[25] on 'Contiguity of the vegetable kingdom and the animal kingdom',[26] and earlier on insists that 'the chain of being is not broken by the variety of forms. The form of a thing is often nothing but a deceitful mask, and the link which appears to be missing perhaps exists in a being already known to us, to which advances in comparative anatomy have not yet succeeded in assigning its true place.'[27] We seem to be faced not so much with the traditional vertical hierarchy as with an area of knowledge laid out before us, awaiting total com-prehension, completion, creation even, by man, who henceforth forms not an intermediate link, but the highest one, the final link in a chain which will terminate in his own understanding.†

The passage from *Claude et Néron* throws further light on this attitude; it continues:

Each cause will gather round it a great retinue of effects; these systems, isolated at first, will merge into one another as they expand; and out of a number of causes there will remain only one which will sooner or later be reduced to an effect. Progress in physics consists in reducing the number of causes by increasing the number of effects.[28]

A question from the same passage indicates what is Diderot's final hope: 'Are the limits of the world within the reach of our tele-scopes?'[29] – the possibility that ultimately we might have before us the total picture. But the answer does not just lie with telescopes, with aids to observation, for observation is only a step towards in-terpretation. This is already recognized in the *Interprétation de la Nature*: 'If we were simply to judge by the empty speculations of philosophy and the faint light of our own reason, we should think that the chain of causes has had no beginning and that of effects will have no end.'[30] Those who are disturbed by the apparently infinite quantity of insignificant causes and effects tend to reject the idea 'because of the prejudice that nothing happens beyond the reach of our senses, and that everything stops happening where we can no longer see it'.[31]

† A rather different emphasis on the Chain of Being and 'fullness' is made by Pope, but with the same equation of fullness and coherence.

> Of Systems possible, if 'tis confest
> That Wisdom infinite must form the best,
> Where all must full or not coherent be,
> There must be, somewhere, such a rank as Man.
> (*Essay on Man*, i, 42)

But the interpreter of nature has a different approach from that of the mere observer: 'he conjectures from what is to what must be; he draws from the order of things abstract and general conclusions which for him have all the evidence of palpable and particular truths; he builds up to the very essence of order'.[32] This passage, as well as any, puts into perspective Diderot's view of the role of observation; it is a step towards the construction of a valid, reasonable picture of reality; this picture is ultimately based not on facts but on *vraisemblance*, likelihood, and this process allows the philosopher to set limits to his enquiry. His picture does not fade off into uncertainty at the edges, but is limited within the firm framework of what is known and what can be induced from that knowledge:

he sees that the *pure and simple* (Diderot's italics) coexistence of a sensitive thinking being with some chain of cause and effect does not suffice to make an absolute judgment about it; he stops there; if he went one step further he would overstep the bounds of nature.[33]

Pending the time when the whole of nature can be reduced to a single system, we can only attack the problem piecemeal, reducing individual areas to order until 'these systems, isolated at first, will merge into one another'.[34] It is all reminiscent of a military operation, or a process of colonization. In the *Interprétation de la Nature*, he says, 'I imagine the vast precinct of the sciences as a huge territory dotted with dark places and lighted places. The purpose of our work must be either to extend the limits of the lighted places or to increase the sources of light in the territory.'[35] One feels that the vision which inspired the apostles of reason in the eighteenth century was not unlike that which must have motivated the explorers and missionaries of the nineteenth.

When Diderot in the *Interprétation* discusses the process by which reason, starting from various points of illumination, moves step by step to annex the whole system of nature, he presumably has in mind a series of scientific problems, ones which can be dealt with by the processes of active perception already discussed, but it is also clear from Diderot's writings that nature itself is characterized by the constant creation of systems, of organisms which only differ from the systems created by our reason in that, on the face of it, they have a limited life, starting as a mere point, annexing matter to themselves until they reach their highest level of organization, and then gradually disintegrating. This process by which a circumscribed system comes into being is described in the *Encyclopédie* article 'Naître':

our life exists in a point which expands up to a certain limit, beneath which life is circumscribed in every direction; this space beneath which we live gradually diminishes; life becomes less active beneath every point of this space; there are even points beneath which it has lost all its activity before the dissolution of the whole mass takes place, and finally we go on living in an infinite number of isolated atoms.[36]

This is the natural cyclical process which Diderot appears to have held to throughout his life, and one which applies not merely to natural organisms, but also has a parallel, which will be mentioned again later, in his conception of the way societies come into being and decay. But with societies, as with scientific systems, the ideal is that, once established, they should become static, resisting the processes of decay which we associate with natural organisms.

I have already suggested that one of the essential but no doubt unintended characteristics of an ordered organism in Diderot's scientific theory is that there is no apparent means by which it can move into ordered activity. It seems to be a purely conceptual notion. Now one of the objections made by some of the eighteenth-century critics of the *plenum* was that it would precisely make movement completely, or else almost completely, impossible. This point is made in various articles in the *Encyclopédie* itself (e.g. 'Création'; 'Matière'; 'Vide'). In 'Création', Formey argues:

If matter is infinite and has a necessary existence, all these changes of position and combinations, the natural effects of movement, will become impossible: the reason being that each part of matter will necessarily have its existence in the part of space which it occupies. It will not be chance which will have set it there rather than anywhere else, nor in the neighbourhood of some parts rather than others: the same reason which makes its existence necessary also causes it to exist in one place rather than another.[37]

What he seems to be saying is that any physical system which excludes the operation of chance also eliminates the possibility of movement. Arguments against the *plenum* crop up in various forms throughout the *Encyclopédie*, not to speak of other works, and it would be pointless to discuss them in full, since Diderot himself never tackled the problem seriously on a strictly scientific level. He may even have preferred to avoid it, as the 'Observation' at the end of the *Interprétation* indicates,[38] perhaps suspecting that his own position would collapse at this level of investigation, or at least that the strict implications of the *plenum* were repugnant to his inmost ways of looking at life. For while he seems to see the whole of nature, at least on a conceptual level, as a *plenum*, when it comes to limited systems, existing separately from the total picture, they seem to be self-contained *plena*, outside of which is a world of isolated and apparently freely moving, not necessarily contiguous phenomena. Outside these systems, chance operates, and it is as though – to put it simply – chance can only operate in empty spaces.

This is in any case how things will look to the researcher who has succeeded in understanding a limited area of the workings of the universe, but to whom the area beyond this remains a mystery. His 'system' will be rational, circumscribed, without gaps; beyond it will be an area in which phenomena appear to be unconnected, obeying no recognizable laws. Nothing shows more clearly the near-identity in Diderot's mind – and perhaps in the thinking of the period in general – between the processes of understanding reality and the processes of reality itself than the fact that he saw the growth of knowledge in the same terms as he saw the formation of systems and organisms in the external world. Just as the mind of the seeker after knowledge starts out from a point of apparent clarity and progressively accumulates more information, using its judgment to assess whether such information fits into the picture until an organized system emerges, so the human body accumulates round a point, like 'this rare seed',[39] the beginnings of d'Alembert as described by Diderot in the *Entretien*,[40] which grew out of molecules originally 'scattered'[41] in the bodies of his irresponsible parents, 'growing by stages'[42] until it becomes the 'writer, physicist and mathematician',[43] which Diderot now has before him. But as becomes clear later on in the *Rêve*, d'Alembert, or anyone else, is only a perfect system when his judgment is in exactly the right relationship of control with the rest of his body, and this relationship implies a state of immobility. The human system is not only doomed ultimately to disintegration by the natural processes of time, it also threatens to lose its status as a separate, efficient unity every time the passions or senses become active.

The conclusion one might draw is that the 'perfect' systems and organisms conceived in Diderot's mind are not thought of as existing in the practical world of reality but are imagined as supports for the judgment, as conceptual yardsticks by which the world of actual people and events can be assessed. Certainly one has the impression that the eighteenth century in general tended to create systems of ethics which were incapable of generating moral behaviour and aesthetic theories powerless to produce beauty; their purpose was simply to facilitate judgment. Such theories – and certainly this can be said of Diderot's – cannot be described as prescriptive, since they cannot tell us what to do, how to act; nor can they be classified as descriptive, since they do not describe an actual state of affairs. The only appropriate word seems to be normative. In fact there is in this kind of thinking, this view of the world, a difference of nature between judgment and action which it is impossible to reconcile. Judgment presupposes a set of conditions which exist in a viable relationship with one another; action, movement, automatically upsets that relationship, whether in reality or thought or art. It would seem that Diderot falls into the same error as those believers in the homogeneity of matter whom he criticizes in a passage already quoted from the *Pensées Philosophiques sur la Matière et le Mouvement*:

they are considering it to be unchangeable at the almost indivisible moment when they contemplate it; they are arguing from the relative state of rest of one aggregate to another aggregate; they are forgetting that, while they are arguing from the indifference of the body to movement or rest, the block of marble is already in the process of dissolution.[44]

Well, Diderot does not forget about the block of marble; nor does he proceed from the same premises as those whom he takes to task; what does happen is that he is forced to recreate conceptually what the partisans of homogeneity take to be a fact; to make ordered perception possible he must assume conditions which he denies in fact.

Given this gap between the conditions necessary for perception and judgment, and the conditions obtaining in the real world of movement, there results on one level a system, or set of systems, which are in perfect equilibrium, like his perfectly healthy man whose judgment operates with complete efficiency while the senses and passions are in a state as it were of suspended animation, or his 'ideal model',[45] which will be discussed more fully in connection with his aesthetic ideas; these are the systems which act as criteria for judgment, as a means of assessing the movements of the real world. On another level, which cannot be sharply distinguished from the former, we find a set of closed systems, like the human being again, or an area of acquired and systematized knowledge, surrounded by a field of disorder; *plena*, areas of fullness, surrounded by what one can only call areas of lesser fullness. This type of system, whether based on a natural system, as in the case of the human body, or founded on a set of laws perceived in a number of phenomena, is constantly threatened by change from within or without. 'There are two kinds of sickness. One is produced by an extraneous cause which brings disorder, the other by too vigorous an organ which upsets the functioning of the machine'.[46] The same kind of influence seems to threaten the hypotheses of the scientist, as described in Sections XLII to XLVII of the *Interprétation*. Either they can be invalidated on closer examination by an illogicality within them, or else they have to be reorientated because of the observation of some new phenomenon. From being ordered systems they become monsters, as defined in the *Éléments de Physiologie*: 'a being whose continuance is incompatible with the existing order'.[47]

What goes before is an attempt to describe the pattern underlying Diderot's thinking about order. It is necessarily imprecise, lacking clear categorization, because this is the nature of Diderot's own thought. One cannot say that his thinking was confused, only that confusion, or contradiction and paradox, inevitably arose because of his wide-ranging efforts to reconcile the conditions for judgment with the intractable phenomena of the world about him, the stability necessary for perception with the movement inherent in reality. The dominant notion which emerges from this examination is that reality, and our understanding of reality, are processes by which isolated phenomena come together to form more or less viable entities. So far the process has been discussed mainly in connection with the formation of organisms and conceptual systems. A parallel process is evident in Diderot's conception of society, both with regard to its origins and its viability.

4

A POLITICAL SYSTEM

Society: its formation and tendency to disintegration

Diderot's ideas about the state of nature and the formation of societies have been thoroughly examined by Jacques Proust (*Diderot et l'Encyclopédie*, Ch. XI), at least as far as his earlier thinking is concerned. For Proust, Diderot's theory is in direct opposition to those of Hobbes: 'The thesis of natural sociability, which he has so often and so insistently made his own, totally precludes the war of all against all' (p. 419),[48] for while Diderot admits a state of anarchy and mutual hostility as a stage in the development of societies, it is an intermediate one, between the essentially peaceful state of nature and the later 'état policé', the civilized state, whereas of course Hobbes's state of war is the initial and natural condition of man. There is no denying this difference between Hobbes and Diderot, but to establish too sharp an opposition between the two tends, I think, to distort the nature of Diderot's own ideas and to obscure analogies which do exist between the two thinkers. One of Diderot's best known descriptions of the original coming together of men to form societies is in Section XXVIII of the *Mémoires pour Catherine II*, and here we find a scheme which corresponds quite closely to that described in the preceding pages of this study:

In the so-called pure state of nature, men were scattered across the face of the earth like an infinite number of small, isolated forces. Now and then some of these small forces would happen to meet, collide too heavily and break. The lawgivers, witnessing these accidents, sought a remedy for them, and what did they imagine? To bring the small forces together and to construct a fine machine out of them which they called society.[49]

A slightly fanciful picture perhaps – who were these lawgivers wandering about in the state of nature? – but apart from that it is the same picture of a kind of *plenum* being formed out of a number of isolated units, previously free to move about at random, 'scattered across the face of the earth'.[50] Diderot even sees a parallel process operating in the formation of what he probably regarded as the highest form of society known to man:

What is an academy? A body of scholars which comes into being by itself, just as human society came into being, the latter in order to struggle more advantageously against nature, the former from the same instinct or the same need: the acknowledged advantage of combining one's efforts against ignorance.[51]

The later stages in the development of civilization are, as one might expect, more complex, or at least more subject to conflict and disorder than the formation of an organism, though not necessarily of a system of ideas. In his views on the motivation which drives men together Diderot follows Montesquieu, and the best expression of the parallel comes in the article 'Besoin'.[52] In this article we first see man 'created and cast into this universe as it were by chance',[53] feeling first hunger and then other needs which lead him to draw closer to his fellows, and while the initial experience of fear may encourage men to avoid each other, the more generalized awareness of fear brings them together. But out of this coming together there does not immediately arise an efficient organism: on the contrary, 'the state of war begins',[54] society makes it easier for men's basic needs to be satisfied, but also creates more complex ones, 'and perhaps makes them more unhappy together than they would have been apart'.[55] This is a version of the fairly common view that society, as it grows more complex, develops in man a greater potential for evil as well as good, greater possibilities for disorder as well as order.

The *Mémoires pour Catherine II* contain a fuller, but broadly similar account of the formation of societies to that given in 'Besoin'. Here Diderot sees the union of men against the common enemy as a very early development. 'This enemy is nature and man's struggle against nature is the first principle of society'.†[56] And the description of the result of this formation also runs on the same lines, except that the account shows a closer analogy to Diderot's general ideas on the movement of matter:

in that fine machine society, the little forces, inspired by endless different and contrary interests, acted and reacted against one another with all their might, and for one moment of accidental war there resulted a veritable state of permanent war in which all the little forces, weakened and exhausted, did nothing but cry out, and more of them got broken in one year than

† 'Nature' here of course is used in a specific sense to mean the phenomena which threaten survival: wild animals, climatic conditions and so on; but this is only one aspect of nature considered in its broader sense as that which obeys the laws of movement, and which, as such, is a threat to man's existence as a rational being.

would have broken in ten, in the original isolated state in which the only law was that a collision would be felt.[57]

Here we have a kind of organism in a state of disorder, functioning in accordance with the laws of cause and effect, it is true, just as the whole universe does, but not in a way which is satisfying to reason.

At this point it is worth stressing what has already been touched on in earlier pages: that the mere recognition that the universe as a whole, or any system within it, obeys comprehensible laws is not a cause for satisfaction, or a recognition of order; rather the opposite. Order lies in control, and determinism is a threat to that control. Diderot's ideal of an ordered personality is an attempt to annex the processes of nature in order to recreate an organism which is in control of itself, to construct, so to speak, a man-made man. It is not surprising to find the same ways of thinking in operation when he deals with the state. Here too, Diderot the observer and Diderot the theorist and reformer work along parallel lines; as already indicated, the processes of normative thinking are directly analogous to the analysis and interpretation of what actually happens.

Two points need to be borne in mind when we examine Diderot's political thought. The first, in connection with what has just been said, is that eighteenth-century thinkers would not be inclined, as we are now, to see a sharp distinction between man as a natural creation and the state as an artificial one. Their political thinking was largely motivated by a rejection of the theory of divine right and the underlying assumption that the state is God-given, an imperfect approximation to the divine or 'natural' purpose. The idea that the state should be created by men for men is of the same order as the notion that individual man should be able to control his own destiny. The implicit denial of original sin and the explicit rejection of divine right are complementary, each a necessary consequence of the other.

The second point is that one of Diderot's dominant concerns in politics, as in so many other areas of his thinking, is with potential disorder: the fact that any organism is initially formed from elements which tend to disorder, and, however highly it evolves, will constantly threaten to revert to it. Allusions to the initial state of mutual hostility in any society are frequent. For example in the article 'Grecs', Diderot tells us that the early Greeks had much of what we associate with civilization, but no overall leader, no conventions, so that 'if they were restrained, it was not so much by public authority as by the fear of individual revenge';[58] for without laws 'tumult reigns, and, with tumult, crime; and it would be better for men's security for them to be scattered than to be free and together'.[59] In his *Apologie de l'Abbé de Prades*[60] a similar picture emerges: 'Now men are in proximity to one another, more in a herd than a society [an important distinction for Diderot, as for Rousseau], by the attraction of their own advantage, and by the recognition of their own similarity';[61] and the result, since there are no laws, is that 'all being inspired by violent passions, all seeking to appropriate to themselves the common advantages of union, according to the talents, strength, cunning, etc., which nature has distributed amongst them in unequal measure, the weak will be the victims of the strong'.[62] Whatever happens, inequality will destroy 'the beginnings of a bond which their own advantage and their outward similarity had suggested for their mutual preservation'.[63]

This recurrence of the idea of the inevitable hostility of men living together and of the chaos which results surely shows a closer analogy with Hobbes than Proust suggests, and while it would be difficult, and in any case outside the terms of reference of this study, to assess the direct influence of Hobbes on Diderot's thought, it seems likely that the Englishman's ideas had a certain affinity with the greater French awareness of the precarious nature of government, the dangers of tyranny at one end of the scale and of mob violence at the other. The fear of public disorder, so real during the Wars of Religion and the Fronde, recurring during periods of weak government, or economic disturbances, seems to haunt the French mind throughout the seventeenth and eighteenth centuries, and must have been a powerful force in shaping Diderot's own thought where politics was concerned. One of the purposes of the Commission listed in the *Mémoires pour Catherine II* is:

To protect against those tumultuous times when there are regencies and minorities, times when the minister is weak and destructive, when everyone listens to his own interest at the expense of the nation's; when it is important to have a body representative of sovereignty, not to bring about destruction, but to prevent it; when, as we know from experience, without a legislative power which can stand up to the depositaries of sovereignty, a structure built over many centuries can collapse.[64]

In another passage from the *Mémoires* he sees a parallel between the deep sense of political insecurity which characterizes the Russians and that which exists in France.

There is a suggestion of panic in people's minds: it seems to be the result of a long succession of revolutions and a long period of despotism. They behave all the time as though an earthquake were about to strike or had just struck, and they seem to be wondering whether the earth has really settled beneath their feet ... I am sure that we felt the same as the Russians after the Ligue, after the deaths of Henri III and Henri IV, and after the Fronde. And I well remember that after the events of the eve of Twelfth Night [he is referring to the attempted assassination of Louis XV by Damiens in 1757] we all had a look of alarm, as if a comet were about to descend upon our globe.[65]

It is impossible to understand political thinking in France at this time without realizing how much the whole structure of the state was felt to depend on the simple physical existence of one person, of the sovereign as a guarantor of order.

When Diderot writes of civil disorder he is not always referring to the extreme form of it which follows on the loss of the sovereign. His *Apologie de l'Abbé Galiani* of 1770 is partly an appeal for realism in the recognition of the disorder which can occur during grain shortages:

you have not the first idea of what happens in times of shortage ... There is a tumultuous conflict of fear, greed and cupidity. Some want four times as much as they need for the moment because they do not know what tomorrow will bring; some make away with it or buy it at any price; others close their granaries and wait for a higher price.[66]

The most cherished values of the time, certainly of Diderot himself, collapse in the face of tyranny, or *raison d'état*:

the sacred rights of property are unfortunately, if you want to know my opinion, nothing but visionary nonsense. Is there any sacred right when it comes to public affairs or general utility, whether real or pretended? I am made to carry a musket, my liberty is removed, I am shut away on a mere suspicion, my field is cut in half, my house knocked down. I am ruined by being forced to move, my harvest is left to the animals, my purse is emptied by a ridiculous tax, my life and fortune are put at risk for a crazy war. Put all your fine ideas into a utopia, they will look well there.[67]

In *Diderot's Politics* Strugnell stresses the increasing realism in the development of his political ideas and quotes *L'Apologie de l'Abbé Galiani* as an early example of this. It is true that Diderot's political works show a growing concern with the realities of human behaviour, but it can also be said that these disenchanted views of individual and governmental conduct spring, despite occasional assertions to the contrary, from a basic disbelief in man's ability to see what is good for him. 'Who has any precise idea of what public utility is?'[68] he asks, in the *Salon* of 1767,

It is such a complicated idea, depending on so much experience and so much insight, that even philosophers argued amongst themselves about it ... Ignorance and self-interest, which cloud everything in the human mind, will show the general interest to be where it is not. Everyone having his own idea of virtue, men's lives will be filled with crimes. The people, tossed this way and that by their passions and their delusions, will have no moral standards: for moral standards exist only when the laws, good or bad, are sacred; for only then is there uniformity in general behaviour.[69]

Once again, the diversity, the heterogeneity of men makes order impossible without some superior authority to dictate what the law should be. Even if a man does not act from motives of immediate self-interest, his views will be affected by ignorance, or at least by a different conception from the next man's of what is right.

Diderot makes more or less the same point in his *Observations sur le Nakaz*, where he discounts the validity of evidence as a 'contreforce', a counterbalance, against the arbitrary power of the sovereign. Only a twentieth part of a nation has any enlightenment, and this is in any case ineffectual, for 'the evidence does nothing to prevent the free play of self-interest or the passions; a disorganized trader sees quite well that he is ruining himself, but ruins himself nonetheless. A sovereign will be aware that he is exercising tyranny, either personally or through his ministers, but he will go on exercising tyranny. Was it evidence that was lacking in France during the preceding reign?'[70]

There is no place either in Diderot's political philosophy for Rousseau's compassion, the quality which, coupled with the instinct for self-preservation, was innate in every human being. The nearest approach in Diderot's thought to this notion of a quality which makes us feel other men's suffering in ourselves is that aspect of sensibility which leads us to identify ourselves with others' emotions, and for him this is at best an unreliable factor, as productive of disorder as of order. The simple coexistence of men in society merely multiplies the dangers which are inherent in the senses and passions of the individual.

But however much the theories of Diderot, Rousseau and the other eighteenth-century thinkers differed on the nature of man, and however much these views represent a new departure on anything comparable in the seventeenth century, there is a more striking consensus between individual thinkers, and between the two centuries, where the actual defects of society are concerned. This is perhaps not surprising, since the structure of the *Ancien Régime* was much the same in the early seventeenth century as it was on the eve of the Revolution, and not only the structure but the tensions and abuses associated with it seem to have remained very much the same. For example, the disparity between 'être' and 'paraître', reality and appearance, so regularly stigmatized by seventeenth-century writers, reappears in Rousseau's *Discours sur l'Inégalité* as a key factor in the deterioration of society: 'Reality and appearance became two completely different things, and from this distinction there emerged imposing pomp, deceitful cunning and all the vices which come in their train...'[71] With this he associates a chaotic state of social mobility and tension: 'consuming ambition, the urge to elevate one's fortune in relation to others ... on the one hand competition and rivalry, on the other opposition of interests'.[72] This could as well have come from the pen of a seventeenth-century writer as could Diderot's impassioned condemnation of that supreme sanction of 'the urge to elevate one's fortune in relation to others',[73] the venality of office.

As soon as a handful of public embezzlers began to overflow with riches, live in palaces and parade their shameful opulence, all social conditions became merged together; there arose a fatal rivalry, a senseless, cruel struggle amongst all the orders of society. A curse on him who first made public office venal ... a curse on him who created the seed-bed from which grew this epidemic desire to flaunt one's fortune ... a curse on him who as a consequence condemned merit to obscurity and enveloped virtue and good behaviour in contempt.[74]

These passages described a kind of society with which we are now much more familiar and reconciled than Rousseau and Diderot were: the competitive society. They saw it as something evil and disruptive because it threatened the accepted structure of society as an ideally static organism in which each man has his proper place. The gradual dissolution of this structure, or at least of the belief in its relevance, released not only the possibility of individual and collective action and achievement, but also an awareness of the world around one as a potential obstacle to that achievement, and the obstacles and unpredictable factors which threatened rational activity were not merely the abuses in the social structure, but simply other people. This is surely the attitude which draws Rousseau, Diderot and Hobbes together.

In *Rousseau, La Transparence et l'Obstacle*,[75] Starobinski says that although Rousseau does not, any more than Diderot, follow Hobbes in positing a state of war as the earliest stage in man's development, he does assume that a state of war occurs at a later point. Both assume that human beings, assembled together in a circumscribed area, will naturally tend to conflict with one another, but whereas Rousseau's solution in the *Contrat Social* seems to offer men the possibility of being tied to the state but isolated from one another, salvation for Diderot lies in togetherness. In the important section of the *Mémoires pour Catherine II*, 'De La Capitale', he says:

everything which has the effect of isolating man from man also has the effect of weakening the struggle against nature and bringing man nearer to his original state of savagery; and must therefore be regarded as an evil.[76]

This is the point of course where his thought differs most markedly from Rousseau, but it is very typical of his own thinking, firstly because he sees the answer to the problem in the same terms, the same form even, as the problem itself, that is, that the evil which has arisen because men have come together can only be remedied by keeping them together; secondly because he sees the ideal society as a kind of *plenum*.

The ideal state

He enlarges on this idea in the same section of the *Mémoires*. Men must first of all be united for the simple reason that only unity can enable them to fight their two great enemies, nature and other men,[77] but he pursues the idea further into a field which interests him much more; the internal organization of the state. Unity is a guarantee against the atomization of the state, its reduction to self-motivated individuals. 'What I say of large societies is borne out by the state of small ones when division is introduced into them; the general bond is broken, each man works for himself and the state of savagery is reborn.'[78] Furthermore, disunity among the people provides the right conditions for tyranny, which, Diderot says, 'desires individuals and not corporate bodies, nobles and not nobility ... subjects and not a nation; which is to say, by the most absurd of consequences, a society and men in isolation'.[79] For both Rousseau and Diderot a despotic society was a reversion to a more primitive stage in man's development, but whereas this stage is for Diderot the earliest – for the idea of men scattered over the surface of the earth as a series of isolated phenomena has no attraction for him – for Rousseau it is a later one, since his isolated man is the repository of innocence and freedom. What characterizes them both – and probably the age in general – is the double fear: of the excesses to which a strong central control is subject, tyranny and arbitrary rule; and of the anarchy and violence which ensue from a lack of it. At least as far as Diderot is concerned the antidote to both threats is the same: that the members of society should be united.

When we come to examine precisely what form this unity should take, we find that Diderot, as so often, is not very specific. He does not go into the kind of detail we find in the *Contrat Social*; no picture emerges of the complete ideal society. Instead, we get a combination of very general notions interspersed with a variety of apparently insignificant details. It is indeed what we should expect of Diderot, whose mind is not the sort to create coherent, all-embracing schemes, in politics, aesthetics or anything else, but we do become aware of certain themes and leitmotifs which keep cropping up and which can help us to disengage, not a coherent political philosophy, but an underlying set of preoccupations.

Perhaps the most striking of these is the importance which Diderot attached to the fact that people should not simply be together, but should actually live close together. This is an idea which comes up repeatedly in the *Mémoires pour Catherine II*. In section VII, on Saint Petersburg,[80] he asks: 'would it not be possible to populate Saint Petersburg more thickly, to make it more alive, more busy and commercially active by linking this multitude of isolated palaces together with private houses?'[81] For once Diderot is quite specific about how this should be done – it is a project dear to his heart. The new population would be made up of 'workers of all kinds, cartwrights, carpenters, masons, ropemakers, etc., just as it is in Paris'.[82] These artisans would be freed from their bondage to the 'grands seigneurs' in their country estates, and would eventually form a 'tiers état' which would have a civilizing effect: 'This closeness of men binds them together, their contact makes them more gentle and civilized; from these workshops will come all the fine arts, which will then be indigenous and lasting.'[83] The same solution could be applied to Germany:

Never will Germany be civilized or have poets, sculptors, painters, orators, great writers, a language without which nothing worthwhile can be done, polite manners, a kind of urbanity, etc., never, I say, until the imperial house has swallowed up the electorates.[84]

'Draw your subjects together', he insists, 'and by this one action you will have an Empire'.†[85]

The idea that dispersion is in itself a hindrance to the development of civilized values is perhaps not very original, but Diderot has more to say, for a few pages later, he comes back to the subject:

above all force the provinces right up against each other, the towns up against each other, the houses in the towns up against each other.

† It seems likely that this concern to bring people together, to fill up empty spaces, may be linked with the uneasiness about depopulation, as expressed in particular by Montesquieu.

I do not like men to be scattered about, I do not like palaces to be isolated, I like them to be linked by a large number of other private dwellings.[86]

Here a further idea is introduced, that of contiguity, each unit must touch its neighbour, the great palaces must be 'linked'[87] by a series of private dwellings. The reason for this is given in a metaphor based on the idea just mentioned of proximity as a condition of civilized values. 'When the corners of the stones touch, they become rounded and the stones are polished.'[88] Another metaphor is used in the next section of the *Mémoires* where the idea occurs, 'Faire des Rues', 'Making Streets'.[89] The life of savages, he says, is characterized by scattered dwellings, 'without order, sequence or contact';[90] and even if the dwellings were palaces, 'the image of a savage nation, greater and nobler, would still remain'.[91] This image will only be effaced when 'by linking these houses with others in between, the whole will remind me of a beehive'.[92] And in expanding this idea he recalls his theory of the original formation of societies: 'As long as your bees are scattered, you will not have much honey. When your bees are gathered together, they will defend themselves against the hornets.'[93] 'Making Streets'[94], in fact, consists in connecting all the palaces in the capital by means of intermediate dwellings, and when this is done, the next step should be: 'Circumscribe the capital. Give it a wall.'[95] In this way 'the bees will all go inside the wall, and gradually the cells of the hive will become contiguous'.[96]

The result is one of those visual, or spatial utopias dear to the eighteenth century where each element is organically linked to the next, and the whole clearly demarcated from the surrounding chaos: a monument of order and a delight to the reason. It is in effect nothing other than a circumscribed *plenum*.

In fact Diderot seems to have a similar plan in mind for the whole country.[97] The passage already quoted in which he speaks of drawing the towns and provinces close together[98] is complemented by a section on boundaries. Once men have acquired the only legitimate right to property, by their work, they will want to fence it in. Diderot approves of this natural tendency because it creates an attitude towards property.

What was the effect of this enclosure on his senses, his mind, his imagination? To accustom him to regarding himself as being at home within this enclosure, and as away from home outside his enclosure.[99]

In an ideal society, the boundary comes to be regarded as something sacred. So enthusiastic is he about this that he even discusses the form which these boundaries ought to take, and comes down in favour of light wooden fences. 'These barriers or light fences will soon have their original effect: to accustom the peasant to regard as his own all the space enclosed within these barriers which he has himself erected';[100] and another advantage will be that of putting an end to territorial disputes between landowners. The idea of the whole of Russia being divided up into portions of land with light wooden fences around them is perhaps somewhat Utopian, even if Diderot does admit that it would take time for people to get used to it, but it is more realistic, more based in physical realities than the 'fine paradox'[101] advanced in his comments on the *Temple du Bonheur* of 1769:

I am convinced that there cannot be any true happiness for the human race except in a social state where there would be neither king, nor magistrate, nor priest, nor laws, nor yours, nor mine, nor landed property, nor vices, nor virtues.[102]

But this, as he says, is 'damnably ideal',[103] a pipe-dream which presupposes a state of equal enlightenment amongst all citizens, whereas his proposal for Russia, recognizing the inevitable differences between people, gives them enough room to be themselves, but not enough for them to encroach on the individuality of others.

Another point which seems partially to contradict what Diderot says in his *Mémoires* appears in his *Apologie de l'Abbé Galiani*, written three years before. Here, while admitting that 'the right to property is sacred as between individuals, and if it is not sacred then society must disintegrate',[104] he sees the situation quite differently where the rights of individuals in relation to the state are concerned.

The opposite is the case where the individual's right is considered in relation to society. It is nothing, for if it were anything, nothing great or useful to society would be achieved. Because the property of a few private individuals would constantly conflict with the general purpose, it would result in its ruin, since the property rights of a few individuals would constantly conflict with the conditions of its wealth, strength and safety.[105]

This second point does not appear in Diderot's advice to Catherine II, but as so often with his various writings, we have to take into account the context in which he was considering the problem. In the *Apologie* he is concerned with the stability and viability of the state, and stability is ensured by firm control; the picture in the back of his mind is the chaos and violence which erupts during periods of grain shortage, the greatest single cause of civil disturbance in his time. In the *Mémoires* his main preoccupation is altogether different.

Catherine II represented for him, as for many others, the possibility not so much of a stable society as of a free one, and by free he meant one in which the rights of the individual were respected, and where the structure of the state would act as an effective counter-balance to the potential tyranny of its central authority.

This explains why Diderot in his writings on the future Russian political system should not have laid much emphasis on the need for power at the top; and it hardly needs to be added that he was dealing with a country where the Czars and the aristocracy had traditionally exercised far more arbitrary power than any French king, and where the mass of the people still lived in varying degrees of feudal bondage. It does not however explain why Diderot should attach so much importance to contiguity, and one reason for this lies in the account already given of Diderot's conception of a viable system. Such a system must be coherent, it must be rational; and a geographical area in which empty, unannexed or disputed places allow room for free arbitrary movement, for the operation of chance, is as repugnant to Diderot the political theorist as an area of knowledge imperfectly understood is offensive to Diderot the philosopher. This kind of freedom is anarchy; it is a freedom which must be eliminated for the sake of survival. But how does Diderot define the freedom with which he replaces it?

Liberty

Undoubtedly liberty is linked in Diderot's mind with the concept of property. In the section of the *Mémoires* entitled 'De La Commission et des Avantages de sa Permanence' he brings to Catherine II's notice 'that where there is no property there are no subjects; that where there are no subjects the empire is poor, and that where the sovereign power is unlimited there is no property'.[106] Some kind of balance is needed between the power of the subjects and that of the sovereign, and this balance is ensured by individual property. The most abject state is that of the slave: 'The soul of a slave is debased; he even neglects himself, since he is not his own property. He is a tenant who allows a house which does not belong to him to fall into decay.'[107] In every properly-run society there must be a guarantee of property. As he points out in the *Fragments échappés du Portefeuille d'un Philosophe*: 'everyone has his head and his property, a portion of the general wealth of which he is master, and absolute master, over which he is king, and which he can use and even abuse as he thinks fit'.[108] Another remark stresses the link between property and liberty: 'The nature of man and the notion of property combine to emancipate him, and liberty leads the individual and society to the greatest happiness they can desire.'[109] Property seems here to acquire a metaphysical dimension, symbolic of an area of man's being which is inalienably his own. The association of liberty and property is also pursued in the distinction Diderot makes between two kinds of happiness, the constant and the accidental (*Mémoires*). There is, he says, 'a constant happiness which depends on freedom, the safety of property, the nature of taxation, its distribution, its gathering and honours the eternal laws'.[110] The point is taken up again in the *Observations sur le Nakaz*, where Diderot, seeing Catherine's reluctance to recognize the principles underlying a free society, is even more insistent than in the *Mémoires*.

Where people are happy, they stay and multiply; and they are happy where liberty and property are sacred. Liberty and property are sacred where all are equally subject to the law and taxation, and where taxation is in proportion to the needs of society and to individual wealth; for the rest, nothing should be tampered with, everything will look after itself and is adequately protected.†[111]

At this point it will be useful to discuss and clarify the main ideas underlying Diderot's preoccupation with property. The point has been made that Diderot, as a comfortably-off bourgeois, and as a leading light in a primarily bourgeois climate of thought, regarded the right to ownership of land, or other effects, as indissociable from the stability of the state, or of a state fit for bourgeois to live in, and he tends to be contrasted in this respect with Rousseau, the land-less wanderer, the 'loner', for whom the ownership of property represented the root cause of social corruption. However that may be, both thinkers regard property as a key factor in any discussion of society, and it would seem useful to try to understand not so much how personal circumstances make different thinkers react diversely to the idea of property as to discover what role the concept plays in the general pattern of their thinking.

In the account so far given of Diderot's views, two ideas emerge with particular clarity: one is that a state should ideally consist of a series of contiguous properties, with the emphasis not on equality in size but on clear demarcation of boundaries; the other is that property is associated with liberty, one of the essential liberties in fact of man in society. As far as the first is concerned, there is very

† The confidence that 'everything will look after itself' is an interesting illustration of the belief that once things are rationally organized, are seen 'as they are', then moral good will follow of itself.

little evidence in Diderot's writings that his view is based on a detailed, scientific examination of the problem. Certainly he would have noticed that people were more scattered in barbarous Russia than they were in civilized France, but the nearest indications of a practical approach to the problem are the point that people will be able to defend themselves better from attacks from outside and the analogy already quoted where individuals are compared to pebbles getting their rough edges smoothed away by contact with others.

Both points are valid; neither is peculiar to Diderot, or even to the eighteenth century. What is more characteristic is the emphasis on the units of society being linked. Whereas savage life is 'without order, sequence or contact',[112]and the passages quoted suggest that the 'linked'[113] is not merely a question of establishing a climate in which men's sociability can develop to the full, but is for Diderot a conceptual necessity. He cannot imagine that an organized system should not be 'full'. Gaps, whether in one's knowledge, or on the ground, are an offence to reason; areas of inconsequentiality in a system which is essentially conceived of in spatial terms.

But while the state as a plenum may be satisfying to the reason, it does not automatically follow that this structure will produce a viable society; it could in fact produce the state of war which Diderot has recognized as one of the necessary stages in political development. There is however a further dimension in the concept of 'liaison'. In the *Mémoires* Diderot advances a rather strange idea which he admits is 'systematical',[114] but which he considered important enough to repeat in the *Observations sur le Nakaz*. In the *Mémoires* he says:

If I had to bring a nation to an awareness of liberty, what should I do? I should set up in its midst a colony of free men, like the Swiss for example, whose privileges I should strictly preserve, and I should leave the rest to time and example... Gradually this precious leaven would transform the whole mass, and its spirit would become the general spirit.[115]

In the *Observations* he seems to be more convinced of the actual possibility of the idea: having set it out in similar terms, he concludes: 'I know by heart all the objections which can be made to this method; they are so trivial that I am not taking the trouble to answer them.'[116] It is difficult to imagine that Diderot could really have thought that a group of freedom-loving Swiss citizens would readily allow themselves to be planted in one of Russia's empty spaces, there to ferment for the benefit of the unleavened natives, but the project does have a realistic attitude behind it, as well as showing remarkable analogies with Diderot's general pattern of thinking.

Sensibility and the body politic

Diderot's realism lies in his recognition that attitudes are not acquired by rational processes, by logical argument or persuasion, still less by force, but by personal experience; and this of course is of a piece with his general theory of perception. The awareness of liberty, of personal rights, must form an integral part of the personality, like any other knowledge worthy of the name. This is a conviction which is more typical of the thinking of the time than personal to Diderot himself, but what is more characteristic of Diderot's individual thought is the analogy between the awareness of liberty and the development of sensibility in matter.

The mass of the Russian people is inert and can only be brought to active political life by contact with elements which are already active. The acquisition by a nation of political awareness is another, higher form of the process by which inert matter is brought to active sensibility by contact with matter which is already 'sensible'. Moreover, just as sensibility is the basis of consciousness in the individual, liberty is also, for Diderot, a matter of consciousness. The essential point is that the members of a state must have an *awareness* of being free. This is what is lacking not only in Russia but, to a large extent, in France. The 'Essai Historique sur la Police de la France' which opens the *Mémoires*, and which is in fact an account of the stages by which France has lost its liberty, describes the present state of the country in terms of a being which has lost all consciousness of itself:

And then I pause for a moment to consider all the vicissitudes by which we have arrived at our present state, or rather our state at that time [for he is ostensibly talking about the Middle Ages], and all the vicissitudes we should still have to experience in order to arrive at anything acceptable, by continuing to abandon ourselves blindly to this dull, obscurely felt movement which plagues us, torments us and makes us twist and turn until we have found a less uncomfortable position; a movement which besets a badly governed empire just as it besets a sick man! But we have even lost this almost unconscious feeling of discomfort. We are no longer aware of ourselves.

In the beginning there was a king, nobles and serfs. Today there is only a master, and serfs parading under all kinds of names.[117]

Elsewhere he emphasizes that a people must *believe* itself to be free. In the same opening section, speaking of the limits a sovereign must place on his own power, he says:

As long as this concession exists unimpaired, the state prospers. The people believe themselves to be free. To attack it is the first act of a despot, to suppress it is the last, and the time nearest the fall of an empire. This is especially true if this innovation is made without bloodshed, for then there is no more resilience, the whole system is slackened and degraded.[118]

A loss of belief in liberty results in the same lack of resistance, of tension, which characterizes an imperfectly functioning human organism.

The healthy nation, then, is one in which an exact balance is maintained between the authority of the sovereign and the rights of the subjects, in the same way that a healthy body depends on a precise degree of tension between the 'centre of the network' and the individual organs. And just as the organs of the body, the senses and the passions have a certain area of activity which is appropriate to them, the individual in society is ultimately defined by the space he occupies and within which he is active. It would seem then that political liberty is conceived of by Diderot as a state of limited autonomy. One of the more distinctive aspects of his and Bordeu's anatomical theories is that the organs can to some extent be thought of as independent elements, but that ideally their autonomy is limited by the power of the nerve-centre.† In the state, individual autonomy is ensured by property, as it were by a physical stake in the body politic, and is similarly limited by the power of the sovereign.

The balance between sovereign and subject is clearly based on the function of each within clearly defined spatial limits:

Sovereignty and liberty do not consist in doing everything one wants to do; sovereignty and liberty are each limited by the same barrier: respect for property on the sovereign's part, and its use on the subject's part.[119]

A few pages later Diderot claims that these limits are not arbitrary or matters of practical convenience, but rooted in the nature of things:

The limits of misfortune or oppression are set by nature. They are marked out in the ploughman's furrow. The earth asks for a share back. Its cultiva-

---

† In the *Rêve* (p. 346) despotism and anarchy are described as the two extremes to which the body is subject, the first where 'the centre of the network commands and all the rest obeys', the second where 'all the threads in the network rise up against their leader and there is no longer any supreme authority' ('l'origine du faisceau commande et tout le reste obéit' ... 'tous les filets du réseau sont soulevés contre leur chef, et où il n'y a plus d'autorité suprême'). As so often in the style and thought of the period, political and anatomical terms seem to be interchangeable.

tor must reserve a second share for himself. The third belongs to the owner. I defy the most hideous of despots to infringe upon this distribution without condemning a part of his people to death by starvation; here is the moment for revolt. I have taken agriculture as my example because in its final consequences all oppression comes back to the land.[120]

It is difficult to see whether this passage represents a rational belief of Diderot's or whether it is a kind of extended metaphor, the poetry of human rights, as it were. What it does show is how much Diderot's political thinking is rooted not just in spatial concepts, but in the earth itself, and how the idea of landed property can become a spatial extension of the individual himself and an expression of his inalienable rights.

It is at this point that the strict parallel between the state and the human body breaks down, for while comparisons can be made, and are made by Diderot, between various bodily disorders and political revolution, it cannot be said that the organs of the body revolt against the 'centre of the network' because the latter has tried to dominate them, has pushed its authority too far. In any case, the analogy between body and state must break down at the point where we become concerned with the members of the state as free individuals: the awareness of personal liberty is clearly a much higher form of consciousness than the sensibility of the organs, and to that extent the state is potentially a superior organism. But we have not finished with the parallels between the two organisms, for there is more to be said on the subject of the sovereign and the 'centre of the network'.

The most striking similarity lies in the detachment which characterizes each of them. The nerve-centre, as we have seen, is ideally uninvolved, its powers of judgment guaranteed by its inability to be moved by the passions, or excited by the senses. Diderot's ideal sovereign is similarly uninvolved in the state on the same level as his subjects by the significant fact that he possesses no property. Imagining himself to be a king, Diderot's first step is to rid himself of his estates.

I sell my estates, because I do not know what private property can mean to one who is supposed to be master of all, and whose purse is in the pockets of his subjects.[121]

He puts it more succinctly in the *Observations*: 'I could not accept the idea of a sovereign having estates of his own',[122] and 'A bad king is one who has an interest separate from the interest of his people.'[123] One of the traditional criticisms of kings was that they subordinated the interests of the state to their own; they became private citizens, 'particuliers'. By having no property the sovereign no longer has a stake in the wealth of the country. On the other hand the members of the commission, the guarantors of the purity and permanence of the laws, and the links between the sovereign and his subjects, are allowed to be private citizens. In fact Diderot does not express himself very clearly in the *Mémoires* on this point.

Let them be isolated in all the districts, only becoming a corporate body as a commission; for when representatives are all magistrates at the same time, when they feel the least discontent as representatives, they cast off their magistrate's robes and the kingdom falls into anarchy.

Occupied and spread amongst different districts, they will never be poor; if they grow rich, they will become the common bond between the upper and lower estates; a kind of amalgam which will unite equally well with the poor nobility and the rich bourgeoisie.[124]

What Diderot seems to have in mind here is that the members of the commission will perform the double function of linking the separate classes in their own areas, creating a kind of organic unity in them, and of conveying to the central authority an impartial account of what is going on. They will be 'particuliers' on their own ground, but will abandon their personal involvement when they meet as a commission. This somewhat individual concept of a separation of powers is thus a way of ensuring for the sovereign a similar relationship with the parts of her empire as the 'centre of the network' has with the parts of the body. The raw impressions, originally experienced in a particular form, as relating to a certain problem in a certain area, are transmitted to the central authority in a generalized form, divested of the personal, emotional involvement which precludes impartial judgment. The relationship which the sovereign has with commission and people is in fact a means of perceiving the true nature of things in the state. Obviously this entails a much more passive role than is usually associated with a ruler, and this seems to be Diderot's intention. This is made clear in a paragraph from the same section:

Whereas our own Parliament took note of the will of the sovereign, it should be the sovereign who takes note of the representations of the commission. Our own magistrates said: We also want what the king wants. Your Majesty and her successors will say: We also acquiesce in what our nation asks of us through our commission; which is very different.[125]

The tendency is for the sovereign to become an organ of perception. The working components of the state are the people, and in order that this situation can be brought about, the sovereign must once and for all alienate a part of his power to the people, that part, in fact, which would define him as a 'particulier'.

Theoretically, then, the state could become a far more highly evolved and efficient organism than the body, since whereas the brain, as an organ like any other, is always prone to revert either to tyranny over the senses and passions or subjection to them, the sovereign, having once and for all alienated a part of his power, would also create the conditions to make it impossible to regain that power, impossible in other words to resume the dangerous status of 'particulier', of an organ like any other. But with this guarantee of order there is associated, as with the human being, the idea of a stability bordering on immobility. It hardly needs to be stressed that the commission is intended to be permanent: 'a physical being, constant, immutable, permanent, eternal... This body made permanent is what I would oppose to the future destruction of my laws and institutions'.[126] Its area of validity is fixed as absolutely as possible.

I would cement in every way possible, for myself and my successors, the alienation of my rights to this body.

I should never convene it in any circumstance foreign to its purpose, lest it be tempted to exceed its rights.

It would not concern itself with war, or politics, or finance.[127]

Its role is thus expressly kept apart from the *actions* associated with the state. This does not mean that it is not active in its own area; it must make itself healthy and vigorous: 'I would use all this time [the period of Catherine's reign] to make it grow strong by the constant exercise of its functions';[128] but this activity is all directed towards the preservation of the laws. 'Its jurisdiction, and its whole jurisdiction, would be limited to the preservation of the existing laws and the examination of those laws which were to be passed or repealed, and of institutions, etc.'[129]

Diderot's state is thus an organism which comes into being naturally, but which can only be perfected and preserved artificially. But because it consists of people and not of organs it has the possibility of lasting life, or at least of staving off the decline and death which is the fate of all natural organisms. 'May they postpone', Diderot says of the American insurgents, 'may they postpone, at least for a few centuries, the sentence passed on all the things of this world; a sentence which has condemned them to have their birth, their prime, their decline and their end!'[130] Its survival is possible because there is a chance that ultimately all its members could achieve an equal awareness of their freedom, an equal degree of consciousness as free citizens with certain inalienable rights. 'A free people differs only from an enslaved people by the irremovability of certain privileges belonging to men as men.'[131] One of these rights is that of opposition: 'The right of opposition seems to me, in a society of men, to be a natural, inalienable and sacred right.'[132] From this opposition, or potential opposition, arises the tension, the precarious equilibrium, without which no order is possible.

The illusion of liberty

Because the permanence of a state depends on such a precarious balance, one wonders how far Diderot really believed in the viability, as opposed to the desirability, of the political structure he proposed for the new Russia. Certainly his proposals are hedged about with frequent realistic insights, for example on the length of time necessary for such a system to become an integral part of people's political attitudes, or on the degree of enlightenment and willpower needed to initiate such reforms. One might also mention his increasing preoccupation with revolution, which has been studied by Strugnell and Benot, but when we are dealing with the structural basis of Diderot's political system, or the general relationship between order and disorder, rather than with the way in which his preoccupations were influenced by a particular time or context, it should be remembered that the possibility of revolution is in any case built into Diderot's conception not only of the state, but of any organism endowed with sensibility. A more important doubt is raised by his mention of the fact that a people must believe itself to be free. In one context, which I have already dealt with, this is a positive idea, in that it insists on the awareness of liberty being more important than its theoretical existence, that liberty is the political equivalent of consciousness, of sensibility in matter. But on another level it implies a negative, pessimistic attitude.

Towards the end of his section on the commission in the *Mémoires* Diderot makes a comment which might seem surprising in the works of a political theorist, and even more so from the pen of the editor of the *Encyclopédie*. He says that if real liberty can not be created then there must at least be a semblance of it:

even if this body were to become in the course of time nothing but a great phantom of liberty, it would nonetheless have its effect on the national spirit, for a people must either be free, which is best, or it must believe itself to be free; for this belief has the most valuable effects.[133]

The implication here is perhaps that real liberty is too much to hope for, and this is borne out by a more striking passage in the *Mémoires*, which is also taken up in the *Observations*, where the illusion of liberty is compared with a spider's web concealing the face of the despot:

between our eyes and the face of the despot was a great spider's web upon which the multitude worshipped a great image of liberty. Those who had eyes to see had long since looked through the little holes in the web and knew very well what was behind it; that web has been torn aside, and tyranny has shown its face for all to see. When a people is not free, the conviction they have of their own freedom is still a precious thing; they had this conviction, and it would have been better to let them keep it. Now they are slaves, and they feel it and see it...[134]

The image is presented in a very similar way in the *Observations*, with the one additional point that the spider's web, the illusion, is equated with the commission.

Either a people must be free, or it must believe itself to be free. Anyone who destroys this national myth is a scoundrel; it is a great spider's web upon which the image of liberty is painted. This image, which draws all the eyes of the people, elevates them, sustains them and gladdens their hearts; a few sharp eyes can see through the holes in this web to the hideous face of the despot. What good is done by the man who tears the web aside? Nothing for the master whose base slave he is; unbelievable damage to the nation which he disabuses, saddens, casts down and degrades by suddenly showing it the hideous face. The body which is the guardian of the fundamental laws of a State is this spider's web.[135]

One can only go on to conclude that the 'fundamental laws' and the spider's web are effectively one and the same.

Here Diderot shows himself to be very much part of a long tradition of political realism, the realism which recognizes that there are certain truths about political power which must not be brought into the open. This is one of Pascal's preoccupations. It is mentioned in a famous passage in Cardinal de Retz's *Mémoires* where he describes the events leading up to the Fronde. After a period of lethargy, he says,

everyone awoke. As they woke, they blindly sought the laws; they could not find them; stricken with panic, they cried out for them; and in all this turmoil the questions they raised, in their efforts to explain them, which had been obscure, and venerable in that obscurity, became a matter for doubt; and as a result, for half of those concerned, odious. The people entered the sanctuary: they lifted the veil which must always conceal anything that can be said, anything that can be thought, concerning the rights of peoples and the rights of kings, which are never so much in harmony as when they are shrouded in silence.[136]

We find it, typically, more openly expressed in Rousseau's *Discours sur l'Inégalité*, where he describes modern society as having originated in a kind of large-scale confidence trick played on the weak by the strong, who 'out of a skilful act of usurpation made an irrevocable law, and, for the benefit of a few men of ambition, were now to subject the whole of mankind to a life of toil, servitude and destitution'.[137]

But a passage which is more telling, by virtue of its very discretion, can be found in the pages of a relatively obscure memoir-writer of the seventeenth century, Nicolas Goulas.

All men are men, the great and the small, and their passions, which they display on the world's great stage, are always the same. It is true that the great conceal them better, and more nicely adjust the masks they take to disguise themselves. Whoever presumes to lift this mask is guilty of a crime, and yet that is what we want the historian and the writer to do, and it is what makes us enjoy and respect what they have to tell. But there are ways of removing the veil: it can be raised gently, without being torn ...[138]

Here, applied like Rousseau's remarks to the power of the 'Grands', not just the sovereign, are the same sentiments as Diderot expresses with respect to the power of government: that to reveal for all to see the secret springs of power, would be to undermine the precarious foundation on which the state rests. The illusion must be preserved, tacitly acknowledged by those who 'know', but never made public knowledge.

What then, for Diderot at least, is this secret? One of the strange features of the passages just quoted from *Mémoires* and the *Observations* is that Diderot takes not the more traditional image of a veil or a mask, but of a spider's web. One does not normally think of a spider's web as an instrument of concealment, but it is of course a familiar image for Diderot, especially in the *Rêve*, symbolizing the power of the central organ over the other elements of an organism, and it seems likely that in using this image he had in mind the continuity which characterizes an 'être sensible', a sensitive being. One could say that the spider at the centre is the authority, while its web represents the ramifications of the organism, just as the commission represents and links the ramifications of the state with the sovereign power. As such it may be nothing more than a representation, that is, a way of looking at the structure of the state, a 'model', and in practical terms an illusion, but one whose slender fabric holds the state together.† This illusion is what masks the total power of the despot, a power which is potentially limitless. To destroy the illusion is to destroy the means by which the state can continue to exist as a rational entity, by which it can be conceived of in rational terms and thereby permit of rational activity within itself. Once the illusion is destroyed, then the civil organism, both conceptually and in reality, either disintegrates into a mass of separate, isolated elements, or eise coheres into a single monolithic monster.

These two extremes between which the state has to steer its dangerous course are both described in the *Fragments échappés du Portefeuille d'un Philosophe*. The first threat is the one which hangs in particular over large democracies and small aristocracies:

> In this case, the harmony of the wills in contact with each other is broken, because they are isolated by terror; between the citizens a moral distance is created, equivalent in its effects to a physical distance; and this moral distance is created by a civil inquisitor who constantly lurks amongst individuals, his axe raised over the neck of anyone who dares to speak either good or ill of authority.[139]

The picture presents itself – as so often, in spatial terms – of a people reverted to a degraded form of the state of nature, to 'isolated forces',[140] and the space created between each member gives free play to the operation of chance, which in this case manifests itself in the form of arbitrary political power. The other extreme is represented by the image of a monastery. Diderot admits that there must be some degree of uniformity in the state, some laws which all must obey, and to this extent the laws of the state must have the inflexibility of those of a religious order.

> But in a monastery everything belongs to everyone, nothing is individually owned by anyone, all goods constitute common property; it is one animal with twenty, thirty, forty, a thousand, ten thousand heads. This is not the case with a civil or political society: here everyone has his head and his

† The point about illusion seems to be borne out by a passage quoted in Léon Schwartz's article, 'L'image de l'araignée...'. He locates Diderot's first mention of the spider image in his *Encyclopédie* article 'Asiatiques', where he quotes the Persian Sufis as believing that the whole of creation is to God as the spider's web is to the spider, able to be extended or re-absorbed at will. 'There is therefore nothing real or effective in anything we see, hear, smell, taste and touch: the universe is nothing but a kind of dream and a pure illusion.' He goes on to say that if the Sufis are asked how it can be that a perfect God can divide himself up into so many bodies and souls, 'they will only offer you clever comparisons ... which are only good for pulling the wool over the eyes of an ignorant people'. ('Il n'y a donc rien ... de réel et d'effectif dans tout ce que nous croyons voir, entendre, flairer, goûter et toucher: l'univers n'est qu'une espèce de songe et une pure illusion' ... 'ils ne vous paieront jamais que de belles comparaisons ... qui ne sont bonnes que pour jeter de la poudre aux yeux d'un peuple ignorant'.)

property, a portion of the general wealth of which he is master, and absolute master, over which he is king, and which he can use or even abuse as he thinks fit.[141]

Certainly then, a perfect society would be difficult enough to maintain, simply because of the hair's-breadth distinctions which its preservation entails, and this is recognized by Diderot in the same *Fragments*, when he asks what the limits are of human happiness and misery, and, more importantly, if such limits are set by nature. On the assumption that what we possess is gained 'by industry and toil',[142] how far are we justified in going?

Should we take from nature all that we can get from her, or should our struggle with her be limited to easing the small number of important tasks to which she has destined us, finding shelter, clothing and food, reproducing ourselves and resting in safety? Might not everything else represent the extravagance of a species, just as everything which exceeds the aspiration after a certain degree of wealth is for us the extravagance of the individual?[143]

The passage ends on a question mark, and one can see from the last phrase how Diderot's reflections on this question are conditioned by the inequalities in the France of his own time. But one can go further and ask whether his doubts about the possibility of order actually being realized in society are not based on more than just the practical difficulties of it.

Enough has been said so far to show that Diderot's ideal state would consist of a mass of private citizens, of 'particuliers', each contained within his own area, in both moral and physical terms, an area whose limits are fixed by the contiguous areas occupied by his fellow-citizens. The perpetuation of this system is guaranteed by the existence of a sovereign who has no status as a 'particulier', who, literally, has no space, that is, no property, and whose relationship with the citizens of the state is mediated through a body of officials who partake at different times of both qualities, who have an existence in their own right as 'particuliers', but who divest themselves of this right when they come together to perform their functions as safeguards of the law. As far as the citizens, the body of the state, are concerned, we immediately come up against the same problem as is presented by Diderot's conception of the perfect human organism: it is completely static. Although the conditions for change or movement within society are already given in Diderot's conviction that the only entitlement to ownership is through work, so that, presumably, a greater or lesser contribution to the well-being of society should result in a corresponding increase or decrease in an individual's rights to property, he never develops this idea; and this is surely because he is chiefly concerned with property as a concept, as a physical representation of the rights which each member of society must regard as inalienable.

Perhaps we can also find a clue to this attitude in a basic aversion to the idea of economic competition as we know it. Rousseau, who does not go beyond the idea of seeing contiguity of property as a source of moral anarchy, says in his *Discours sur l'Inégalité*:

Now when inherited estates had increased in number and extent to the point where they covered the whole earth and all touched each other, none could grow except at others' expense; and those who were left over, those who through weakness or indolence had not been able to acquire any in their turn, and who were poor without having lost anything, since, while all changed around them, they alone had not changed, were forced to accept or to seize their livelihood from the hands of the rich; and out of this were born, according to the different characteristics of each person, domination and servitude, or violence and plunder.[144]

Here are the roots of modern society, which Diderot no doubt saw as well as Rousseau; but what for the author of the *Contrat Social* is the inescapable condition of a society founded on property is for Diderot the intermediate 'state of war' which exists before a balance is set up between the limited authority of the sovereign and the consciousness of freedom and rights to property in the subjects; this 'state of war' corresponds in the physical world to the state where matter is in pure movement, where sensibility, still inert, has not created from it a viable organism. It is the awareness of liberty permeating the structure of the state which offers the same possibility of salvation as does sensibility in the human organism; and the danger in both cases of the organism running out of control can only be counteracted by the separateness and limited autonomy of each part being preserved.

In this way the heterogeneity which Rousseau sees only as a source of anarchy becomes for Diderot a limitation on the power of sensibility, or a safeguard against liberty becoming licence. But this limitation is only achieved by the insistence on a kind of spatial rigidity. Thus, although in a passage already quoted from the *Apologie de l'Abbé Galiani*[145] he says that a state can achieve nothing great if it respects individual rights to property, he leans in his Russian writings more in the direction of the Physiocrats in seeing economic activity as a kind of flow or circulation, comparing the movement of money to and from the capital to the blood flowing to and from the heart,[146] a constant movement which leaves the structure of the organism untouched.

This does not mean that the views put forward in defence of Galiani were later abandoned; they were simply left out of account in a work which is concerned with ideals for the future, not present realities. For this reason there is very little mention of war in the works dealing with Russia, except for the hope expressed in Section II of the *Mémoires* that Catherine's conflict with the Turks will soon come to an end. 'The thinkers are distressed at the continuance of the present war',[147] because war is *par excellence* the activity in which the individual's interests are sacrificed to an objective lying outside the state: Diderot's model of society does not allow for war, any more than his human model allows for action. As soon as the state goes to war – and it should be remembered that the commission has no part in such decisions – the sovereign automatically becomes a 'particulier' in relation to the nation against which war is being waged, and this applies even if he is completely indifferent to his personal glory and motivated solely by the good of the state; for the state now becomes a single unit, 'one animal with ... ten thousand heads',[148] as he says in the *Fragments*, a single space to be preserved or enlarged in relation to other spaces, and its internal structure is subordinated to this purpose, just as the various organs of the body are directed towards a single purpose in the case of a man in the grip of a powerful passion. This seems to be the only conclusion to be drawn about a subject on which Diderot, perhaps significantly, has very little to say.

Diderot's Utopia, then – and this hardly seems an inappropriate description – is a norm, a concept existing at an exact point between internal disintegration, when its individual citizens make war upon each other, and total coherence, when all citizens are merged together in the struggle against an external force. In the same way, an organism is only perfect when its molecules, having once joined together to form it, are in exact balance with one another and are not directed towards some external activity. There is a profound contradiction here between the original purpose of the state and its ideal condition, in that the individuals who initially come together to join forces against a common enemy can only exist *as* individuals when they are not engaged in dealing with the enemy. A state's natural function is to protect itself, but in doing so it automatically endangers the individuality of its members; the body's natural function is to be active, but such action destroys the possibility of perfect balance between its individual parts. Equilibrium is achieved in a state of thought, not of action: 'The thinkers are distressed at the continuance of the present war',[149] Diderot has said: and he adds at the end of the same paragraph: 'the eye of the philosopher and the eye of the sovereign see things very differently'.[150] In the nature of things, a sovereign can never become a *philosophe*. Once again, we have an unbridgeable gulf between the ideal and the reality, and the nature of that gulf is made clear by the nature of the ideal sovereign.

I have already drawn attention to the fact that Diderot's sovereign has no property, no stake in the wealth of the state, and thus, occupying no space, is a person of a different order from his subjects. The same point could be made about the 'centre of the network',[151] which 'has ... no sense that is its own ... it emanates from a soft, insensitive, inert substance, which acts as a cushion on which it is enthroned, hears cases, considers its judgment and pronounces verdicts'.[152] Its role, too, is subject to the same hazards as that of the sovereign: 'the slightest pressure makes the judge suspend his sitting'.[153] A comparison suggests itself with the opening lines of the *Rêve*, where d'Alembert admits to Diderot:

I grant you that a Being who exists somewhere but corresponds to no one point in space, a Being with no dimensions yet occupying space, who is complete in himself at every point in this space, who differs in essence from matter but is one with matter, who is moved by matter and moves matter but never moves himself, who acts upon matter yet undergoes all its changes, a Being of whom I have no conception whatever, so contradictory is he by nature, is difficult to accept.[154]

The qualities of the God which d'Alembert is encouraged to reject seem to have passed into the 'centre of the network' and the sovereign. The ideal, the norm, can only be realized by a restoration of the conditions which had been ensured by the concept of the two substances. In both the human and the political organism, 'this sensitivity that you substitute for him'[155] has to be neutralized, reduced to a condition of potentiality, so that order can come into being. Does order then have any status as a reality rather than as a concept? As a general problem this requires further examination, but as far as the state is concerned the answer would seem to be no; and yet this fact makes it all the more imperative that we should believe in it, that the concept should remain alive in the face of the reality which denies it. Order in the body politic is an illusion, but one which must at all costs be preserved, and it is the duty of those who have power, or knowledge, to preserve it. On this level the web which conceals the face of the tyrant is like the semblance of reality which conceals the hand of the artist. The state is as artificial a creation as a work of art; each depends for its survival on the strength of the illusion it creates.

5

A SYSTEM OF AESTHETICS

Artistic illusion and artistic order

It is in Diderot's writings on aesthetics that the problem of illusion gets its most thorough treatment. In his political theory the question is only rarely dealt with explicitly, even though it is implicit throughout; but when we come to aesthetics the matter can be dealt with more openly, since we are concerned with fiction, with invention. But first it will be useful to establish what relationship there is between political and aesthetic illusion. The illusion necessary in a political organism is that the state is based on principles of order, that its members can perceive a rational liaison between the events which occur within it, and that the power which governs it is subject not to arbitrary whims, but to reason. If we substitute the artist for the sovereign, and the public for the citizens, we would seem to be on the way towards a close parallel between politics and aesthetics; but are we dealing with the same kind of illusion?

At first sight it might appear not, since artistic illusion is usually regarded as an illusion of reality, whereas political illusion consists in a belief that order operates within a structure which is already there, but on closer examination the distinction is not so clear-cut. In *Diderot et la Mystification* (p. 139), Jean Catrysse quotes Georges Blin in support of the point that artistic illusion is not in fact an illusion of reality at all: 'there is no illusion of reality; but on the one hand an illusion which deceives no one, and on the other, reality':[156] the novel (for this is the genre he is talking about, but the same could be said of any narrative work) 'is founded on a pact made in bad faith, or more precisely, a kind of faith is appealed to which is discredited at the very moment it is agreed to. Everyone involved, whether author or reader, is pretending.'[157] The point is perhaps obvious enough if one thinks about it, but it is easy to be misled by the use of such works as 'realism' or 'vraisemblance', or by many statements by practising artists and critics, into assuming that a work of art is based on an illusion of actual reality. What we, the public, need to be convinced of is surely not that the artist is showing us something real, which we know he is not, but that he is obeying a set of standards which we ourselves regard as reasonable, that he is not exploiting his unlimited powers in the same way as might the despotic ruler of a state. In other words, we demand not reality, but a kind of order, and the kind of order we demand is conditioned by the complex mass of moral and aesthetic preconceptions which, in a given society at a given time, govern our way of seeing the world about us.

The question of artistic illusion was inevitably undergoing a thorough reassessment in the eighteenth century, as it created new forms in the effort to cope with new areas of reality, and there is no doubt that Diderot was acutely aware of the complexity of the problem, all the more so because of his personal convictions about the essential diversity of people's reactions to the world about them. In one of his most important texts on the subject, the section of *De la Poésie Dramatique* entitled 'Du Plan de la Tragédie et du Plan de la Comédie', he says:

There are perhaps not two individuals on the whole surface of the earth who have the same standards of certainty, yet the poet is condemned to create the same illusion in all of them! The poet is exploiting the reason and experience of the educated man in the same way as the governess exploits the stupidity of a child. A good poem is a story worthy to be told to sensible men.[158]

A poet, and, presumably, any other kind of artist, has the task of playing a confidence trick convincing enough to fool as many people as possible, and in this respect artistic practice is of the same order as any other activity. The artist creates the same kind of 'paraître', appearance, in his works as does the state in relationship to its members, or an individual in relation to his fellows. However, the awareness that artistic creation, or any kind of relationship set up with other people, involves some kind of illusion, does not, for Diderot, necessarily imply a tongue-in-cheek approach on the part of the artist; rather it is a recognition of the elusiveness, perhaps purely subjective nature of such concepts as truth and beauty, and in Diderot's works, more than in those of any of his contemporaries, we find an extraordinary range of attitudes towards aesthetic problems.

Two points should be made, however, which help to define and mark the limits and nature of the aesthetic attitudes of Diderot and his contemporaries. One is that, although they recognized that tastes alter under the influence of local conditions, they did not abandon the belief that this should not be so; their belief in the relativity of aesthetic, or any other values, did not extend to a denial that absolute values should and could exist. This is made clear when Diderot speaks of the 'Modèle idéal', the 'ideal model', in the *Salon* of 1767.[159] Although, he says, the 'modèle premier', the ideal of perfect beauty, has no counterpart in reality, and cannot even be reconstructed from elements existing in reality; and although the particular conditions of our own civilization allow no-one but the occasional genius to catch a glimpse of it, Diderot still allows for the possibility that this model could be understood 'by a return to the barbaric state',[160] for in this state people are without preconceived ideas. This is 'the only state in which men, convinced of their ignorance, can make up their minds to move forward slowly; the others remain second-rate, precisely because they are, so to speak, born learned'.[161] Even if perfect beauty was concealed from them by their degenerate state, the belief that the ideal existed enabled them to carry on the search for it, to construct systems which would allow them to approximate to it as closely as possible. They therefore stood in a kind of halfway position in aesthetics, just as they did in every other field of thought, simultaneously recognizing both absolute and individual, relative values, both striving towards stability and acknowledging the primacy of movement, seeking a final point of rest and perfection in a world which could only offer the provisional and the relative.

For this reason, side by side with their concern with aesthetic systems, with theories and ideals of beauty, we find the eighteenth century preoccupied with the problem of introducing reality into art, of enabling art to cope with the relative, the particular as opposed to the general. As far as literature is concerned, the tendency is for dramatic theory to lean in the direction of the general, while the particular is associated with the novel. This is necessarily an over-simplification, particularly in the case of Diderot, but it is generally based on the fact that drama, as a public art-form, was traditionally associated with public order, accepted morality and permanent values, while the novel dealt increasingly with the private side of life, with the personal problems of contemporary people; as such, it claimed to represent things 'as they are', to give a 'true' picture of society and human behaviour, and many novels – thus contributing to the impression that art provides an illusion of reality! – went so far as to pretend that they were authentic stories, memoirs, exchanges of letters, or transcripts from accounts given by real people. Certainly we find in Diderot's writings an effort to bring these two conflicting worlds together; but the conflict was so deeply rooted in the pattern of thinking, the two kinds of nature – the ideal on the one hand and the 'facts' on the other – so essentially different in kind, that the dualism remains. It is essential to bear these two faces of reality in mind when we examine Diderot's aesthetics. It would be misleading to say that all his utterances on art form a coherent whole (though this does not mean that there is not a coherent explanation), and pointless to try to create one out of them. Just as there is a gulf between Diderot's normative human being and the realities of human behaviour, or between his model society and the vicissitudes of political life, so his system of aesthetics – for such a system can be discerned in his works – cannot account for or embrace the whole practice of artistic creation and perception. His theory of beauty cannot, and is not intended to cope with *Jacques le Fataliste*, any more than his political and moral theory can contain Rameau's nephew.

As far as Diderot's theory of beauty is concerned, one of his chief preoccupations – and this is hardly surprising – is to discover the exact relationship between nature and art, and one of his most interesting statements on the subject comes at the end of his article 'Beau'. Beauty, he says, is not always

the work of an intellect: sometimes the movement of nature can set up, either in one object considered in isolation, or between several beings considered in relation to each other, an extraordinary multitude of surprising relationships ... These relationships are in such cases the result of chance combinations, at least so far as we are concerned. On a hundred different occasions nature gratuitously imitates the products of art; and one might ask ... how many relationships one would need to observe in an object to be absolutely sure that it is the work of an artist; under what circumstances a single defect in symmetry would prove more than the whole sum of relationships; what link there is between the duration of the chance cause and the relationships observed in the effects produced; and if, except in the case of the works of the Almighty, there are examples where the number of relationships can never be balanced by the number of chance causes.[162]

This passage raises a host of questions. Jacques Chouillet, in *La Formation des Idées Esthétiques de Diderot* (p. 321), describes it as 'this formula which deposes all aesthetic theories then known'.[163] It is a grandiose idea, in that it envisages the possibility of calculating on a spatio-temporal basis the exact point of division between art and nature, the man-made and the natural, order and chance. The passage comes at the end of the article, like an afterthought, but it might be more accurate to say that it is an idea which haunted

Diderot, but which he found it difficult to integrate into a more conventional discussion of aesthetics. The idea is paralleled in his philosophical writings. The possibility of order arising out of an immense number of 'jets', chance causes, is discussed as early as 1746 in the *Pensées Philosophiques* where he concludes that 'the difficulty of the event [here the creation of the universe] is more than adequately balanced by the multitude of chance causes';[164] that nothing is more repugnant to reason than that 'matter having been in motion from all eternity ... none of these admirable dispositions should have come about amongst the infinite multitude of those it has successively assumed'.[165]

Here of course we are concerned with the formation of the order of the universe out of primeval chaos. Elsewhere Diderot looks at things on a different scale, seeing, in the *Lettre sur les Aveugles* of 1749, the possibility of a number of universes coming into being and disintegrating at different times and in different places:

How many crippled, failed worlds have disintegrated, formed again and disintegrated, perhaps at every moment, in distant space ... but movement continues and will continue to bring together masses of matter until they have achieved some disposition in which they can endure.[166]

In this passage, each world is seen as an approximation to order emerging out of chaos, and, like the monsters which play so large a part in Diderot's thought, returning to chaos when they prove to be incapable of survival. On a smaller scale, and only a few lines away from this passage, the world itself is also seen as a chaos with its own temporary moments of order.

What is this world...? A structure subject to revolutions which all indicate a constant tendency to destruction; a rapid succession of beings which succeed one another, displace one another and disappear; a fleeting symmetry; a momentary order.[167]

And in his commentary on Hemsterhuis Diderot refers to the undiscovered causes which 'maintain within the whole and always will maintain this passage or perpetual flux from one order or coordination to another'.[168]

Here we have one of the dominant elements in Diderot's ways of looking at things: the concept of an apparent disorder producing, by apparent chance, successive moments of order, a concept which carries over into his aesthetic ideas. It is certainly a pre-rational concept, because it contains conflicts not only within itself, but also with much of his aesthetic thought. For example, there is a shift of emphasis in the *Paradoxe sur le Comédien*. Here he admits that

nature can produce beauty, 'its sublime moments',[169] but he has res-
ervations about the artistic reproduction of these moments: 'I think
that if anyone can be relied upon to grasp and preserve their sublimity, it is someone who, having first felt them through his
imagination and genius, can then render them in cold blood.'[170] It is
not then the total event which will be reproduced but its 'sublimity'.[171] The second speaker objects that 'a wondrous spectacle'[172]
could arise from a crowd of men being suddenly faced with some catastrophe. True, admits Diderot (if we can safely assume him to be
the first speaker): 'But could this spectacle be compared with one
which would result from a well-judged harmony, the harmony
which the artist will introduce into it when he conveys it from the
street-corner to the stage or the canvas?'[173] There is nothing here to
suggest that the original is faithfully imitated at any point; it is not a
question of art seizing on a moment in nature and prolonging it or
developing it, but of the moment merely suggesting something
which art can do much better.

In any case, you are talking to me about something real, and I am talking to
you about an imitation; you are talking to me about a fleeting moment in
nature, and I am talking to you about a work of art, planned, followed
through, with its own development and duration.[174]

There is no evidence that there must be a point at which art and
nature exactly coincide.

Why then does Diderot at times think of nature producing perfect
beauty? There are two possible reasons. One is his belief that nature
alone is perfect, and this is a logical consequence of his determinism,
even if, as we have seen, his aesthetic inferences are not always so
logical. 'There is nothing imperfect in nature, not even monsters',[175]
he says in his article 'Imparfait'. 'Only in art is there imperfection,
because art has a model existing in nature with which its creations
can be compared.'[176] Another version of this approach to the
problem can be found in the *Essais sur la Peinture* of 1766: 'Nature
makes no mistakes. Every form, beautiful or ugly, has its cause; and
of all existing beings, there is not one which is not as it must be.'[177]
Now it might be said that the type of perfection he is talking about
in these two passages has nothing at all to do with aesthetic judgments, that he is simply making the point that the artist, dealing
with a limited area of reality, is ignorant of the multiplicity of causes
and effects which lie behind each phenomenon and is therefore
obliged to produce a distortion of the truth. This is certainly true,
but one cannot go on to assume that Diderot regards art and nature

as being inevitably divided because of this: there is no essential qualitative difference between art and nature, only a gap corresponding to our own ignorance of nature's workings. 'If causes and effects were evident to us, we should have nothing more to do than to represent things as they are. The more perfect the imitation was, the closer it reflected the causes, the more satisfied we should be.'[178] And, he continues, if an artist did imitate nature perfectly, going against the rules and conventions we have established to make up for our ignorance, he might still succeed 'by that subtle intuition which comes to us from continuous observation of phenomena, which would make us aware of a hidden connection, a necessary link between these deformities'.[179]

Reading this last remark, one is reminded of one of the sections of *De l'Interprétation de la Nature* which deals with the methods of experimental science. Diderot quotes the example of Socrates, who 'judged men as people of taste judge the works of the mind, by intuition';[180] the same applies, he goes on, in experimental physics to the

instinct of our great experimental scientists. They have seen nature at work so often and so closely that they can guess with a fair degree of accuracy the path she may take ... Therefore the most important service they can provide for those whom they are training in experimental philosophy is not so much to instruct them in methods and results as to inculcate in them that spirit of divination by which one can so to speak *smell out* new methods, novel experiments and unknown results.[181]

Scientist and artist alike have this same task of acquiring an instinct, a feeling for the processes of nature which will make it possible for them to penetrate its mysteries. The important point here is not so much the particular kind of approach called for, which has already been mentioned, but the fact that Diderot makes no distinction between the activities of the scientist and the artist. Both are working in limited fields; both are in a sense creators of limited systems; but the instinct they develop should enable them, within their area of activity, to create something which does not conflict with the vast area which remains unknown to them.

Whether he is dealing with science or art, Diderot is inspired by the same conviction that there is no chance in nature, that our impression of chance only arises from our ignorance of causes; and behind it all lies the dream that, in a universe in which 'everything holds together'[182] we might one day be able to evolve a set of moral and aesthetic principles in total conformity with nature. As he writes to Sophie Volland:

if once the principles of morality were firmly established, this trunk would put out innumerable small branches which would attach even the most insignificant virtues to it ... if the principles of taste were established, they would extend to every trivial thing down to the fringes of a coquette's finery.[183]

Here we have the most all-embracing form of Diderot's aesthetics, where it is implied that nature itself, not an ideal of beauty distilled from it, defines the terms of aesthetic theory and practice, and where it is further implied that there is no ultimate distinction between aesthetics, science or ethics.

The second reason is one to which I have already referred, and that is Diderot's idea of nature producing intermittent moments of order during the changes it undergoes. These moments are perhaps a temporal equivalent of those 'lighted places'[184] which provide occasional areas of illumination in the 'vast precinct of the sciences'[185] as described in the *Interprétation de la Nature*, but as well as suggesting that the artist can use these moments as starting points for his own creation Diderot also seems to think that the temporal pattern itself should be reflected in the artist's work. Applied to painting, this notion expresses itself in the necessity of choosing the most significant moment in the representation of an event. When he discusses Challe's *Cléopâtre expirante* in the *Salon* of 1761, he objects that Challe ought to have chosen the moment before Cleopatra applied the asp to her breast, not the moment after. 'The choice of the moment of her death does not give us a Cleopatra, it merely gives a woman dying from a snake bite. It is no longer the history of the Queen of Alexandria, but an accident of life'.[186] The implication here is that in each event there is a characteristic moment which carries more significance than any other, and which contains within itself something of the past and the future, transcending the limitations of the 'instant fugitif de la nature'.

Every action is made up of several moments ... the artist has only one, no longer than a glance ... there may remain, in the moment the painter has chosen, either in the attitudes, or the characters, or the actions, surviving traces of the preceding moment.[187]

This might be considered simply a commonsense piece of advice to any narrative or historical artist were it not for the fact that the idea also crops up in Diderot's dramatic theory in the form of the *tableau*. This will be more fully discussed later in this chapter, and it will be enough for the moment to say that Diderot's ideal play should proceed from *tableau* to *tableau*, from one moment of highly charged significance to the next. Moreover the quality of each of these moments can be assessed by the ease with which one could imagine it transferred to a canvas. The artist, having understood the processes of nature, is apparently required to reverse them in his own creations: in place of the constant movement, the indiscriminate scattering of energy which characterizes the natural world, he must attempt to give us moments of concentration, moments when past and present are drawn together in a simultaneous spatial representation which transcends the passage of time. There is a close parallel here with the emergence of the thinking, perceiving individual out of the dispersed molecules of matter described in the *Rêve de d'Alembert*, or the formation of the perfect state from a mass of separate individuals in Diderot's political theory.

Problems of realism

Much of Diderot's writing on aesthetics seems to present a more traditionalist view of art as creative of order. In a passage from the *Entretiens sur le Fils Naturel*, Dorval is made to say:

there are no lasting forms of beauty save those founded on relationships with the phenomena of nature. If one imagined phenomena in a rapid process of change, every painting representing just a fleeting moment, all imitation would be superfluous. Beauty has in the arts the same basis as truth in philosophy.[188]

This seems at first sight a strange statement to come from Dorval. Chouillet (*ibid.*, p. 473) calls it 'homage paid by movement to stability',[189] and attributes it to Diderot's failure to reconcile two views of nature: the Aristotelian, of nature as a principle of truth, and the Heraclitean, of nature as a principle of movement. In what Dorval says here, the idea of nature in a state of flux is rejected in favour of something corresponding to 'the truth in philosophy'.[190] And what is truth? the passage goes on: 'What is truth? The conformity of our judgments with phenomena. What is beauty in the imitative arts? The conformity of the image with the thing itself.'[191]

This, as the surrounding discussion shows, is a plea for realism, but it is still not easy to see exactly what kind of realism is being advocated. A little before the piece just quoted *Moi* has suggested that unity in character does not exist, and Dorval has agreed, but, to *Moi's* conclusion that to demand unity of character in a play would be to abandon truth, he points out that since a play only deals with a single action, it is reasonable to suppose 'that a man has kept the same character'.[192] But what happens, then, in the epic, which covers a variety of incidents over a long stretch of time? To this Dorval replies:

I think there is a lot to be said for representing men as they are. What they ought to be is too systematical, too vague to serve as a basis for an imitative art. There is nothing so rare as a completely wicked man, unless perhaps it be a completely good man.[193]

This seems very traditional, Aristotelian in fact, with its description of the man whose perfection is limited by some fault, and this is borne out by the example Dorval chooses: 'When Thetis steeped his son in the Styx, he emerged with a heel like that of Thersites.'[194] Yet Dorval is clearly criticizing the literature of the immediate past, and, presumably, of his own time, as is shown by his insistence that art must concern itself with worthwhile things: 'the imitation of nature, and of nature at its most powerful'[195] and not 'an absurdity'[196] or 'a fable'.[197]

What Diderot seems to have done here is to set up an Aunt Sally, an exaggeratedly unrealistic concept of the theatre of his time in order to replace it with one which would admittedly be more realistic in its elimination of the mythical and academic elements of traditional drama, but not in its conception of character. To modern eyes it may seem disappointing that of all people Dorval, perhaps the most 'pre-romantic' of Diderot's creations, should be allowed to put forward a theory of dramatic and epic character in such opposition to Diderot's beliefs about human nature. But Diderot's ideas on dramatic structure – and I stress the word 'structure' – are strangely unrevolutionary. Despite what he says and does in other fields, he is not prepared to incorporate the concept of movement, or chance, or the inconsistency of human character into his dramatic theory.

To find confirmation of this it is first of all necessary to ask what innovations Diderot did propose, and to set them in the context of his time. Very conveniently, Dorval draws up a short summary of the work that remains for modern drama to do.

To create domestic and bourgeois tragedy. To perfect the serious genre. To substitute the conditions of men for their characters, perhaps in all genres. To associate mime closely with dramatic action. To alter the stage; and to substitute *tableaux* for *coups de théâtre*, a new source of invention for the poet and of study for the actor. For what use is it if the poet imagines *tableaux* and the actor remains faithful to his symmetrical positioning and his stilted acting style? To introduce real tragedy into the lyrical theatre. Finally to convert the dance to a real poetic form, to be written down, and distinguished from any other imitative art.[198]

116

All of this can be said to amount to a plea for realism, as opposed to formality and academicism; realism in the choice of subject-matter and its treatment and an attempt to bring dramatic art closer to the life of its public. Examined more closely, in the light of the discussion throughout the *Entretiens*, this realism looks like an effort not so much to enlarge the field of drama as to enclose it within fairly well-defined limits.

This is especially true if we concentrate, as Dorval does, on the 'serious genre',[199] which he regards as the basic form of drama, like the nude in painting and sculpture, on which the other forms – 'the burlesque, the comic genre, the tragic genre, the fantastic'[200] – are variations. It is a kind of 'ideal model' which fixes the original nature of things, and which must be properly understood before an artist can depart from it to try his hand at other forms. One gets the impression indeed that it is the only really worthwhile form of drama, and that the others are only included because they already exist. The 'genre sérieux' is defined, for example, not so much by its ability to generate comedy and tragedy as by its exclusion of them. Diderot seems to be aware of this as a possible criticism, and tries to forestall it: 'The serious genre has this advantage, that being placed between the other two, it has possibilities whether it rises or falls',[201] and later, claiming a specific set of poetic values for the genre, he adds 'and the poetics of it would also be very extensive',[202] but when, immediately afterwards, he lists some of its characteristics, they tend to be negative and exclusive in nature. The genre lacks colour and variety; it must not contain elements which are too comic or tragic; it must not contain valets or episodic characters; the main character must not initiate action; the plot must be simple and domestic. It seems to be a recipe for boredom, and such it often turned out to be, but these principles were seen by Diderot not to be prime characteristics of the genre but conditions which would enable it to produce its particular appeal.

What Diderot wanted to eliminate were the elements which distract the audience from the essential subject and the essential purpose of drama; and the subject was human nature in its most powerful and universal expression, while the purpose was to uplift the audience morally through the emotional impact created. The limitations in the scope of the genre act on three levels: the play must create an illusion powerful enough to carry total conviction; it must be concentrated enough to generate intense emotions in the characters, and therefore the audience; it must be universal in its reference. The first two categories explain Diderot's retention of the three

117

unities. His insistence on eliminating the 'fantastic',[203] the burlesque, the conventions, some of the *bienséances* (proprieties) and
rhetorical delivery applies to all three. In this way dramatic energy is
centred on the portrayal of 'great causes, great passions'[204] and will
at the same time produce 'the complete picture of the misfortunes
which surround us ... a real background, authentic dress, speeches
adapted to actions, simple actions, dangers which you cannot fail to
have feared for your relations, your friends, yourself'.[205] Seen in this
light, the 'serious genre' is not so much a revolutionary concept as a
logical step in a development in serious drama which has been
taking place since the seventeenth century.

In the second half of that century tragedy was already well on the
way towards the portrayal of human passions in a simplified setting.
Certainly the mythical and historical trappings, the rhetoric and
declamation were still very much present, but the public desire for
the spectacular and the lyrical was being increasingly catered for by
opéra-ballets and machine plays, while serious drama, like historio-
graphy itself, was less concerned with history or myth than with the
presentation of ordinary human beings caught up in some extreme
predicament, and in this the three unities played the same double
role of intensifying both the characters' passions and the dramatic
illusion. Even the view expressed by Dorval about the dramatic
function of the hero echoes seventeenth-century practice:
'movement almost always detracts from dignity; therefore your
main character should rarely be the activator of the plot in your
play'.[206] One has only to think of all the seventeenth-century plays
in which a plot is set in motion against a monarch or father, or both,
by an impetuous son or rival, to see how traditional this view is.

The idea of movement being destructive of dignity is all the same
a strange thought for Dorval to express if we think of him as
the romantic enthusiast, genius, the forerunner of the heroes of
Chateaubriand and perhaps, as Vernière asserts (*Oeuvres Esthétiques*, pp. 73–4) an actual portrayal of Rousseau, though Chouillet
convincingly disputes this (*ibid.*, pp. 426–7). Two points must be
made here. Firstly, the 'serious genre' has a moral intention; it may
portray passion, including its 'inarticulate cries',[207] but in an age
which was still highly conventional and formal by our standards it
could not help but conform to received ideas of human decency.
Secondly – and this is much more important – Dorval's raptures
over nature, his enthusiasm, his lyrical outbursts, are only remotely
connected in Diderot's mind with the philosophical idea of nature in
movement. We have already seen that his dramatic theory does not

go far at all towards representing the kind of views Diderot expresses about human nature in the *Rêve*, still less in *Le Neveu de Rameau* or *Jacques le Fataliste*. Chouillet (*ibid.*, p. 472) associates Dorval and all he represents with the Heraclitean aspect of Diderot's thought. 'Nature-in-movement, as he conceives it', he says, 'is conflated with the violence of the passions'.[208] This is true on one level; but not, I think, 'as he conceives it'.[209] When Chouillet goes on to establish Dorval and the Ariste of the *Discours sur la Poésie Dramatique* as a contrasting pair: 'All that concerns violence and enthusiasm goes by the name of Dorval. All that revolves round the idea of observation, logical rigour, the portrayal of conditions and morality is linked with the character of Ariste',[210] he is making a distinction which certainly has a large amount of truth in it, but which would almost certainly not have been made by Diderot himself.

To understand Dorval and the whole attitude towards nature which he represents one must distinguish clearly between it and the concept of nature in movement. The confusion can arise partly from a problem of vocabulary: in both attitudes the word 'passions' figures largely, but the passions which arouse Dorval's enthusiasm are essentially a subjective experience, felt either within oneself or vicariously in others (note the emphasis on audience-identification in the theory of the 'serious genre'), while the passions in the other sense are the human equivalent of movement in matter. Consequently, the typical responses to these two versions of passion are quite distinct. To the first kind, Dorval's kind, the response is positive; the passions represent natural, original man, unspoilt by the vices of civilized society, and are therefore to be associated with the unspoilt nature round about us. A quotation, not from the *Entretiens*, but from the *Discours*, shows the typical association.

Is human nature good then? Yes, my friend, indeed it is very good. Water, air, earth, fire, all is good in nature; both the hurricane which blows up towards the end of the autumn, shakes the forests, and, beating the trees against each other, breaks and separates their dead branches; and the tempest, which beats the waters of the sea and purifies them; and the volcano which pours out from its gaping flanks the floods of glowing matter, raising into the air the vapour which cleanses it. It is the wretched conventions which pervert men; it is not human nature which should be blamed.[211]

All this is said in the context of a plea for 'the honest'[212] in the theatre. This is the 'good' nature, which inevitably smacks of finalism and touches off a reaction in the sensibility.

Now Chouillet makes the perfectly valid and significant point that Diderot's use of this argument is totally inappropriate (p. 459). In the first place it is not a description of human nature; in the second it describes the effect of violence, of chance, on an effete order in nature itself, and seems to have very little connection with 'the wretched conventions'. And yet Diderot does not appear to see any contradiction. 'All this is said ingenuously', as Chouillet says (p. 459), 'and all in one breath, as if the arguments went without saying.'[213] Perhaps the argument seems self-evident to Diderot because he is moving in the familiar territory of the opposition between the natural and the artificial, or nature and civilization. What he is really talking about is the true order of nature, the original perfection, which in man and the whole creation has been obscured and corrupted by the passage of time, by movement in fact. What he has actually done is to conflate the perfection of nature with the violent activity which reveals it. He seems to have been carried away by his enthusiasm. Dorval is in fact both a human representative of this perfection and the agent which produces an awareness of it in Diderot, so that even if the passage does not stand up to logical analysis it does at least offer a close analogy with Dorval's role in the *Entretiens*.

When Diderot considers the passions in terms of nature in movement, however, the response is either neutral or negative; neutral when looked at from a scientific point of view as motive forces in man and society; negative when seen as a disruptive force, an obstacle to rational endeavour. As such, they are unpredictable, irrational and, whether within oneself or others, productive of that 'surprise' which the rational mind must seek to avoid, and, as both the *Entretiens* and the *Discours* show, this 'surprise' is equally to be avoided in the spectacle of dramatic action. One of the most remarkable aspects of Diderot's dramatic theory is his emphasis on the *tableau* at the expense of the *coup de théâtre*. The point is more fully made in the *Entretiens*.

An unforeseen incident which takes place in the action and abruptly changes the situation of the characters is a *coup de théâtre*. An arrangement of these characters on the stage, so natural and so true that, faithfully rendered by a painter, it would please me on a canvas, is a *tableau*.[214]

Surprise is to be avoided in favour of a convincing scene in which all is visible. In the *Discours* the point is made that the emotional effect will be far greater if the audience knows what is coming.

The poet, by hidden means, contrives a moment of surprise for me; if he had confided in me he would have exposed me to a long period of tension. I shall only pity for a moment someone who is struck down and overwhelmed in a moment. But what becomes of me if the catastrophe is held up, if I see the storm building up over my head, or the head of another, and hanging over it for a long time?[215]

What the *tableau* tries to achieve is a balance between emotional involvement in the characters' plight and emotional detachment brought about by foreknowledge of events. Dorval justifies the *tableau* on the grounds of reason and taste:

I should much prefer *tableaux* on the stage, where there are so few, and where they would produce such a pleasing and reliable effect, to these *coups de théâtre* which are brought about in such an artificial way and based on so many peculiar suppositions that for one of these combinations of events which is felicitous and natural, there are a thousand which are bound to displease a man of taste.[216]

But the appeal to taste and reason does not by any means involve the exclusion of powerful emotions.

The sort of *tableau* which Dorval has in mind is difficult to achieve in contemporary drama not merely because playwrights do not favour it, but because the formal style of the actors makes it impossible; impossible, that is, not to achieve the effect of a picture, but to convey intense emotion.

Is it possible that people are not aware that misfortune has the effect of bringing men closer together; and that it is ridiculous, especially in moments of turmoil, when passions are carried to extremes, and the action is most violent, to stand in a circle, isolated, at a certain distance from one another, and in a symmetrical pattern?[217]

And this brings him again to the comparison with painting: 'Dramatic action must still be very far from perfection, since one sees hardly any scenes on the stage from which one could make a tolerable composition for a painting.'[218] The *tableau*, then, is a moment of intense emotion which, because we have been fully prepared for it, gives added significance to what precedes and what follows, whereas the *coup de théâtre*, by unexpectedly putting things into a different perspective, destroys the balance between ourselves and the spectacle, alters the distance which should be preserved between us and the action, a distance which is all the more necessary when violent passion is being portrayed.

It seems that the ideas put into the mouth of Dorval very closely foreshadow those which will be more thoroughly worked out in the *Rêve* and the *Paradoxe*. It is with all this in mind that we must interpret Diderot's plea for 'wildness' in the arts, not just through the

words of Dorval, but also in the long list of subjects in the section
'Les Mœurs' of the *Discours*[219] which are summed up in the statement: 'poetry demands something enormous, barbaric and
savage':[220] or in the *Essais sur la Peinture*: 'the imitative arts need
something savage, crude, striking and enormous';[221] or the many
references in the *Salons*.[222] We are not concerned here with nature in
movement but with good nature and natural man, stripped of the
enfeebling, corrupting conventions of contemporary civilization,
and academic art.

This exaltation of nature will lead in some writers to the conviction that nature is in all ways, including the aesthetic, superior to
art, but Diderot never goes as far as this. Although, as we have seen,
the ideal of the artist achieving a total understanding of nature as a
whole is likely to remain an ideal, the good artist's portrayal of the
limited area of nature open to his vision will be an improvement on
the raw material offered by nature. This point is made in the article
'Beau', when he compares the constraint of a park with the freedom
of a forest. Beauty, he says, is inseparable from the idea of freedom,
the 'innate feeling, this dominant taste for independence';[223] nature
is only great if it is, or appears, free. If we compare a park and a
forest:

one is the prison of luxury, languor and boredom; the other is the refuge of
roving thoughts, lofty contemplation and sublime enthusiasm. On seeing
the captive waters of Versailles and the leaping waters of Vaucluse hurtling
through the rocks, we can say of each: *that is beautiful!* But we say it of the
effects of art, and we feel it where the activities of nature are concerned: this
is why art, which subjugates, performs the impossible to hide from us the
constraints it imposes on it, and in nature left to itself, the painter and poet
take good care not to imitate accidents which might lead us to suspect traces
of servitude. Excellence in art, in its moral as well as its physical aspects,
consists in surpassing nature, in applying more intelligence to the composition of its scenes ... Notice how the most terrible accidents of nature,
tempests, volcanoes, thunderbolts, are more terrifying still in the fictions of
the poets.[224]

Against the formality of Versailles Diderot sets not the unfettered
freedom of nature itself, for this is not as unfettered as it appears,
but an art which can recognize the freedom concealed in nature and
give expression to it. This is the theme which he will develop, and
which we have already seen in his ideas on drama, that of throwing
off those civilized conventions which deform nature; but as in
drama, this does not mean that nature can be left to itself: it must be
processed in such a way that its essential nature is freed, for it too
can give an impression of 'servitude'.

The argument here may seem confused unless we remember that both civilization and nature in their present state are felt to embody imperfection, degeneration from some original 'model', and that the artist's task is to discern and recreate that lost perfection. 'Servitude' in nature, as in society, represents domination by the arbitrary forces of matter in movement. For the eighteenth-century mind, the search for truth involved going back to origins, finding the timeless essence beneath the distortions of history. This stripping down to essentials can also be described as an elimination of the contingent elements which hide the true nature of phenomena, and these elements can arise not only as a result of civilization, but, as the article 'Beau' shows, by the processes of nature itself. Here we see how Diderot's aesthetic thought fits into the general pattern of his thinking. The natural man, who is revealed in moral thought by a return to the state of nature, is revealed in painting and sculpture by arriving at the 'ideal model'[225] described by Ariste in the *Discours*,[226] to which I shall return, and in the *Salon* of 1767: 'by a plan ... to impart to him ... a character free of all the forms of servitude in our puny, meagre, mean and wretched lives',[227] and in drama by creating a milieu in which no external, irrelevant factors distract from the interplay of characters and passions. Dorval draws the parallel quite clearly:

If the serious genre is the easiest of all, it is on the other hand, the least subject to the contingencies of time and place. Take the nude to whatever place on earth you like; it will arouse interest, if it is well drawn. If you excel in the serious genre, you will give pleasure at all times and amongst all peoples.[228]

Universality, then, is the object, a universality achieved by freeing the subject-matter from the contingent features which mask its true nature. At this point it is possible to define the relationship between order and chance in this aspect of Diderot's aesthetics. In art chance is eliminated, not to produce order as an end in itself, but so that the resultant order will create the right conditions for art's purpose, which is the release of truth. The inarticulate passion which Dorval would have us witness on the stage, the 'something savage, crude, striking and enormous'[229] which Diderot would like his painters to imitate cannot be described as order in any of the generally accepted senses of the word, but in the particular artistic climate of Diderot's times, they represent a closer approximation to the truth of nature than formal drama or academic painting. As in the case of ordered perception, the representation is brought closer to the thing itself.

To refer back to the article 'Beau', 'excellence in art ... consists in ... applying more intelligence to the composition of its [nature's] scenes'.[230] Nature can at times come near to beauty, but art makes sure of it by what looks very much like a rational process.

The rational element

Just how rational the process is can be seen in some of the other comments Diderot makes on drama and the visual arts, particularly in connection with the control which the artist must exercise over his subject-matter. 'The dominant idea, carefully conceived, must exercise its despotic sway over all the others. It is the motive force of the machine which, like that which holds the celestial bodies in their orbits and bears them along, acts in inverse ratio to distance.'[231] And this insistence on a strong central control follows immediately upon a description of the balance necessary between reason and the imagination.

Expression demands powerful imagination, impassioned enthusiasm, the art of raising phantoms, bringing them to life and magnifying them; composition, in poetry as in painting, assumes a certain combination of judgment and enthusiasm, warmth and wisdom, intoxication and calm, of which there are few examples in nature. Without this strict balance, according to whether enthusiasm or reason predominates, the artist will either be extravagant or cold.[232]

The imagination can only function effectively in a rational framework. A more specific reference to the 'great idea' comes in the *Salon* of 1759; Diderot is speaking of Vien's *Résurrection de Lazare*:

These people think that all one needs to do is to arrange the figures; they do not know that the first point, the important point, is to find a great idea; one must walk up and down, meditate, put down one's brushes and rest, until the great idea is discovered.[233]

The work must exhibit unity and this unity can only come from the total control, intellectual control, which the artist exercises over it: only thus can chance be eliminated.

Another related point which Diderot considers important is that the dramatist must ensure that a fixed distance is maintained between play and audience:

if the action grows more complex, if the incidents grow more numerous, there may easily be some which will remind me that I am in an auditorium; that all these characters are actors, and that this is not a real event which is taking place. The narrative monologue, on the other hand, will transport me beyond the stage; I will follow its every detail. My imagination will bring them to life just as I have seen them in nature.[234]

The spectator must neither be so detached that he remembers he is a spectator of a fiction, nor so carried away that his imagination takes him beyond the limits of the scene before him. Like the artist, he must neither be 'extravagant' or 'cold'. A comparison which Diderot makes between drama and painting is interesting here. In the *Discours* he says that when he is uncertain how to judge a scene in a play he sometimes imagines it transferred to a canvas. 'One way of making up my mind . . . is to gather the objects together in my imagination, to transfer them from nature to canvas, and to examine them at that distance where they are neither too close to me nor too far away.'[235] A picture, set at an ideal distance, can give the right measure of objectivity, a mean between detachment and involvement.

The frequency with which Diderot draws analogies with painting suggests that in some ways a picture is for him the ideal form of art. This is certainly implied in a remark he makes about the tableau in the *Entretiens*:

Dramatic action must still be very far from perfection, since one sees hardly any scenes on the stage from which one could make a tolerable composition for a painting. How is that then? is truth less essential here than on a canvas? . . . My own view is that if a dramatic work were well made and well performed, the stage would offer the spectator as many real *tableaux* as the action would contain moments suitable for a painting.[236]

The painting is self-sufficient, self-contained, a world in itself with its own laws, and this is the advantage of a *tableau* over a *coup de théâtre*. Diderot makes much of the need for works of painting and drama to be self-contained, to stand by themselves, and the point is most neatly made in a letter to Sophie Volland: 'If, when one is doing a painting, one imagines spectators for it, then all is lost. The painter comes out of his canvas, as the author who speaks to the audience comes off the stage.'[237] There must be no visible link between the work and the world outside; it must have internal coherence, its own logic: 'It is the same with a play as with a well-ordered society, in which everyone sacrifices some of his original rights for the good of the whole',[238] he says in the *Paradoxe*. And, as in a well-ordered society, a work of art must run according to rational laws, so important events must not be set in motion by trivial causes, even though this happens in real life; the poet 'will make use of this incident, if it is given in history, but he will not invent it. I shall judge his methods with more severity than the conduct of the gods.'[239]

As for the permission to use such trivial incidents if they are sanctioned by history, this hardly seems in keeping with Diderot's general aesthetic, but first of all it must be seen in the light of the tradition which sees serious drama as a form of history, and secondly it falls into place if we remember that the artist is above all trying to establish a convincing illusion. If he invents unlikely incidents, he loses our acceptance; he has created a situation which is repugnant to our sense of what is reasonable; the objection disappears if we know that the incident has actually taken place. He makes his attitude on the subject clearer in the *Discours*, when he speaks of the conditions under which a poet may describe unusual events. Since these 'rare cases'[240] do occur in nature he may imitate them.

Either he seizes upon these extraordinary combinations of events, or he imagines similar ones. But whereas the connection between events often escapes us in nature, and, being unaware of the total picture, we see only an inevitable concomitance in the facts before us, the poet on the other hand requires that there should prevail throughout the texture of his work a clear and perceptible connection, such that there is less truth but more verisimilitude in his work than in the historian's.[241]

And then he adds that some liberty is permissible for the tragic poet: 'the things he invents gain in verisimilitude from those which are already available to him'.[242]

The rule is only broken, then, in the genre which traditionally deals with historical fact, but there is no doubt that Diderot was happier about an artistic structure which followed logic rather than facts.

To recall a necessary sequence of images such as they follow one another in nature is to reason according to the facts. To recall a sequence of images such as they would follow one another in nature if such and such a phenomenon were given, is to reason according to a hypothesis, or to suppose; it is to be a philosopher or a poet, according to the purpose one has in mind.[243]

And this even applies to history itself:

We read in history what a man of Henri IV's character did and suffered. But how many possible circumstances are there where he would have acted and suffered in conformity with his character, and in a more extraordinary way, which history does not offer to us, but which poetry imagines.[244]

In such a case the logic of art gives greater freedom than reality in that it offers a range of possibilities, but, as we should expect, in any one work the number of possible elements is limited by the internal logic of the work itself. In the *Essais sur la Peinture* he tells painters not to put things in their pictures if they are too far away to be distinguished for what they are; for example a dog must not be in danger of being confused with a wolf. This is a case 'where one must no longer paint according to nature'.[245] And he goes on to give a general rule:

The whole range of possibilities must not take place in good painting any more than in good literature; for there are certain concatenations of events whose possibility cannot be denied, but of which one can see, when they are placed together, that they have perhaps never taken place, nor perhaps ever will. The possibilities which one can make use of are the likely possibilities, and the likely possibilities are those where the odds are in favour of their having moved from a state of possibility to a state of existence within a certain time bounded by the action.[246]

This artist's guide to *vraisemblance*, loosely based on the law of probabilities, seems at first sight only to have a tenuous connection with the example of the dog – or wolf – which leads into it; but the fact that they are linked in Diderot's mind does reveal the general drift of his thought. A work of art is a closed system within which every element must be clear, must have the force of evidence to the rational mind. The animal in question is problematical: the perception has insufficient evidence to recognize it for what it is. The animal belongs to another system – in this case a painting executed from a position nearer to it. Just as in a given narrative work there is not time for certain events to be considered likely to take place, so, in a visual work, there is not the space: our perception can only cope with a limited quantity of phenomena in either time or space without rebelling in the name of reason. The last quotation is reminiscent of the final section of the article *Beau* quoted earlier in this chapter:

one might ask ... how many relationships one would need to observe in an object to be absolutely sure that it is the work of an artist ... what connection there is between the duration of the chance cause, and the relationships observed in the effects produced.[247]

Having infinite time and space, nature can produce anything allowed for by the laws of the material universe; the artist, with limited time and space, must limit the possible events he can portray. In nature, we do not understand the relationship of individual causes and effects because the scale is too great for us; but such understanding becomes possible within a limited spatial and temporal framework in which the quantity of causes is scaled down to the limits of our intellect. The artist, like Leibnitz's God, creates a series of possible worlds in which everything is in a rational proportion: 'I will judge his methods with more severity than the conduct of the gods.'[248]

It is on this level that the relationship between art and the materialist universe becomes evident, in that art produces a small-scale model of what is assumed to be the total reality before us. But one cannot, because of this relationship, say that Diderot's aesthetics are therefore materialist. Certainly the concept of a work of art as a self-contained world (which is not of course purely an idea of Diderot's, although he developed it more rigorously than his contemporaries) is a result of his conception of the universe, but art for him could be better described as the partial fulfilment of a dream, the possibility of total understanding. This dream is sometimes revealed when, as in the passage quoted from the *Essais sur la Peinture*, he says that a skilful artist might be successful in faithfully portraying nature as it is, for 'if causes and effects were evident to us we should have nothing more to do than to represent things as they are'.[249] But the dream goes further, because the understanding Diderot seeks is not just of causes and effects; his aesthetics assume meaning in the universe, and nothing in materialist determinism can suggest that complete knowledge would reveal any kind of moral purpose.

It would be more accurate to say that art, for Diderot, is not merely a compensation for our ignorance of the total world about us, but a form of resistance to it, almost a challenge, based on a recognition of its nature. In this resistance there are three stages, which might be called limitation, control and liberation. The artist selects a limited area of nature, which might resemble a chance moment of order produced by the contingencies of movement; by a combination of insight and reflection he arrives at his 'great idea', his unifying principle, which, once established, will define the laws and proportions of this possible world; out of this world, from which chance has been excluded, artistic and moral truth will be free to emerge, to have free play within a rigid framework which excludes all contingency. Thus man and nature acquire the meaning which the material world denies them, but which Diderot, at least on this level, is anxious to preserve.

I have said that Diderot's aesthetic theory does not arise directly out of his materialist philosophy, and it might be appropriate here to make the point that this does not imply a criticism of Diderot on the grounds of inconsistency. When Diderot looks at the processes of the universe he sees them in terms of monist determinist materialism, and, in the absence, as a marxist would say, of the dialectical

approach, all that can be logically developed from such a philosophy is in fact monist determinist materialism. His ideal man and
his ideal state are not logical consequences of this philosophy, but
attempts to resist its consequences, attempts to establish forms of
order and stability in opposition to a world which contains neither,
and which by definition cannot generate any system of action, any
kind of order which is not completely arbitrary, and has no more
claim to definitive status than any other.

It is this awareness which leads to the preoccupation with the
possible, or more specifically, the range of possibilities which open
up in a universe from which a providential order is banished. To the
speculation, which recognizes the necessary interplay of cause and
effect throughout the universe, there is only one possibility, and
that, as far as the past is concerned, is given in history; to the individual observer, seeing things from his own particular corner of the
universe, the possibilities seem infinite. To quote Diderot's example
of Henri IV, the materialist will say that the events of his reign came
about necessarily, they could not have been otherwise; to the contemporary observer the possible events are limitless. Between these
two extremes the poet and the philosopher operate, setting strict
spatial and temporal limits to the world they choose to deal with, so
as to offer us a complete picture of the workings of cause and effect
within it. The order they create is part way between the chaos of the
world in movement which we see evolving around us and the
abstraction of a universe in which all is necessary and consequential:

whereas the connection between events often escapes us in nature, and,
being unaware of the total picture, we see only an inevitable concomitance
in the facts before us, the poet on the other hand requires that there should
prevail throughout the texture of his work a clear and perceptible connection, such that there is less truth but more verisimilitude in his work than in
the historian's.[250]

There are two kinds of illusion here: the illusion of reality which
satisfies the senses, and the illusion of order which satisfies the
reason. Clearly this is a rational system, and the comments already
quoted show that it is also a closed system, a self-contained one; but
to what extent does this involve that kind of creation which we
normally associate with the artistic process?

The limits of creation

I think it is possible to say that in Diderot's aesthetic theory – and
the emphasis is on the word theory – the work of art is a creation to

exactly the same degree and within the same limits as the ideal man or the ideal society. The artist has the task of creating the conditions for his work by the exercise of control, dominating his imagination and arriving through a rational process of thought and meditation at the 'great idea' which will make of his work a unified, self-contained whole. Its nature will be such as neither to involve the spectator's imagination to the point where his critical judgment is impaired, nor to preclude his involvement to the extent that he is reminded that he is confronted with an artificial creation. This point was made in the *Entretiens*,[251] and is developed again in Diderot's imagined conversation with the *abbé* in the *Salon* of 1767.[252] The *abbé* is led to see that when he watches a play he is two people at once: 'I play two roles; there are two of me; I am Le Couvreur and I remain myself. It is I Le Couvreur who tremble and suffer, and it is I, just I, who enjoy it. Very good, abbé', answers Diderot approvingly, 'and there lies the limit for the imitator of nature. If I forget myself too much, and too long, the fear is too great; if I don't forget myself at all, if I remain completely myself, it is too weak: it is this exact balance which causes delightful tears to flow.'[253]

The idea is developed here in the sense that a more accurate physical basis for the 'exact balance'[254] has been established: a separation is recognized between the critical faculty and the emotions, or the 'centre of the network' and the diaphragm. It should be added that this balance between detachment and involvement applies as much to the artist as it does to his public. Similarly the ideal man, or rather his mind, his judgment, is sufficiently detached from the rest of his body to exercise control over it, but sufficiently involved in its nature not to let that control be a product of arbitrary speculation or the imagination; he creates himself, but only within the terms set by the nature and limitations of his own being. The sovereign is in the same situation *vis-à-vis* the state, potentially able to exercise unchecked control, but ideally prevented from such arbitrary use of power by a structure which forces him to recognize the true nature of the state itself. All three organisms are therefore creations but creations within strict limits, and those limits, as in the cases of the human being and the state, are fixed at the precise point where the activity of perception threatens to become action, to become part of the world of movement.

In the case of artistic 'creation', this impression is borne out by the role of the 'ideal model' as defined by Ariste in *De la Poésie Dramatique*.[255] The context of his discussion foreshadows that of the *Rêve de d'Alembert*. The starting point is the heterogeneity of mankind:

'There are perhaps not two individuals in the whole human race who bear a close resemblance to each other.'[256] What is more: 'Within the same man everything is in a constant process of change ... It is only by virtue of our memory that we are the same individual for others and for ourselves. At the age I am now, there is perhaps not one molecule left of the body I brought with me at birth.'[257] Since, given these conditions, we can never make the same judgments as other people, or even as we ourselves did at some point in the past, should we conclude that there are no objective values such as truth, goodness and beauty? 'Are these localized, momentary, arbitrary things, words without meaning?'[258]

Ariste's answer does not lie in either affirming or denying the existence of such objective values, but in defining the method by which we might best come to know them. The method consists in creating outside oneself 'an ideal man whom I shall create for myself, to whom I will present the objects, who will pass judgment, and for whom I shall be no more than the faithful echo...'[259] This is the only way, but in practice Ariste admits that it is impossible. In the first place this model would be an extension of himself, and any attempt to make up for its subjective origin by accumulating objective facts would be beyond the scope of an individual: he would need the powers of a god. 'But this ideal general model is impossible to create, unless the gods grant me their intelligence and promise me their eternal life...'[260] But there is a partial solution – and this is the strangest part of the passage – a man can form for himself an ideal member of his own profession, and having done so he will make the same use of it 'that painters and sculptors have made of their own. I will modify it according to circumstances.'[261]

There seems to be some obscurity in Diderot's reasoning here. He has said that sculptors 'have created a model according to their profession',[262] but the preceding paragraph, and common sense, would suggest that this model is not that of the ideal sculptor but of the perfectly proportioned human figure. This is confirmed by a later paragraph where Diderot talks of the various modifications which the sculptor can make in his ideal model.

Study bows the shoulders of the man of letters. Exercise gives the soldier a firm tread and an upright bearing ..., and so on. Observations such as these, endlessly multiplied, provide the sculptor's training and teach him how to alter, strengthen, weaken, deform and diminish his ideal model from the state of nature to any other state he wishes.[263]

It seems that Diderot's passion for analogy has been pursued here at the expense of logic.

But beneath the non-sequiturs of the argument one can discern two typical features of Diderot's thought. One of them starts from the familiar point that any kind of judgment presupposes a norm; and the model conceived by the sculptor is indeed a norm, a fixed entity to which he can refer and against which he can assess the changing phenomena of the world about him. But Diderot wants to develop the idea further. Although in practice there is no ideal man, since we are all born different and further modified by the contingencies of our lives, might it not be possible to pin down these variations, so as to see exactly what happens in the conformation of the body when a man spends his life in study, when a woman becomes pregnant or when someone gets angry? 'It is the study of passions, manners, characters, habits, which will teach the painter of human subjects how to alter his model, to convert it from the state of being a man to that of being a good or bad man, a calm or irascible one.'[264]

The attempt to fix the nature of the passions is no individual concern of Diderot's, it is practically an obsession of the period, from Montaigne, through Descartes, La Rochefoucauld and Vauvenargues to Diderot's own chapter on the passions in the *Éléments de Physiologie*[265] which, unusually for him, contains what seems to be an attempt at a comprehensive list and definition of the passions. But the particular mark of Diderot's approach is that he should have tried, and believed it possible, to define all the movement of human life in tangible terms, or to put it more precisely, in physically quantifiable terms. In 1771 he wrote to a Doctor Petit[266] asking him to describe in minute detail the internal and external changes which would take place in a man who, having spent the first twenty-five years of his life in complete inactivity and having thus preserved 'the outward forms of the strictest proportions, just as they appeared at the tip of Raphael's crayon',[267] successively became 'highway robber',[268] 'debauched and apoplectic',[269] 'jealous or envious',[270] and finally 'limping or hunchbacked'.[271] Armed with this information Diderot would then demonstrate to the artists of Saint-Petersburg the necessity of a profound knowledge of anatomy.

The answers provided by Petit and another doctor[272] could hardly have been very satisfactory to Diderot, but his question does show how the 'ideal model' is used to convert any contingency into an essence. What he had hoped for from the doctors was a description of the perfect 'highway robber', followed by the perfect 'highway robber turned to debauchery', and so on. The 'ideal model' is arrived at by eliminating the contingent elements which make men different and indefinable, but once it is arrived at we can generate from it a series of modifications which will abolish the contingent altogether: it can reinstate in an ordered form (that is, a rationally comprehensible form) the same elements from which it had to be divested in order to come into being. In practice only art, or philosophy – for on this level they are one and the same – can achieve this conversion of chance into order, the real world being too complex to allow the effects of human activity to be quantified; they are lost in the nexus of cause and effect which constitutes our total experience. But the artist and philosopher, working in a deliberately limited world of 'possibles', can achieve it. The advantage which art has over nature, then, does not consist in offering us a world of a different, purely aesthetic order, but in realizing, and operating within, the same order which we sense obscurely in the world but which the world hides from us. In this the philosopher, the critic and the artist all have the same function, one depending essentially on the use of judgment. This provides a partial explanation of the apparent confusion in Ariste's account of the 'ideal model'.

The second point is that, while it is clear enough how the effort to formulate the contingencies of human experience in ordered form presupposes a model as a standard of assessment, it does not explain why the man of letters or the philosopher should create models not of man in general, but of themselves, as expressed in their professional activity. In a sense this is a compromise, born of the impossibility of ever arriving at a perfect conception of man. But it also has its positive side. Ariste does not give any justification for basing his choice on his own profession, beyond the fact that he is dealing with something he knows about, but a little more illumination can be found in the *Entretiens*,[273] where Dorval introduces his revolutionary idea of basing his *dramatis personae* not on distinctions of character but on 'conditions': 'it is no longer, properly speaking, characters which we should place on the stage, but conditions'.[274] He puts this plan forward when *Moi* points out that 'the little differences which are evident in men's characters cannot be so successfully dealt with as can distinctive characters'.[275] If the stylized characterization of traditional comedy is to be avoided in the interests of realism, then something must replace it. 'However little exaggeration there was in the character, a spectator could say to himself: that is not me. But he cannot avoid noticing that the station in life being represented before him is his own; he cannot be unaware of his own duties. He must necessarily apply

what he hears to himself.'[276] Linked with the realism is the moral
purpose of drama, not just comedy, for it turns out that Dorval has,
as always, the 'serious genre' in mind: 'these subjects do not only
belong to the serious genre. They will become comic or tragic,
according to the genius of the man who adopts them.'[277] Moreover,
he sees drama as having primarily a social purpose, and although he
does not make this explicit, his insistence on 'conditions', together
with 'all the relationships: the head of a family, the spouse, the
sister, the brothers'[278] indicates that the social purpose is not in the
first place to teach men simply to be more moral, but quite specifically to carry out their social duties, and to understand those of
others.

The new drama would therefore be based on characters who were
defined not by the particular passions which predominate in their
make-up, but by their social function; and this is certainly one of
Diderot's chief contributions to dramatic theory. He is not so much
concerned to alter the structure of drama as to integrate it into the
lives of his fellow men, and to strengthen its social and moral role.
And as is so often the case, his originality here lies in his pursuit to its
logical conclusion of an idea which is both present in the attitudes of
his time and reflected in other areas of his own thought. There is no
need to stress the point that the theatre was regarded as having a
social function, that it was *par excellence* the art form which, as a
formal public spectacle, should improve – and, in the eyes of the
Church, could worsen – the moral standards of the public. If we
consider, together with this, the deeply rooted conviction that each
man had his proper place in society, and that that place defined his
social duties, then we can see how much Diderot's new conception
of drama reflected the spirit of his time.

As for the parallel with other aspects of Diderot's own thought,
the link can be found in the concept of function. For him, men are
essentially social beings, and in the social organism their roles are
fixed by the particular contribution they make. This is why it should
be quite logical for Ariste to make his ideal model a perfect version
not of his character, but of his objective function in society.
Moreover, this pattern also characterizes the human organism, and
the whole world of sentient matter. The two things which enable
Diderot to see the beginnings of order in the natural world are the
fact that matter can come together to form organisms and that these
organisms are characterized primarily by a relationship between individual organs each exercising a different function. This, one might
say, is the basic content without which no order is possible, and this

is the content which Diderot has attempted to incorporate into his new drama.

It is perhaps too much to ask of any writer's aesthetic theory that one should see it clearly and directly translated into his creative works. Certainly there are very clear parallels between Diderot's dramatic theory and practice because he was consciously evolving a new kind of drama, and some of these I shall deal with in the next chapter, but as far as the rest of his fictional work is concerned, especially the great dialogues, the gulf between theory and practice is immense. Where Diderot's finest works are concerned the parallels are only discernible at a deeper level. Here all his thinking, of whatever kind, is governed by the same preoccupations, formed in the same mould. Moreover this conceptual structure – the subject of this study – itself creates the gulf between theory and practice. Diderot's ideal of artistic creation moves between the two poles of the 'ideal model' and pure imitation, detachment and involvement, reason and sensibility. Operating only within these limits, it allows only for an art which is judged in the same terms as the reality it represents. What we now understand by artistic creation, the creation of another world, and by the specific nature of aesthetic pleasure, has no place in it.

Perhaps there is no better example than the aesthetic theories of the seventeenth and eighteenth centuries, which seem to us to by-pass so many important issues, of the way in which the minds of a given age can be imprisoned within a pattern of thinking which will not allow them to account for their actual experience of reality. For there is no doubt that Diderot and his contemporaries were aware of the problem. The consciousness of a type of aesthetic pleasure which could not be encompassed by their theories is often revealed in discussions of the sublime, and to this I shall return in the final chapter.

III

SOCIAL AND
INDIVIDUAL VALUES

6

PUBLIC ORDER
AND PRIVATE DISORDER
IN DIDEROT'S WORKS

Drama and the realization of order

If we look for examples of the realization of order in Diderot's artistic practice, then the best are undoubtedly his two plays; and this is as it should be, since the theatre is traditionally, as a public spectacle and a moral spectacle, the home of order. This was its function in the seventeenth century and it continued to have this role in the eighteenth. The plays of Corneille end in the triumph of order and so, formally at least, does *Le Mariage de Figaro*. Throughout the period, dramatic plots present a situation which either contains within itself the possibility of a return to order – usually the fact that the characters are under a misapprehension as to their proper social or political roles – or else can be engineered by the dramatist to produce the desired ending. This association of the theatre with public order seems to have been one of the dominant attitudes of the age, and some aspects of this attitude will be clarified in the discussion which follows of Diderot's own dramatic efforts. Chouillet (*La Formation des Idées Esthétiques de Diderot*, pp. 457–8) has drawn attention to the frequent echoes of Corneille in the dialogue of his two plays. One can also see a parallel in their structure, perhaps more obviously in *Le Père de Famille*.

Here we have the spectacle of a family whose members are at odds with one another. What should ideally be a closed system, that is, an organism in which each member has a proper function relating to the whole, is apparently threatened by one outside element, Sophie, who seems to have led Saint-Albin astray, and actually threatened by another, the Commandeur, who exerts an evil influence on the father himself, M. d'Orbesson. This latter is by rights the central authority, the guarantor of order, and he possesses the attributes of good authority (or of a good sovereign). We see him dispensing justice and putting the welfare of his dependants before his own: 'Their needs are more pressing than my own; and it is better that I should be short of money than they'.[1] He has tried to arrange a career for his son which will be in accordance with his nature: 'I have based your future life on your talents and tastes'.[2] He respects social order: 'Should I then, by my shameful weakness, countenance social disorder, the confusion of blood and rank, the degradation of the family?'[3] But M. d'Orbesson steps outside the limits of his proper function, his conception of what is 'right' being obscured partly by social convention and partly by the influence of the Commandeur. Moreover, social convention has set up barriers between the members of the group, since both pairs of lovers believe their union to be unacceptable to M. d'Orbesson.

This situation is, of course, much more domestic than anything we might find in Corneille, but if we leave aside the subject-matter, the structure is strongly reminiscent of those seventeenth-century plays in which a tyrannical sovereign, or father, or both, is set against a youthful rival or an impetuous son, and in which order is finally restored when the dominant figure is led to see his true role. Schérer (*La Dramaturgie Classique en France*, pp. 20–32) has pointed out how frequent this structure is in classical drama, and the pattern seems to continue into the next century, always with the underlying assumption that good consists in order and stability, but that the agent which enables us to perceive that order is a disruptive influence either within the system or outside it. In *Le Père de Famille* M. d'Orbesson has, for most of the time, the role of the tyrannical father, the obstacle to the happiness of the younger characters. Saint-Albin is the typically impetuous, '*sensible*' son, who poses an apparent threat to the order of the family. The role which would, in a political play, have been taken by the 'evil counsellor', is assumed here by the Commandeur, ostensibly encouraging d'Orbesson to assert his rightful authority, in fact working for his own ends.

As Joly points out (*Deux Études sur la Préhistoire du Réalisme*, pp. 95–6) there is really no need for the Commandeur as far as the plot goes; the situation could be resolved without him. But he still has an important role, as does Sophie. These are the two characters who act as outside influences on the family unit; they belong to no group themselves, but represent the two opposing principles which are operating within the family, and which tend to operate in any organism. The Commandeur is an agent of tyranny, of separation. As M. d'Orbesson says:

His ambitious plans, and the authority he has assumed in my house, grow daily more irksome to me . . . we used to live in peace and unity. The restless and tyrannical temper of this man has divided us all. We fear and avoid each other, and I am isolated; I am alone in the bosom of my family, and I am dying...[4]

But as the principle of order and authority fades away, another influence is secretly acting as a leaven on the members of the family in the person of Sophie. Contact with Sophie awakens the sensibility of one after another of the members of the family: first Saint-Albin, prepared to go with her in defiance of the 'wretched conventions':[5] then Germeuil, who describes her to Cécile as 'a hapless woman to whom you could not refuse your sympathy if you saw her',[6] a prediction which is confirmed when Cécile's initial resistance to the idea of hiding her in the house breaks down. 'Here anxiety gives way to pity in Cécile's heart',[7] says the stage direction.

In the final scene order is restored. Sophie, the apparent threat to the family, is revealed as an agent of unity; the Commandeur, the agent of atomization and disorder, is ejected, and the father is restored to his true position of authority. His blindness to the truth had turned him for a time into a tyrant: 'For the first time my father is in agreement with this cruel uncle',[8] Saint-Albin had said in the second act. His role closes with him seeing things as they are: from being an active agent of tyranny he reverts at the end to being a guarantor of happiness and stability; events have enabled him to become an instrument of ordered perception, not an agent of disruption.

It is worth stressing that the chief element which distinguishes Diderot's play from the more traditional forms of serious drama, apart from the more obvious points dealt with in his theoretical writings, is the character of Sophie, who is the means by which sensibility, in the form peculiar to Diderot, is introduced into the action. It seems that Sophie, by her mere presence in the household, is able to awaken the sensibility of the other characters, and in this her influence is exactly parallel to that of sensibility in matter, which breaks down barriers and awakens the sensibility inert in surrounding matter by contact with it. One could also compare her with the colony of Swiss whom Diderot imagined settling among the Russians so that the latter would develop an awareness of freedom. Sophie has the role of both agent and symbol of the awareness of natural rights which enables the play to proceed to its conclusion.

The Commandeur, too, has his counterpart in Diderot's political theory in the despotic force which causes the break-up of states into isolated individuals, the force described in the passage already quoted from the *Fragments échappés du Portefeuille d'un Philo-*

sophe: 'between the citizens a moral distance is created ... and this moral distance is created by a civil inquisitor who constantly lurks amongst individuals...'[9] A final parallel can be drawn with Diderot's political thought in that the enlightenment which finally brings order into being is only made possible by the goodwill of the characters concerned, especially that of M. d'Orbesson.

Chouillet, comparing Diderot with Molière, (*ibid.*, p. 470) remarks that despite the similar structure of *Le Père de Famille* and many plays by Molière, M. d'Orbesson is distinguished by his selfless desire to be a good father: 'M. d'Orbesson, unlike Molière's fathers, is open-minded and tries to understand.'[10] Catherine II, on the other hand, turned out not to have the desire to understand which Diderot had hoped for; his ideal for Russia depended as much on the enlightenment of the sovereign as the happy conclusion of *Le Père de Famille* depends on the inherent goodness of the head of the family. The parallel drawn here with Diderot's political thought does not of course imply that his plays are intended to put across political ideas. The point is that his underlying pattern of thought is the same, whether he is thinking about the problems of the family, the problems of the state, or for that matter any problem involving the relationships of organisms.

In fact it would seem here again that the play is more comparable with those of Corneille than with Molière's. Like many of Corneille's kings and fathers, M. d'Orbesson already has within himself the potential to be a good head of a family: the conditions for the satisfactory conclusion are planted right at the beginning, and the playwright's task is to engineer the scenes so that the moral problems are brought to the fore. Indeed, Diderot may well have had Corneille in mind when he wrote *Le Père de Famille*. In *De La Poésie Dramatique*, writing of the possibility of 'a sort of moral drama'[11], he says: 'What would be the aim, in fact? So to arrange the poem that the events came about of themselves, like the abdication of the empire in *Cinna*.'[12] Moreover, one of the factors which leads M. d'Orbesson to his eventual enlightenment is, as in the case of Auguste, his increasing isolation.

But there is no denying that the events of *Le Père de Famille* are contrived to an extent which makes a mockery of Diderot's theories of *vraisemblance*, as Joly observes (*ibid.*, p. 97). His further point, however, that Diderot's theories are made unrealizable by his 'manichean and tendentious metaphysics' (p. 96)[13] needs some qualification. His philosophy may be manichean if one can apply the term to a conviction that the good is associated with stability and permanence, while evil is identified with movement and disruption. But the play does not seem tendentious in the sense that, as Joly suggests (pp. 90–3), Diderot is striking a blow, consciously or unconsciously, for the bourgeois values of liberal economy. We have already seen that the Commandeur is a 'domestic' version of the traditional evil counsellor to the sovereign, and that, on a more profound level, truth can only emerge from the collision of an existing order with some disruptive element. In Diderot's dramatic theory perhaps the most telling comment in support of this view comes from the *Discours*: 'In comedy, men must play the role which the gods play in tragedy. Fatality and wickedness, these are the foundations of interest in the respective genres.'[14]

To see the reason for this it is not enough to say that Diderot, having a bourgeois axe to grind, needs to show his main characters as virtuous. We are concerned here with the fundamental opposition between stability and movement, and between reality and appearance. The discussion from which the above quotation is taken centres on the question of dramatic illusion, but the sentence which immediately precedes it is: 'If there is anything that can move us, it is the spectacle of a man suffering guilt and misfortune through no fault of his own'.[15] This is an expression of what is surely one of the most important of eighteenth-century attitudes. Whatever variations there may be in different thinkers' conceptions of natural man, all are agreed that he is innocent. Whether he is the vulpine predator of Hobbes or the naive savage of Rousseau, he carries no burden of sin. The unity of his character is not threatened by an innate flaw, only by the movements of the elements which make up his own organism and the whole world about him.

If we look again at the question of our relationship with the world around us, as seen by Diderot, we, and for that matter all organisms are constantly being forced to change in the effort to adapt themselves to the shifting pattern of the external world. Any satisfactory adaptation can only be momentary: what at one instant is 'reality' becomes at the next 'appearance', when the world no longer corresponds to our conception of it. We strive, by a kind of moral inertia, for permanence, for that 'repos', that state of calm which, it seems, can alone ensure the unity of the self, but self-preservation demands that we should constantly adapt to change. The forces which compel us to change will inevitably seem to be chance phenomena, products of disorder. As d'Holbach put it in his single-minded attempt to take the mystery out of nature, the *Système de la Nature*:

Disorder, for any being, is never anything more than its passing into a new order, a new mode of existence, which inevitably involves a new sequence of actions, or movements different from those to which this being had previously been subject.[16]

and: 'The pattern of what we call *order* or *disorder* exists only in our minds'.[17]

Disorder, then, is both an evil, from the point of view of the individual experiencing it, and a necessity in terms of the general order of the universe, and this truth perhaps reaches its highest expression in the person of Mephisto in Goethe's *Faust*, but we can also see it in *Le Neveu de Rameau* and even in *Le Père de Famille*. In this play, the Commandeur, a gratuitously evil character, is allowed to hasten the disintegration of the family to the point where it becomes aware of the truth and is able to form itself together again into a harmonious whole. Having fulfilled his role he is then eliminated from a scene in which he no longer has any function, a scene in which reality and appearance once more coincide. It is he who acts 'the role which the gods play in tragedy', and who represents 'wickedness'. But this 'wickedness' is dramatically interesting not because it is the dominant feature of the Commandeur but for the effect it has on M. d'Orbesson, who is fixed in a conventional way of thinking and fails to recognize the true nature of either the Commandeur or Sophie. The play is in fact built round the person of the father: 'I wanted the father to be the main character. The plan would have been the same, but all the episodes would have changed if I had chosen as my hero either the son, or the friend, or the uncle.'[18] This device, which gives unity to the play, is inevitably false to Diderot's picture of real life as a never-ending, all-embracing process of change and adaptation. As the play proceeds the viewpoint does shift away from M. d'Orbesson towards other characters, but the end is engineered so that it returns to him, with all the characters seeing things in the same way, except of course for the Commandeur, who is removed entirely. The final scene presents us with a family which has become a unified organism, and although the order thus restored is contrived and artificial in terms of real life, its very artificiality is what makes it possible for us to get in proper perspective the truth which has been revealed in the course of the play.

Conflict and disorder are allowed to operate for a short space and then the tensions are resolved; the dangers of tyranny, passion and sensibility are briefly displayed, but are checked before they can run their full course, to bring about destruction or else become submerged in the constant confusion of the surrounding world. This

process is comparable to the awakening and subsequent neutraliza-
tion of sensibility which takes place in ordered perception. In both
cases the agents of disorder are arrested in a state of potentiality,
becoming immobilized as they are revealed for what they are. The
final satisfaction which we are intended to feel at the suspension and
resolution of the conflict coincides with the moment when the father
sees things 'as they are', so that he becomes a kind of extension of
ourselves and we in our turn are included in the pattern of order.
Here a comparison suggests itself with Diderot's ideas on painting.

In his article 'Composition' in the *Encyclopédie* he writes: 'If you
make a torrent fall from the mountains and you want me to feel terri-
fied, imitate Homer, place a shepherd in the background among the
mountains, who will listen with terror to its noise.'[19] The spectator
in the picture acts as an intermediary between the world within the
frame and ourselves. Although Diderot insists, as we have seen, that
a picture should be self-contained, it is perhaps a condition of its
self-containment, its existence as a unified, rational system, that its
impact should be made on the right level. The presence of an
observer within the picture recalls the well-known passage from the
article 'Encyclopédie':

if we banish man, or the thinking and reflecting being from the face of the
earth, this moving and sublime spectacle of nature is no more than a dreary,
silent scene. The universe speaks no more; silence and night envelop it. All is
transformed into a vast solitude where everything takes place in darkness
and obscurity. It is man's presence which gives interest to the existence of
natural beings... Why should we not introduce man into our works, as he
is placed in the universe?[20]

But the man who is introduced into Diderot's painting is not
exactly the 'thinking and reflecting being' of the *Encyclopédie*; he is
afraid at the sight before him. It seems that where a work of art is
concerned, the relationship between it and the observer must
involve two stages; the impact on us must be mediated by a human
presence within the system itself. The shepherd experiences the
'terror' of the scene itself and we experience it at one remove. Like
the *abbé* in the *Salon* of 1767, watching Le Couvreur and being Le
Couvreur and himself at the same time, we have the experience, but
its direct impact is channelled off into the sensibility of the actor or,
in the case of a picture, the observer within the frame, leaving our
own judgment unimpaired. In the case of a play, unfolding in time –
and here *Le Père de Famille* is again a good example – the system
which threatened to disintegrate, the family, is restored to itself and
becomes a self-contained unit as the principal figure, the head, is

able to 'see' his proper role. At this point his view of things and ours become identical: M. d'Orbesson becomes the link between us and a perfect system or organism which, being complete in itself, can be comprehended, in the fullest sense of the word, by our intellect.

An analogous role is played by Dorval in *Le Fils Naturel*: starting out as a man of great sensibility whose personality threatens to become submerged in his own problems and those of the people around him, he slowly raises himself above these problems with the help of Constance, first divesting himself of his personal wealth at the end of Act III (as Diderot would do if he were king), and at the end of the next act deciding to set things right by the exercise of virtue. Thus he 'has raised himself above fate'[21] – to use *Moi's* phrase in *Le Neveu de Rameau* when he described the satisfaction which comes from performing a good action – and in so doing he has set himself apart from the other characters, placed himself halfway between them and ourselves. From the vicarious experience of emotion and passion in the various characters in the play we move, through the mediation of Dorval, to the direct experience of a closed, ordered system.

One can say that Diderot has, in these two plays, pushed the dominant dramatic structure of his age to its logical conclusion. Dorval rises above his fate like Auguste in *Cinna* and M. d'Orbesson is led towards his true role like Prusias in *Nicomède*, but Diderot takes us a step further in providing the means whereby we can identify more closely with his central character, so closely that the ultimate attainment of order becomes so to speak our own experience. This is the point made by Dorval, speaking in the *Entretiens* of the dramatic advantage of replacing characters with 'conditions':

However little exaggeration there was in the character, a spectator would say to himself: that is not me. But he cannot avoid noticing that the station in life being represented before him is his own; he cannot be unaware of his own duties. He must necessarily apply what he hears to himself.[22]

That the experiment was not successful must be partly due to the fact that Diderot failed to recognize the true nature of dramatic experience, which depends – as he would have conceded himself in other contexts – on a constant distance being set between ourselves and the characters, and on those characters having a convincing existence in their own right.

Public and private worlds

It is perhaps for this reason that the *Entretiens sur le Fils Naturel* are so much more interesting than the play itself. The Dorval who failed to achieve life in the *drame* now achieves it, paradoxically, in conversation with his creator, and in a conversation largely concerned with the ill-defined boundaries between fiction and reality. Here the order which was achieved in the play is once more called into question.

> The performance was so life-like that, forgetting at several points that I was a spectator, and an unseen one, I was about to leave my place and add a real character to the scene. And then, how was I to reconcile what had just happened with my ideas? If this play was a comedy like any other, why were they unable to play the final scene?[23]

Order was never realized not just because its dramatic restoration in the final scene did not take place, but because throughout the performance, Diderot, the unseen spectator, is frequently tempted to become a part of the action himself. The distance between spectator and play without which the spectator can never achieve the right critical relationship with it is never established; nor for that matter are the actors in the play sufficiently in command of their roles, that is, emotionally uninvolved in them, since they break down when Lysimond appears. Sensibility everywhere triumphs over critical detachment.

Diderot seeks an answer to the problem he poses at the beginning of the *Entretiens*, but it is difficult to find one in the subsequent discussion between *Moi* and Dorval. If one were anxious to discover a chronological progress towards certainty in Diderot's thought, one might say that the problem not solved here eventually finds its solution in the *Paradoxe sur le Comédien*. In this work a clear distinction is made between the kind of performance which can be put on for a private gathering, in a *salon*, and the kind which is suitable for the theatre. Diderot maintains – seems to take it for granted, in fact – that the rules governing poetic or narrative delivery in a private performance are different from those called for in a public one. The subject is dealt with early on in the *Paradoxe*[24] and he returns to it later.[25] His view is that a theatrical experience is of a totally different kind from what is felt in a private gathering. In the first, the actor is, in keeping with Diderot's general thesis in the *Paradoxe*, detached from his role; he has learnt it down to the smallest detail and is able to reproduce it at will, in order to elicit the desired reaction in his audience. In the second, it is a case of performer and audience being equally moved as he recites a passage which

147

he will never again be able to utter in the same way. Whereas the actor on the stage has overcome the inevitable process of change by dissociating himself, or rather his sensibility, from the part he is playing, the reader in the *salon* has not; he is as involved as those who listen to him, and the performance he gives will be lost as soon as it is delivered.

It would seem then that the performance of *Le Fils Naturel* which so moved Diderot and those who acted in it is of the second kind: a private performance in which the involvement of the actors generated a similar involvement in the spectator. It is presumably for this reason that the first speaker in the *Paradoxe* seems to be claiming that a *salon* performance of drama is not possible.

I understand you, [says the first speaker to the second] you involved your audience, you amazed them, moved them, produced a great effect. All that is true. But transfer to the theatre your familiar tone of voice, your simple expression, your domestic apparel, your natural gestures, and you will see how feeble and inadequate you become.
... Do you imagine that scenes from Corneille, Racine, Voltaire, Shakespeare even, can be delivered in your conversational voice and in the same tone as if you were sitting at the fireside? No more than your fireside story can be related with the stress and declamatory force of the stage.[26]

Moreover, the private performer will be emotionally exhausted by his delivery: 'your spirit is exhausted, you have no more sensibility, warmth or tears to give'.[27] And he goes on to explain why.

Why does the actor not experience the same exhaustion? Because there is a great difference between the interest he takes in a freely invented story and the interest you take in your neighbour's misfortune. Are you Cinna? Have you ever been Cleopatra, Merope, Agrippina? What do these people matter to you?[28]

It emerges that the real difference between private and public performance is not just that the latter is subject to a number of theatrical conventions which set a distance between audience, actor and play, but that the actual subject-matter is assumed to be different. What we experience in the *salon* has the force of reality, it is close to our own lives, whereas what we see on the stage are 'the imagined phantoms of poetry ... spectres in the style peculiar to a certain poet',[29] which do not even correspond to the historical figures they are supposed to portray: 'they would cut a poor figure in history: they would draw peals of laughter in literary circles or any other social gathering'.[30] In fact not only the subject-matter but the form is different, for the type of work which is listened to in an intimate circle is most often referred to as a 'tale',[31] of the same order as 'your fireside story'.[32] The fundamental distinction that

Diderot is making is that between everyday reality and formal art, between ordinary language and rhetoric, between facts and fantasy. The interesting point, however, is that the values of order, as so far discussed, seem to belong with formal art, with the unreal. The formal restrictions of art, the rules and conventions, may act as an essential check on the poet's imagination and the actor's sensibility, but the result is still far removed from life as we live it.

When Diderot returns to this problem later in the *Paradoxe*, he makes the point that a work intended for public performance cannot by its nature attempt a perfect imitation of nature. If a poet, he says, were to write a scene to be performed on the stage just as it would be delivered 'in a social gathering',[33] not even the most accomplished actor could do it: 'if he managed it once, he would fail a thousand times. Success depends on such minute factors!... It is forbidden, on pain of being insipid, dreary and odious, to descend by one iota below the simplicity of Nature.'[34] The truth of nature can occasionally be achieved, but it is very much a matter of chance, and in any case something to be avoided, since the kind of emotion involved is characterized by total disorder:

Let us suppose I have a rather moving tale to tell, a kind of turmoil seizes my heart, and my head; my speech is muddled; my voice grows hoarse; my ideas melt away; my words will not come out; I stammer, and I become aware of it; tears flow down my cheeks, and I fall silent.[35]

Such a display may succeed 'en société', never in the theatre:

neither dramatic convention, nor action, nor the poet's words could adapt to my stifled, broken, sobbing speech. You see, it is not even permissible to imitate nature, not even beautiful nature, the truth, too closely, and there are limits within which one must confine oneself;[36]

and these limits are set by 'good sense, which requires that one talent must not detract from another. Sometimes the actor must sacrifice himself to the poet.'[37]

Here we are back with the concept of the ordered society, in which each member sacrifices something of himself for the general good, where people are considered in terms of their function rather than as individuals; and what is sacrificed is not merely a part of an individual's personality, but the truth of nature.

In the ensuing conversation, the possibility is touched upon of 'another sort of tragedy'[38] which would allow for the natural expression of the emotions – a sort which, one imagines, might not be unlike *Le Fils Naturel* or *Le Père de Famille* – but the first speaker is reluctant to commit himself on the subject: 'I don't really know

what you would gain from it; but I do know what you would lose.'[39]
It is difficult to say whether Diderot is, with hindsight, implying that
the new kind of drama with which his name is associated should be
confined to drawing-room performances, but there is no doubt that
behind this discussion between the two speakers of the *Paradoxe*
there lies a problem which is fundamental to the social attitudes of
the period. To return for a moment to the introductory pages of the
Entretiens sur Le Fils Naturel, there is a passage where Diderot
describes himself walking away from the unfinished performance,
deeply moved and saddened, and saying to himself: 'I must be a fool
to get upset like this. All this is just a comedy. Dorval made it up out
of his head. He wrote the words from his imagination, and today
they were amusing themselves acting it out.'[40] Diderot tries to
imagine that the play was a fiction but fails; and yet, on another
level, the play is a fiction, and so is Dorval.† In this passage Diderot
is establishing an ambivalent approach which will reach its finest
expression in *Jacques le Fataliste*: preventing the reader from establishing any fixed relationship with what he is reading, calling into
question the assumptions which both public and author like to
preserve about artistic illusion. This tendency to question the status
of order, which has produced Diderot's two most fascinating works,
Le Neveu de Rameau and *Jacques le Fataliste*, illustrates better than
anything his awareness that order is – there seems no better way of
putting it – of a different order from the world of everyday reality,
from the direct experience of life.

Public and private writing

No eighteenth-century writer has dealt with this problem so
thoroughly – pehaps Voltaire comes nearest – but it is important to
remember that such awareness of the qualitative gulf between order
and the 'real' world, between stability and movement, is an essential
feature of the attitudes of the seventeenth and eighteenth centuries
towards the world about them. The point tends to be forgotten
when we read the works of thinkers like La Mettrie, d'Holbach or
Helvétius, or even Rousseau. The attempts of these men to produce
systems of thought which would encompass the whole of human
activity and banish the irrational from our lives obscures the fact

† J. S. Siegel makes a parallel point in 'Grandeur–Intimacy...' (p. 252): 'Whether
Diderot knows it or not, he is leaving the world of the stage, and even the boards of
the salon, and is crossing the threshold into the suggestive world of pure imagination, the world of the novel.'

that duality continued to define men's ways of seeing the world.

The point has already been made in connection with Diderot's science of man. It is evident too, in his attitude to his own work and can, I think, help to clarify the much discussed problem of his published and unpublished works. Of the views which have been advanced on this subject, the most common centre round the two factors of censorship and posterity. The theory that Diderot was more concerned with fame in the future than in the present, chiefly supported by what he says in the *Lettres à Falconet*, is expressed in a fairly representative way by Wilson in the Epilogue to his biography, 'The Appeal to Posterity'. The chief argument is that Diderot considered the judgment of posterity to be more reliable than that of his contemporaries, but one might object that if Diderot was so concerned that his work should be judged by posterity, he would surely have taken more careful steps to ensure that they saw it. Kempf in *Diderot et le Roman* (pp. 33–4) points out that as well as addressing many of his works to a specific reader, he had a general 'uneasiness in the presence of the reader or the unseen spectator'.[41] 'Diderot chooses an audience for the future, which is to say that he rejects the real audience.'[42] Kempf adds that this attitude seems unique to Diderot: 'This is an attitude of which no other examples are known in the eighteenth century.'[43]

This last point does indeed present a problem, and suggests that Diderot may well be a unique case, and that the reason lies in his personality. And yet we have the *Encyclopédie*, surely one of the greatest efforts ever made until then to achieve widespread dissemination of ideas, and one in which Diderot did not try to conceal his own participation either as editor or as a writer of articles. Diderot's persistent championship of the *Encyclopédie* illustrates not only his willingness to be read, but also the fact that he was not necessarily made cautious by his incarceration at Vincennes. The claim is made by Hélène Vianu (*Nature et Révolte dans la Morale de Diderot*, p. 66) that we are not seeing the real Diderot in the *Encyclopédie*, for he was too mindful of his responsibilities towards it to endanger its future by being too audacious. 'For this reason, Diderot, the author of so many articles in the *Encyclopédie*, chooses his words with care, in the knowledge that this care will ensure their effectiveness.'[44] This may well be so, especially after the criticism raised by 'Autorité Politique', but these self-imposed limitations, if in fact they exist, as well as Diderot's reluctance to publish much of his work, could equally well be explained by the fact that he had, in common with the whole period, a fairly definite conception of what could and what could not be published. Bénac, in his introduction to the *Œuvres Romanesques* (p. ix) is perhaps nearer the mark when he discusses the non-publication of all but a few of his narrative works.

Diderot regarded them as a form of relaxation or as confidences reserved for his close friends. It has been noticed that Diderot's ideas are much more daring in the works he did not publish than in the others: we should not therefore be surprised if we find in the novels a purely intellectual element, born of the author's hypotheses and paradoxes, and, for this reason, more closely connected with his philosophy than his art. We must not forget either that, unlike Voltaire's *Contes*, all this philosophy remains purely speculative and is not intended to be practised.[45]

But here again, a point seems to have been missed. The problem is discussed at some length by Dieckmann in the first of his *Cinq Leçons sur Diderot*. He recognizes Diderot's desire for a closer contact with an ideal reader as the most significant factor, and points out the modernity of this attitude, but not its links with tradition. I have quoted the views of a number of scholars on this question, because this diversity of opinions in a fairly limited area of Diderot studies illustrates, I believe, a failure to take into account the deeper attitudes of the period and in particular a feeling about order in its social context which is very different from our own.

To identify these attitudes as they affect authorship in general, we have to distinguish first between theoretical works, those which are specifically about religion, philosophy, politics and so on, and literature proper. As far as the first category was concerned, orthodox, unorthodox and frankly subversive works were regularly published throughout the *Ancien Régime* and the only check – a powerful one, it is true – on publication was official censorship, which resulted in the more heretical works being published abroad, mostly in Holland. Where literary and historical works are concerned, the situation is more complex. Certainly they were equally subject to official censorship, but in the seventeenth century in particular there seems to have been in addition a fairly clear distinction between what one might call public and private literature. This was a distinction not imposed from without but accepted as apparently self-evident by writers and the reading public in general. I say the distinction was fairly clear, because the genre which was placed rather uneasily between the two categories was the novel and especially, as time went on, the realistic novel.

Public literature corresponded roughly to the traditional genres; it was produced almost exclusively by professional writers, and its subject-matter was almost as limited as its form. One of the features which distinguished it most sharply from present-day literature is that it was impersonal. It was inconceivable that a writer should seem to express his own feelings in such works; they were felt to enshrine certain values sanctioned by society; they represented in short a conception of order which might be called 'official'. But we must leave aside the modern association of the word with governmental propaganda, because public order for the *Ancien Régime* was associated with an outlook which went deeper than any single pronouncements which might be made by Church or state; it would be better defined as a tacit pact that life should and could be conducted according to rational criteria, that these criteria were sanctioned by an underlying order in the universe, some kind of providence, and that the preservation of such criteria, whether by individuals or government, was a public, even a political matter.

The literary form most closely associated with this concept was of course the theatre, and in particular serious drama, and the force of the concept is illustrated by the survival of classical drama in France right through the eighteenth century, and also by the failure of Shakespearian drama ever to strike any powerful chord in French literary sensibility until the nineteenth century. The genius of Shakespeare was acknowledged, just as it was acknowledged that, in fact, life did not necessarily obey the rational laws associated with order, but it seems to have been generally held that to make a public admission of the objective existence and validity of the irrational by embodying it in a work of art meant for public consumption would be to open the floodgates to disorder and anarchy. For this reason we find in the France of this period an extraordinary dichotomy between public and private values, not so much those values which could be expressed in religious or philosophical terms, but those which represented a total view of social, human reality.

Georges May, in an article whose title sums up his thesis – *L'Histoire a-t-elle engendré le roman?* (Did history give rise to the novel?) – suggests that the type of history which may have been particularly influential in shaping the novel is the memoir, a genre widely practised during the period, but one which was to a large extent personal in its approach. It is a feature of these memoirs, from the time of the Fronde onwards, that their authors often claim both to be giving a personal, authentic view of events as they were experienced, and at the same time to be writing something which is intended, not for publication, but only for the eyes of a few intimates. It is as though, beneath the monolithic 'official' view of events, enshrined in standard histories and historical drama, there

153

existed a range of individual reactions, very often insisting on a different set of values, in particular on human self-interest, on the irrationality of human behaviour, on the unpredictability of events, in short on the absence of any rationale governing the process of history. Perhaps the nearest we can get to this attitude in the better known works of the period are the Maxims of La Rochefoucauld, and even these are couched in a form which had no place in the hierarchy of literary genres. Moreover, as W. G. Moore stresses in his book on La Rochefoucauld, these reflections owe a good deal of their inspiration to the events of the Fronde, which also produced a considerable body of personal memoirs.

In such works the prime concern is not with the values of public order but with those of the private individual. As May says of the development of the novel (*ibid.*, p. 172):

This particular development of the novel under the influence of history, and especially memoirs, can, thanks to the intimate nature of these works, give us a foretaste of the change in sensibility which will suddenly lead men to prefer individual happiness to the public good.[46]

There is no denying that individual happiness becomes an increasing preoccupation of literature as the period progresses and that the novel is the literary genre best adapted to express it. As such, the novel represents an attempt to expand the scope of literature written for the general public to include the concerns of individuals, of 'particuliers'. But, by virtue of being a work of fiction, the novel is still able to disguise its import, to present the truths it conveys not directly, but by implication. This is not so of the memoirs, which claim to relate true personal experience and the opinions and reactions of one individual, and this kind of writing is as absent from the 'public' literature – as opposed to the memoirs and confessions – of the eighteenth century as it is from the seventeenth. The underlying assumption seems to be that individual concerns are not just likely to be, but are *necessarily* opposed to public values, to order.

To compare memoirs and confessions with the unpublished works of Diderot, the *Rêve, Le Neveu de Rameau, Jacques le Fataliste*, might seem to be stretching comparison, or even analogy as favoured by Diderot, a little far. Quite apart from the immense difference in form between the two sets of works, it could be objected that there is no clear line of separation between the subjects of Diderot's published and unpublished works or the manner of their diffusion. In the matter of publication we have examples of works which were published openly, in the normal way, some which were secretly published or else printed with 'tacit permission', a considerable number circulated in the *Correspondance Littéraire* and therefore meant for the eyes of a select few, and finally some which were never disseminated at all. It would probably not be possible, or profitable, to establish a direct correlation between the form, subject-matter and method of publication of all Diderot's works, especially as the eighteenth century was a period of great experiment in literary forms, precisely because it was generally felt that subjects which had formerly been beyond the pale as far as literature was concerned should now be brought within it. Nevertheless, it can be said that Diderot recognized a point beyond which a work could not be considered suitable for general consumption, and his criteria were based not so much on specific questions such as politics, religion or decency as on that of order, the kind of order which ensures the continuance of rational activity within society.

A part of Diderot's attitude can be illustrated by reference to the *Entretien d'un Père avec ses Enfants*, where it is admitted that wise men can be above the law, but only if there are not too many of them; or the *Supplément au Voyage de Bougainville* where the wise are enjoined to speak out against bad laws, but, pending their reform, to submit to them for: 'Anyone who, on his own initiative, offends against a bad law, authorizes everyone else to offend against good laws'.[47] But there is a lot more to the problem than this. Enough has been said in the chapter on politics to show that Diderot conceived of order as something which may not have an objective existence, and which by its nature cannot be translated into action but which must nevertheless be believed in, acknowledged as an active force, if society is to survive. The necessary condition of this belief is, as we have seen, a belief in liberty, the 'phantom of liberty'[48] of which he speaks to Catherine II, and this liberty, when examined more closely in a social context means the freedom of the individual within certain clearly defined limits, the limits of his social function. This concept of freedom guaranteeing and guaranteed by order is of course a key feature of Diderot's thought in every sphere, but as far as the individual's role in society is concerned, it is more general to the whole period. The triumph of order in the classical drama of the time, as well as in the domestic drama of Diderot, consists precisely in the establishment of the characters in their proper social roles, or else, if they prove irredeemable, in their complete elimination from the scene. In the final moments the characters are released from the bondage of the passions and enabled to fulfil their 'true' function. Even the *Mariage de Figaro* ends in this way, although here we are made aware of the artificiality of the process: 'It all ends up in a song.'[49]

This inseparability of order and form, the framework and structure which alone can permit rational activity, is perhaps one of the dominant assumptions of the period, and while eighteenth-century thinkers, with Diderot in the forefront, tended increasingly to try to extend the area of order to embrace the whole of experience, Diderot at the same time, and far more acutely than any of his contemporaries, recognized that the world of order and that of chance, of freedom and of 'servitude', still preserved their separate existence side by side, equally valid and equally irreconcilable. Theories which abolished the two substances did not eliminate duality: they merely recreated from one substance the conditions which had formerly been explained by two, relocating in human perception what had formerly belonged with God. How far Diderot realized this last point is very difficult to assess. Certainly he was not aware of all the implications arising out of the persistent dualism in his thinking, but he was aware of the co-existence of two disparate moral, if not physical worlds, and deals with the problem most acutely in *Le Neveu de Rameau*. He realized too that, even though order no longer has an objective sanction in God, or the sovereign, men still aspire to it, must aspire to it. This is implicit, but no more than that, in the *Rêve*, where Diderot not only provides a psychological theory which shifts the centre of order from God to the human mind, but also a moral theory which overturns the standards of his own society and perhaps any viable society. It is therefore not surprising that in the letter where he speaks of the completion of the *Rêve*[50], he talks of 'a disorder which goes far beyond the freedom of conversation',[51] and calls it, significantly, 'this formless, dangerous creation',[52] one which would not only ruin his reputation, but which is, by its nature, the kind of book which must not be released to the general public: 'there is a speculative kind of teaching which is not meant for the mass of the people, nor for practical use ... if, without being insincere, one can refrain from writing everything one does, one can, without being inconsistent, refrain from doing everything one writes'.[53]

And no doubt he did not see any inconsistency in writing books like the *Rêve* and the *Supplément*, while remaining an upholder of the public virtues, as in his letter of 1772, exactly contemporary with the latter, where he condemns the moral tone of both authors and actors in the theatre of his time:

Today they breathe into the hearts of our citizens a double poison, vengeance and love, a poison equally fatal to religion and to society ... if evil and suffering are deplored it is only to arouse desire and not repentance. Libido sentiendi.[54]

The remarks which precede this condemnation suggest that he saw the purpose of tragedy and comedy as primarily and directly moral. Tragedy should teach us 'patience in adversity',[55] 'moderation in prosperity',[56] and so on, while comedy 'rebukes the infamies of avarice; senseless prodigality; the evil face of slander; the stupid impertinence of fops, etc.'.[57] The general intention is the same as it was fourteen years earlier in the second and third sections of *De la Poésie Dramatique*. If we call this double standard hypocrisy, then it is the hypocrisy of a whole age, and one which was recognized, more or less obscurely, and in their actions rather than their thoughts, by most, but with much greater awareness by Diderot. Behind it all is an attitude which sees change, movement, heterogeneity, both as an essential part of the nature of reality and yet as something inherently dangerous, which, once openly acknowledged, can submerge man as a free, rational being. The culmination of that process by which the concept of perfect order has been removed from God and reconstructed in the mind of man has left the official, public simulacrum of order where it is; not only that, it has made its preservation and continuance even more necessary because the spread of enlightenment has revealed the uncertain structure on which any kind of order is built.

The dialogues

In his search for the nature and limits of order, in his attempt to establish the areas in which rational activity is possible, Diderot was, therefore, forced to the conscious realization of a truth of which his whole age was less consciously aware, that order ultimately exists only as a concept, operating on a different level from the realities of individual experience. These realities he examined most thoroughly in *Le Neveu de Rameau* and in *Jacques le Fataliste*. In the first – and here I commit myself to a view of the roles of *Moi* and *Lui* – Diderot in the role of a stock philosopher is brought face to face with reality at its most intractable; in the second, the philosopher is joined by the creative artist in being subjected to a similar experience. In both works the boundaries between one and the other, between the thinker/creator and the reality before him are deliberately obscured, firstly because Diderot in each case introduces a representation of himself into the work, secondly because the relationship between this representation and the other elements of the work is never stable.

Both these aspects need careful examination because they are closely linked with the idea of order. The intrusion of the author into his own work is not only a feature of the two works just mentioned but also of the *Entretiens sur le Fils Naturel* and the *Rêve de d'Alembert*, and a case could also be made for the inclusion of the *Paradoxe sur le Comédien* and the *Supplément au Voyage de Bougainville*. All of these are to a certain extent an examination of boundaries, or limits: the first, of the boundaries between art and reality, and between the artist and his material – and in this sense it offers a foretaste of *Jacques le Fataliste*; the second, of those between the self and the rest of creation, and between the moral and immoral; the third defines the limits within which an actor, and by implication anyone, can play his role successfully; and the last deals with the limits which European civilization imposes on sexual morality, and discusses whether any such limits can be found in nature.

Much has been written of Diderot's predilection for dialogue form,† rather less, perhaps, of its corollary, his tendency to project himself, or some character which might be construed as himself, into these dialogues. The immediate effect of this practice is to obscure the normal distinction between subject and object: his works do not, once created, assume an existence independent of their creator, they preserve their relationship with him, and in this they recall the process which for Diderot constitutes the acquisition of scientific knowledge: the process in which the subject experiences an aspect of reality at first hand and subsequently absorbs it into his mind, making it a part of himself. The subject is split: the reflecting self (or author) is detached from the active self which experiences external reality (projection of author); but the whole nevertheless remains something personal to the author. This is the primary sense in which *Le Neveu de Rameau* and *Jacques le Fataliste* can be called, as Lester Crocker has called them, moral and artistic experiments.

One can say, then, that Diderot is attempting in his dialogues to make art corrrespond more closely to reality as experienced by the individual. The effect of placing a representation of the author within his work is to reflect more accurately the position which Diderot and perhaps his readers felt they occupied in relation to the

† See Peter France's chapter on Diderot in *Rhetoric and Truth in France* for a fuller discussion of this question.

world in which they moved and thought. Instead of presenting us with a self-contained world – of the kind his aesthetic theory favours – he gives us, in various forms, himself observing himself dealing with a reality outside him. As such, his dialogues parallel the situation in which a thinking, creating self looks on, Godlike, at an active self playing a part in the created world. The shifting relationship between the two reflects our awareness of being of the world and yet not of it.

The pattern is less obvious, certainly less central, less exploited, in the structure of some dialogues than others. Without embarking on an exhaustive analysis of all the works which consist wholly or partly of dialogue, it is illuminating to examine the relationship between the two speakers in some of them from the point of view of Diderot's involvement as author. In the *Entretiens sur le Fils Naturel* our first impression is of Diderot talking to a friend about a play written and produced by the latter and based on an actual occurrence. We are also aware that Diderot has projected himself as dramatist into the person of Dorval (who has written *Le Fils Naturel* and is planning *Le Père de Famille*), and that the events which inspired the play are fictitious. We thus have Diderot discussing various problems of dramatic illusion with an aspect of himself; but the effect of pretending that the play is written by someone else and is based on actual happenings is to give a more immediate impression of reality than does the play itself; yet what we find ourselves reading is not a series of events but a critique of the artist's relationship with his material.

Moi, that is, Diderot, abstracted from any kind of creative involvement with reality, has the role of questioner and critic; he sees problems and raises doubts. Dorval is more positive, both as an advocate of the new type of drama and in his views on form and technique. At the same time he is forced by Diderot's questions to acknowledge a distinction between traditional theatre and his own play, and to admit that *Le Fils Naturel* is really only fitted for private performance. This is partly explained by its conception as an essentially personal experience, partly by the fact that his raw material, the members of the household, have persuaded him to include certain elements which conflict with dramatic convention. For example, Dorval has given a part to Charles, the valet, because he feels he deserves it,[58] although when pressed by *Moi*, he readily admits that there would be no question of doing such a thing in a play meant for public performance. 'I should forget about my moral scruples, and take good care not to give importance on the stage to creatures who are of no account in society.'[59] The inclusion of Constance's declaration of love[60] again leads Dorval to maintain that what would offend in the theatre has in fact pleased in the *salon*. 'Leave the boards behind; come back into the drawing-room; and admit that Constance's speech gave you no offence when you heard it there.'[61] Moreover, it transpires that a first draft of the play was submitted to the characters, who made alterations in their own parts in order to show themselves in a better light than was possible in the heat of the moment. But this was not Dorval's intention: he had shown them the draft 'so that each of them could add to their parts, or remove portions of them, and portray themselves even more accurately'.[62] But, as he says,

something happened which I was hardly expecting, but which is really quite natural. It was that, being more concerned with their present than their past, they softened an expression here, and moderated a feeling there.[63]

One of the results of this was Constance's declaration.

The situation is thus quite complex. Dorval had created a first impression of the action; he had then gone back to the raw material in order to check this impression against the reality. Thus far the process seems the same as that prescribed for scientific research in *De l'Interprétation de la Nature*; but the reality to which he returns is now no longer the same as the one he was describing, and so the play in its new form presumably reflects the characters' own correction of Dorval's impression of what they said and did at a certain point in the past. Although the result is still more real – and less observant of the rules of *vraisemblance* and *bienséance* – than a standard theatrical production, we are still not seeing what actually happened; this is lost without trace. And this is not all, for, as we are told in the 'Introduction', we are not even reading the conversation between *Moi* and Dorval as it took place:

But what a difference there is between what Dorval said to me and what I am writing!... There is no point in my seeking within myself the impressions made on me by the spectacle of nature and the presence of Dorval. I can no longer find them; I can no longer see Dorval, I can no longer hear him. I am alone, amid the dust of books and in the darkness of my study ... and the lines I write are feeble, sad and cold.[64]

Diderot seems to be telling us at the outset that any attempt to recapture the moment is doomed; and the ensuing conversation bears this out.

Nevertheless, the fiction upon which the *Entretiens* are based: a Diderot who separates himself into two characters, one of whom has tried to recapture a series of incidents – themselves fictional – in which he himself was, and is, involved, tells us more about the elusive nature of reality as we experience it than a conventional drama based on historical events. We do not see a finished product but a character, appropriately designated *Moi*, constantly adjusting himself to the revelations which Dorval makes about the play, drama in general, the subjects of his play and his own role in it. It is not just a question of *Moi* having to adjust his ideas, but his actual relationship with Dorval. At one point,[65] they are discussing the relative merits of the *coup de théâtre* and the *tableau*. They have together arrived at an approximate definition of each and *Moi* is led to quote an example from *Le Fils Naturel*: 'What a fine *tableau*, for it really was one, I think, was made by poor Clairville, lying on his friend's breast, as though it were the only refuge left to him...'[66] but he is interrupted by Dorval: 'You may well think of his troubles, but what about mine. How cruel that moment was for me!'[67] Dorval, reminded by *Moi* of a situation in which he was involved, has abandoned his role of dramatic critic to revert to that of participant in the play, or rather in the reality on which the play is based. *Moi* is forced to alter his perspective on things, to readjust his sights, as it were, and this is brought about by what is a minor *coup de théâtre*, an unforeseen change in circumstances which is typical of life as we live it, but, as it happens, not at all what Dorval prescribes for its dramatic representation, since he advocates the use of *tableaux*.

The general theme which emerges from this confused, shifting picture is the gulf between private life, 'real' life, that is, and public drama, a theme which is one of the explicit subjects of discussion and is also embodied in the relationship between *Moi* and Dorval, as well as in Dorval himself, as, in response to *Moi*'s questioning, he moves between his conflicting roles of dramatist and participant in life, and from upholder of many of the values of traditional drama to being a man who is so absorbed in his immediate sensations that, having been 'under the spell'[68] he cannot remember the experience a moment later. What constitutes the ultimate interest of the *Entretiens* is that they are a commentary on the way, or ways, in which we perceive reality, with the implicit conclusion – disguised but certainly not invalidated by the final lines in which we are told that the play was in fact true to the actual characters it portrayed – that it is in the nature of reality to be unattainable in art.

The *Entretiens* are Diderot's first serious experiment in the fruitful area of the dialogue, which allows him to explore the problems of our relationship with the world about us; and already the form has established its value as a way of conveying a certain kind of awareness of reality and the way it impinges on us. I have said that one of the effects of Diderot's particular kind of dialogue is to obscure the distinction we normally make – or, for practical purposes, assume – between subject and object, the assumption that a fixed, unchanging subject can, at a given moment, perceive an object in its total reality. Each of his dialogues presents a different kind of relationship between the speakers and Diderot himself: in the *Entretiens* both are overt representatives of some aspect of their creator; in *Jacques le Fataliste* neither are, but Diderot as their author intrudes as a separate element; in the *Neveu de Rameau*, to judge from the diversity of scholarly reactions, many interpretations are possible ranging from both to neither, but it would seem reasonable to suppose that *Moi*, as I have said, represents Diderot in the role of philosopher; the position is less clear in the *Paradoxe* and the *Supplément*, but we do find that one of the speakers in these two dialogues tends to play a more passive role, enquiring, but rarely asserting, learning, but hardly ever instructing; in general he has the function of inciting the other to express or clarify his views, but this does not hold for the more complex dialogues. In these the parallel which might be made with Socratic dialogue is no longer possible. Whereas the two speakers in the *Paradoxe* and the *Supplément* are convenient conversational partners, in the *Neveu*, for example, they have evolved to the extent of representing separate principles.

One could make a very rough distinction between two categories of dialogue: the didactic and the exploratory, with *Jacques* and *Le Neveu* falling into the second. In the first category are those dialogues in which one speaker is used as Diderot's mouthpiece to put forward a fairly definite point of view while the other serves as a 'feed'. In the second, the speakers are functionally equal in status and their positions irreconcilable on the level at which they are disputing; the purpose of these dialogues lies in the opportunity offered the reader to see a truth of a higher order arising out of the conflict. The distinction, as I have said, is not clear-cut, since some of the 'didactic' dialogues, especially the *Paradoxe*, open out onto problematical areas, but certainly *Jacques* and *Le Neveu* are works of a different order and plunge far deeper into the contradictions of life than others.

The realism of *Le Neveu de Rameau*

The *Moi* of the *Neveu de Rameau* is not just an individual *philos-ophe*, or philosopher, he represents the attitude, the stance which the typical philosopher must adopt. From the beginning he presents himself as self-sufficient, content to discuss problems with himself, to look on as life proceeds around him.[69] His inclination is to see things not as an individual, but *sub specie aeternitatis*: 'let us look at the really interesting side of it and forget for the moment the point we occupy in time and space; let us cast our eyes over the centuries to come, the most distant lands and nations yet to be born. Let us think of the good of our race.'[70] It is this feature of his character which *Lui* finds least sympathetic: 'For my part I don't look down from that height from which everything looks the same';[71] *Moi* can hoist himself up on his 'epicycle of Mercury'[72] if he likes; 'it's your business, and I'm not interested. I am in this world and here I stay'.[73] *Moi* goes so far as to claim that the one person who is exempt from the 'dance which makes the world go round'[74] is the 'philosopher who has nothing and asks for nothing'.[75] His ideal achievement would be to emulate Voltaire or *le père* Hoop in performing an out-standingly selfless action: 'You are people to be pitied if you can't see that we have risen above our human condition, and that it is im-possible to be unhappy with two good deeds of this kind to make one secure'.[76] True happiness for him lies in raising oneself above the contingencies of this world.

But for all his independence *Moi* seems to need *Lui*, or people like him.

They interest me once a year when I run into them because their characters contrast sharply with other people's and break the tedious uniformity that our social conventions and set politeness have brought about. If one of them appears in a company of people he is the speck of yeast that leavens the whole and restores to each of us a portion of his natural individuality. He stirs people up and gives them a shaking, makes them take sides, brings out the truth, shows who are really good and unmasks the villains. It is then that the wise man listens and sorts people out.[77]

Moi seems to regard such people as phenomena, rather than indi-viduals in their own right. They swim into his ken from time to time. They are the equivalent in civilized society of monsters in the natural world.

This comment by *Moi* on *Lui* shows how Diderot's conception of dialogue has developed into a form which represents not just the way we apprehend reality, but the two principles which govern our general relationship with the world around us, the two poles between which our responses to life fluctuate. *Moi*, as a man, strives to observe the static principle, while *Lui* belongs essentially to the world of movement. For one, the ideal is detachment; the other makes a virtue of involvement. But although, seen in this light, the two figures have a symbolic value, they constitute at the same time one of Diderot's most ambitious attempts at realism, an attempt to convey the true nature of our experience of life in the context of human society. As such the *Neveu de Rameau* is far removed from Diderot's system of aesthetics, but much closer to another of his statements on the subject of realism and artistic illusion. This is what is sometimes referred to as the 'warts and all' theory, and it is worth setting down here in its most familiar form, as expressed at the end of *Les Deux Amis de Bourbonne*, since it is an important statement both of Diderot's views and of an aesthetic attitude of the period, as well as being a passage which has given rise to much comment. Diderot is speaking of the 'historical story-teller',[78] as opposed to writers of 'fantastic tales'[79] and 'comic tales':[80]

The latter's purpose is to deceive you; he is sitting at your fireside; his object is the strict truth; he wants to be believed; he wants to interest you, move you, involve you, stir you, bring you out in gooseflesh and make your tears flow; all effects which cannot be achieved without eloquence and poetry. But eloquence is a kind of lying, and there is nothing more destructive of illusion than poetry; both of them exaggerate, overvalue, magnify and inspire distrust: so how will this story-teller go about deceiving you? Like this. He will scatter through his story little circumstances which are so closely linked to the subject, features so simple, so natural, and yet so difficult to imagine, that you will be forced to admit to yourself: My goodness, how true! you don't invent things like that![81]

Diderot then goes on to give an example from painting which in fact seems to illustrate a different kind of procedure altogether:

A painter executes a head on the canvas. All its features are strong, generous and regular; it is the most perfect and the most rare of compositions ... I look for its model in nature, and I don't find it ... it is an ideal head; I feel it; I tell myself so. But let the artist show me a small scar on the forehead, a wart on one of the temples, an imperceptible break in the lower lip; and, from being ideal, the head immediately becomes a portrait; a smallpox scar in the corner of the eye or beside the nose, and this woman's face is no longer that of Venus; it is the portrait of one of my neighbours.[82]

Diderot scholars have pointed out that the ideas expressed here are both inconsistent with the rest of his thinking and absent from his practice. Jacques Proust, in his edition of the *Quatre Contes* (p. xxxvii), says, 'The study of *Mystification* shows ... that the story teller's secret is not the one he reveals to us in the postface of *Les Deux Amis*.'[83] In a more thorough study of the subject, Joly shows that Diderot here contradicts his own notion of the 'ideal model' as well as his theory that a single defect affects the whole organism; and that, as far as his practice is concerned, Diderot's method is not to invent a character or story and then to add one or two realistic details; on the contrary, he does not so much invent as reorder various elements selected from the reality of his own experience. Now it may well be that the wart should benefit from a much more liberal interpretation than it is sometimes given. Both Vivienne Mylne in *The Eighteenth-Century French Novel, Techniques of Illusion* (p. 195), and following her, Jean Catrysse in *Diderot et la Mystification* (p. 135 et seq.) suggest that what is meant are not so much small visual details, as aspects of behaviour, speech and gesture. Certainly this is where Diderot's realism lies, and an interpretation of this kind would link the theory to the practice not only of the novels and tales, but also of the plays, but one wonders if this is not falsifying Diderot's own attitude to the problem.

If we examine Diderot's statement more closely, we see that he assumes an opposition between rhetoric and truth. This is part of a traditional attitude, based on the more general opposition felt between emotion, the speculative imagination and abstract thought on the one hand, and reality, experience, the facts, on the other. On one side we have poetry, eloquence, the tendency towards form and idealization; on the other, 'the strict truth', the facts of life as we experience it. Moreover, it seems, the details have a kind of validity as truth whether they actually happened or not: detail, as raw, unprocessed material, is automatically factual. This explains the apparent contradiction in 'the latter's purpose is to deceive you ... his object is the strict truth'. One could say that Diderot is merely making the obvious point that a story containing a few convincing details will be more likely to be realistic than one which does not; that detail can create the illusion of truth; but there seems to be more to it than this.

Diderot's theory is a manifestation of an attitude towards the 'two substances'. The credibility of a story is guaranteed not so much by whether it really took place or not, but by the extent to which it is anchored in a world which resembles the one we can see and touch, in the world of matter and not that of mind. Mind on the other hand covers all phenomena which cannot be seen and touched: not just thoughts and theories but the emotions and passions. Thus far, it is true, we are roughly in line with the views of the two critics mentioned above: poetry and eloquence give free rein to the imagination, therefore, in a play, for example, one's characters must not only speak, they must also have facial expressions and gestures which enable us to visualize them; they must be involved in everyday activities which link them to ourselves. But it is interesting that the example Diderot takes to illustrate his point is not taken from literature at all, but from painting, and the head he describes does not appear so much to be a product of free poetic imagination as an example of a superior kind of order: 'All its features are strong, generous and regular; it is the most perfect and the most rare of compositions ... it is an ideal head'.[84] What is more, the scar, or the wart, the detail which will bring the picture down to earth ('the portrait of one of my neighbours' and not 'that of Venus'),[85] is an accidental feature, something which will destroy both the symmetry and the universality, an element of chance.

Here we surely have two very different kinds of realism. One is the kind which clothes an idea with flesh and blood, which integrates a product of the imagination into the visual world ('little circumstances which are so linked to the subject'),[86] and brings us out of the realms of fantasy into the world of reality. This, as other statements of Diderot have shown, is largely a quantitative matter: the more unusual your subject-matter is, the more you must compensate it, 'save' it, with factual detail. A section of *De La Poésie Dramatique* develops this point, and can be compared with what Diderot says in *Les Deux Amis*, even though, in the latter, the details counteract the formal elements of eloquence and poetry, whereas in his dramatic theory Diderot is dealing with unusual subject-matter. 'The more these cases [he is referring to "rare cases in the general order of things"] are rare and unusual, the more art, time, space and ordinary circumstances he will need to make up for the fabulous element and provide a base for the illusion'.[87] It is a question of probability: the improbable must be balanced by an adequate proportion of the probable; deviations from the norm must be compensated by a sufficient dose of the normal; poetic language must be weighted with factual material; all this in the interests of creating a 'possible' world. But the other kind of realism, in which Diderot resorts to painting for his example, is not a quantitative matter at all, but rather a juxtaposition of two extremes, the ideal and the real, the universal and the particular. It is also, as we have seen, a method which does not have any very obvious application in Diderot's works.

Why then should he have mentioned it, and included it in his discussion of realism, without apparently noticing that he was speaking of two different things? One answer is that Diderot is not the kind of thinker who always makes clear distinctions between concepts. A further, and more important point, is that for him, as for his period, the concepts of the ideal, the imaginary and the extraordinary are linked together by the same kind of associations, all partaking to some degree of the unreal, whether it be the fabulous (and sometimes ideal) world of the novelist's imagination, the 'systems' and hypotheses of the traditional philosophers or the religious and political dogmas of traditional authority, and all partake too, however contradictory this may seem, of the fixed and stable, just as their opposites, the facts of everyday experience, partake of the world of change, contingency and unpredictability. The ideal head of the painter, the fabulous events of legend and the imaginings of novelists and poets have a kind of stability precisely because they are unreal, because, as products of the mind, they are untouched by the contingencies of real life.

Here we are very much in the realm of the two substances, and it seems that the wart theory, although apparently advanced by Diderot as a piece of practical advice, might be better regarded as a kind of shorthand example of the fact that the ideal must always be combined with the contingent, or order with chance, if it is to be convincing, and that our mental processes operate between a striving for the ideal, which we can control, and a permanent awareness of the chance factors which are beyond such control. In fact the work which best embodies an expression of these two extremes is *Le Neveu de Rameau,* but with a marked difference of emphasis. The ideal which bulks so largely in the painting is reduced to the character of *Moi,* who moreover represents a striving for the ideal rather than the ideal itself, while the wart expands out of all proportion to embrace the obtrusive figure of *Lui,* an embodiment of all that conflicts with *Moi*'s sense of order.

This is one way in which the passage from *Les Deux Amis* contains in a rudimentary form the same attitudes which underlie the structure and content of *Le Neveu de Rameau.* Another feature of the passage is its description of the 'historical tale' as an essentially private communication. The narrator 'is sitting at your fireside'. The phrase has already been used by Diderot in the *Paradoxe*[88] where he distinguishes between the conversational tone of 'the story told at your fireside'[89] and 'the stress and declamatory tone of the stage'.[90] The emphasis is on the relaxed, natural, intimate atmosphere which contrasts with the formal rhetoric of the stage and which for that reason alone carries a convincing appearance of truth. A similar atmosphere and similar associations are conveyed a century earlier, in a passage from the *Memoirs* of

Goulas (already quoted on the subject of political illusion) written sometime in the 1660s. In defining the nature of his memoirs he says:

Finally, bear in mind that this is neither history, nor memoirs [he presumably means official memoirs], nor commentaries; it is a conversation between two people who trust each other, the uncle and the nephew having an after-dinner talk. You are in the armchair, by the day-bed in the salle de la Mothe, and I am sitting on this little bed, leaning on a cushion, without ceremony, in complete intimacy. I am relating to you what I have seen and heard, and you are listening to someone you consider worthy of belief.[91]

Here, as with Diderot, we find the assumption that an informal account, delivered in an atmosphere of privacy, can bring with it a guarantee of truth, whereas an official, formal history does not. The difference between Diderot's method and that of the informal memoir-writer is that the latter is telling a story to an intimate about himself and his experience in the past, while Diderot elevates the actual conversation to the position of subject-matter. The intimate memoir-writer had broken new ground by recounting not a series of events, but a story of himself grappling with these events; the events were seen not as objective phenomena but as an integral part of his personal experience. Diderot takes the process a long way further: not only does the hypothetical listener to the memoirs become an active participant, he takes over the role played in a story or a set of memoirs by the events. Thus in the *Neveu de Rameau* we have Diderot projecting himself, or an aspect of himself, into a setting in which his exchanges with his conversational partner are not a commentary on a story, but the very substance of the work.

This is an extreme and brilliant development of a practice which grew out of a need, felt long before Diderot's time, to create a kind of literary art which would not replace the traditional, formal genres, but would provide a vehicle for another kind of truth, whose measure was that of the individual and whose form was fixed by the varying extent of that individual's experience. But Diderot's experiment in literary form, although it is in the tradition of the memoirs, and perhaps of all the writings generally known as humanist, whose greatest exponent was Montaigne, would not have been possible without the development which led to the eighteenth-century novel; the process by which the essentially factual, eye-witness quality of memoirs was channelled into fiction; the general realization that the interest lay not just in a thirst for authentic facts but in a need for a certain kind of experience, of which facts were simply one element. The types of literary interest which the new 'factual' fiction tried to provide were, as it turned out, to cover a wide field, for it is in the nature of personal experience to produce either deep involvement on the part of the listener or reader, or else an attitude of critical enquiry; which is perhaps only to say that the actions of our fellow-men can either impose themselves on our feelings and arouse our emotions, or present themselves as behavioural or ethical problems and lead us to question them. Formal literature, insofar as it reflected 'official' attitudes, aimed to elicit an emotional and intellectual adherence to a certain kind of order, but aesthetic order, as Diderot himself was well aware, exists in a precarious balance between the total involvement of the sensibility and the critical detachment of the intellect.

Two options thus lay open to the novelist and *conteur* and there is no need to resort to a detailed analysis of examples to show that both were taken up by eighteenth-century writers; one only needs to mention the sensibility of Rousseau's *Nouvelle Héloïse* and, at the other extreme, the cerebral wit of Voltaire's *Contes Philosophiques*. It is equally obvious that Diderot himself ventured along both paths. We have on the one hand his *Éloge de Richardson* ('Richardson! whether one wants to or not, one plays a part in your works, one intervenes in the conversation, one shows approval, blame, admiration, irritation, indignation');[92] his enthusiasm for Greuze and his 'moral painting'; his own story, *La Religieuse,* and his two plays. But we owe most of his masterpieces to the other option, in which he exploited the dialogue form to examine a broad range of problems relating to human experience.

Herbert Dieckmann, in the third of his *Cinq Leçons sur Diderot,* says that Diderot chose the forms of the *conte* and dialogue to express certain problems which did not admit of a rational solution. 'Dialogue', he says, '... to a certain extent allowed Diderot to give a direct representation of the movements of his thoughts in all their unexpected changes of direction'; Diderot 'needed, to convey this movement, a form of expression which would admit the unforesee-able and would above all enable the mind to abstract itself from its ideas and set itself at a certain distance from them'.[93] And of the *conte* he writes: 'The story replaces thought; the mind escapes from an impossible situation by means of artistic creation.'[94] The obstacles to the solution of the problem become part of the story and are resolved on an artistic level. Intractable problems thus become events and characters: as Dieckmann concludes: 'by turning his ideas into the beings which people a story, Diderot frees himself from the conflicts in which his thought was becoming trapped'.[95]

This might look like the romantic conception of art as the objectivization of a personal conflict, but I do not think – and nor, I believe, would Professor Dieckmann – that this phenomenon is especially 'pre-romantic'. At least in the case of the great dialogues, and probably in his *contes* too, Diderot is not so much delivering himself of a personal burden as seeking a means to express various aspects of experience which defy ordered thinking and order itself, and which are an offence to the rational mind. And here it is worth recalling that the irrational, once recognized as such, falls into the realm of informal writing. Rameau is an obvious case, but Diderot's most brilliant attempt to deal not merely with a specific problem but also to incorporate that problem into an appropriate artistic form is of course *Jacques le Fataliste*. It is in this work that the consequences of the ambivalent status of order, as Diderot sees it, are most fully worked out.

Order called into question: *Jacques le Fataliste*

Fictional characters and events – one might even go so far as to say all the elements of a work of art, whether literary or visual – have a significance beyond themselves, they have their place in a total pattern which transcends them. In the traditional view of the world this was also felt to be true of people and events in real life: they were working out their destinies within a divinely ordained framework, even though the nature of that destiny was hidden from them. On this level there was therefore no barrier, no difference in kind between art and reality; the work of art reflected or celebrated in a heightened and more comprehensible form the role of man on earth. But once the transcendental sanction for human activity is felt to be lacking, as it increasingly was during the seventeenth and eighteenth centuries, it can either be replaced by something else – by a doctrine like optimism, or a belief in final causes – or else the world must be seen, from the individual's point of view, as a domain of pure contingency; and this is the view which is forced on the materialist determinist, for although determinism leaves the individual as helpless to decide his own fate as does the belief in providence, it does not suggest that our steps are guided by some higher purpose. In terms of art, this means that an artistic creation must either present us with a coherent world which can convince us of its validity, a 'possible' world which can impress us as an acceptable form of order – and this is the self-contained work – or else it must try to be a true reflection of the world of contingency as we experience it.

Diderot deals with both types, or to be more accurate, he deals primarily with one, the first, in his theoretical writings, and with both in his fictional work. In an *œuvre* which is singularly difficult to classify in terms of tradition and experiment, one might say that the two plays are the best examples of self-contained works, while the novels and tales are somewhere between the two extremes, and the most striking example of a work which is not self-contained is *Jacques le Fataliste*. By the time Diderot came to write it, the 'realistic' novel was well established, and the devices authors used to give their works an appearance of factual truth, ranging from the introductory note indicating that the story has been found among the papers of X, to the structure in the form of memoirs, diaries or letters, were as commonplace as the realistic elements within the stories themselves. But here again we are dealing with works which are self-contained to the extent that the author deliberately absents himself, ostensibly being replaced by the narrator, whether this person be a key figure in the story or not; the problem remains that the true author is still there, still manipulating characters and events in some scheme which transcends them. This impression is mitigated to a certain extent in *La Religieuse* where the story breaks off on a question mark instead of being rounded off. We are left wondering whether the marquis will help or not, and the novel, issuing onto a problematical reality, thus gives the impression of being a fragment of a complete life. But the real problem, that of the author's presence, is only dealt with in *Jacques le Fataliste,* where the creator comes out into the open, revealing himself with the total freedom he really has, a freedom over a character who, in these circumstances, can only be a fatalist.

It seems worth repeating here the point made by J. Robert Loy, in a book whose punning title, *Diderot's determined Fatalist,* indicates its main purpose. Loy distinguishes clearly and convincingly between fatalism and determinism (p. 60):

there is one fate or destiny which is teleological and has followed its unswerving course through all existence; and another fate which, aiming at no foreordained endpoint, still follows an inexorable chain of causes. The first is Jacques' Great Scroll and properly referred to as Fatalism; the second may best be identified as Determinism.

And a further point is that fatalism assumes some kind of order in the universe, whereas determinism does not.

Having established this, we should perhaps take as our starting

171

point not Diderot's ideas on freewill, determinism, and so on, nor the internal structure of *Jacques le Fataliste* itself, but certain preoccupations, of the kind already discussed, which surrounded the rise of the novel. One of the common features of the 'intimate' story is that it is addressed to a specific listener, which immediately sets it at a certain 'distance'; it is permanently accompanied in the telling by an awareness of a teller and a listener. But Diderot recognizes that the case of a completely silent listener, while not necessarily unrealistic on the surface, cannot represent the mental activity of the ideal listener, who must at various times feel that the story as told does not conform to his desires or expectations, or else raises questions to which he would like an answer. The problem is stated in the opening lines of *Ceci n'est pas un Conte:* 'When you tell a story, you tell it to someone who is listening, and however short the story, it is rare that the teller is not interrupted occasionally by the listener.'[96] But Diderot's reluctance to allow a work to exist in its own right, the urge to present it to us with an accompanying commentary, goes back to the *Entretiens sur le Fils Naturel.* Here, as in the later experiments, the effect is to displace the interest from the emotional impact of the characters and events to a consideration of the problems they raise, problems which are both moral, as they concern the actions of the characters, and aesthetic, as they concern the status of the work in relation to reality on one side and ourselves, the recipients, on the other. Although this procedure would seem to give the listener a more active role, allowing him some rights in the matter, the actual result is to pre-empt our reaction to the story. Our reactions are guided by the discussion within which it is presented.

Diderot is obviously fascinated by this question of the relationship between narrator and listener and has given us quite an anthology of variations on it. In the *Neveu de Rameau*, by making this relationship not the framework but the substance of the work, he creates a situation which seems to evolve by itself and at the same time is able to present us with a character so extraordinary that we should hardly have accepted him in a more conventional story. In *Jacques le Fataliste* he creates a far more complex structure by giving us a combination of stories, discussions and events, all enclosed within a discussion between Diderot and a listener set up to represent ourselves, and in which narrator and listener are involved in a running dispute over their respective rights to tell, or hear, what they think fit. Again, the situation is clearly an illusory one, since in fact the narrator is free to tell us what he likes and we are condemned to listen, so that the relationship adds a further dimension to the question of freedom, or of the illusion of freedom, with which the book is concerned.

In the *Mémoires pour Catherine II* Diderot writes: 'The right of opposition, in human society, seems to me to be a natural, inalienable and sacred right. A despot, were he the best of men, commits a crime if he governs just as he pleases.'[97] And so, we might say, does the man who tells a story 'just as he pleases',[98] even if that story is based on truths which he can guarantee from personal experience. 'Any arbitrary government is bad; I make no exception for the arbitrary government of a good, firm, just and enlightened ruler.'[99] The subject, or the listener, must have a right to counterbalance the freedom of his own master with his own freedom; and this right is all the more necessary if, as we have seen, that freedom is only a 'phantom', if the order we need to assume in the state does not reside in the nature of things.

Awareness of political freedom then consists in believing that the order in which we live is based on a limitation of the sovereign's powers, so that he can only do what is in our interests. The same applies to the illusion in the mind of the listener to a story: he needs a guarantee that the author is telling him the truth, the 'possible', that he is not trying to impose on him a series of events which offend his own conception of what the world of reality should be. Now what Diderot seems to be doing in *Jacques le Fataliste* is to question whether there is, so to speak, any reality in this conception of the nature of reality. Do we not ask for things which our own experience does not necessarily provide, but which we desire in order to feel at ease? A thirst for such details is implied in the first few lines: we like to 'fix' our characters by knowing how they met, what their names are, where they come from, where they are going; in other words we like to see them fulfilling some function, occupying a recognizable place in an ordered system. We also like to think that the story has an internal logic which will enable it to go forward without the help of the author. In aesthetic matters, it seems, we are Cartesians, not Newtonians.

Diderot very quickly disappoints us, not merely by refusing to grant us this illusion, but by having as his hero a man who accepts – as, after all, we do – that life is not like this. Moreover, he has acquired a philosophy to match, for if there were a manifest order in the events of our lives we should have no need to postulate fatality, or the Great Scroll. One thing which very quickly becomes obvious is that what we demand in a realistic story is not in fact what we see in life; another is that the freedom the author offers us is not the kind we want. We do not want to be given choices; we do not want to be distracted from a story we are absorbed in (though once we are properly distracted and our curiosity is aroused, then we want to stay with the new one, and the return to the original one has become a distraction); in fact it becomes clear first of all that we want to be persuaded that neither we nor the author have any freedom at all and secondly that what we really want is a certain rather arbitrary freedom of our own.

This leads to another aspect of personal, or private literature. The two options which it offers are, considered in their extreme forms, that of total involvement and total detachment. The need for a knife-edge balance between the two, as presupposed in the aesthetics of the public work of art, is relaxed, usually in favour of one or other of the options. But in *Jacques le Fataliste*, both options are taken up. We, the readers, are alternately involved in and detached from the story of Jacques' love-life, as well as the adventures of Jacques and his master and the stories told by the other characters. This playful alternation of the two approaches results in a profound discussion of the nature of our relationship with experience, a discussion which is constantly fuelled with examples, forcing us to go backwards and forwards between involvement and detachment, experience and reflection, or, as Diderot puts it in *De l'Interprétation de la Nature*, 'along a chain of experiences spaced out at intervals, in between pauses for reasoning, like weights along a wire suspended at either end'.[100]

Yet *Jacques le Fataliste* seems a long way from this earlier scientific document, and the one obvious difference is that the scientific interpreter is in control of his researches. True, he has no control over what he will find in nature, but he is free to decide where and when he will consult her. This freedom is not among the privileges given us in *Jacques le Fataliste*, or in life; we cannot decide where or when to seek the message it has to give us; nor will that message necessarily offer any relationship with what we already know. When the crowd of peasants appears, after the night which Jacques and his master have spent in the sinister inn,[101] we expect, as Diderot knows we will, that the peasants are after their blood; Jacques thinks so too, but we and Jacques are mistaken. The peasants apparently belong to a different order of things, and we are free to go back to the story of Jacques' love-life. But Jacques is thrown off-balance by it all: 'I don't remember where I'd got to.'[102] The incident had upset him and he cursed whatever motive it was which led him to go off with the keys: 'A curse on the keys and the whim or reason which made me take them with me. A curse on caution, etc., etc.'[103] When it turns out that there is no danger, he is unable to readjust immediately. Jacques' problem is that he is incapable of sticking either to his belief in fatality or to his inclination to act as he thinks fit; neither consistent detachment nor consistent involvement is possible for him, and he loses his peace of mind. The teaching of his captain has destroyed the state of innocence in which he was able to enjoy life directly, without remorse, as he did in his youth with Justine, Marguerite and Suzon. Now he is constantly torn between reflection and action.

There is no doubt that his ideal is one of total involvement, as we see in the comparison of his horse with destiny,[104] but this is just where the problem lies: one can be involved, but one cannot *decide* to be involved without introducing a contradictory element: 'Jacques stopped short, and consulted destiny in his head.'[105] And so he is forced to go backwards and forwards between the conception of life he carries in his head and the things that life does to him. Sometimes he succeeds, sometimes he does not, but Diderot makes sure that we cannot find a criterion for his successes, they are purely a matter of chance, and the whole process, for Jacques and ourselves, is one of constant adaptation to new sets of circumstances. But despite the uncertainties of his existence, Jacques is not presented as a victim, still less as a passive character. The same cannot be said for his master: 'He hasn't many ideas in his head; if he does happen to say something sensible, it's either from his memories or from inspiration.'[106] His philosophy has been fixed at some point in the past; action he leaves to Jacques. He no longer exists as an active principle, 'he lets his life go on',[107] and the passage of time is only marked for him by the progress of the hands on the watch which he so frequently consults. He is a caricature of the stability which comes with 'repos': his state of equilibrium is due to his withdrawal from the twin worlds of action and reflection. His speculations, completed, lie in the past, while action is an eternal potential existing outside him in the person of Jacques. The only actions he performs himself are directed towards a past which went wrong, they are attempts to settle an account, as when he beats Jacques in anger, or, finally, kills Saint-Ouin, setting up another chain of events from which he absents himself, leaving Jacques alone to carry on his own story, a story which can have no end as long as he remains open to the solicitations of life.

Jacques' master is an object-lesson in the boredom which arises from the attempt to avoid the disorders which accompany action and involvement with the contingent, and his plight recalls an unusual passage in which Buffon reflects on the conditions of human happiness. There are, he says, two principles operating in man, the spiritual and the animal, and we are least happy when they are operating together. When the 'reasonable faculty'[108] is uppermost we go about our affairs calmly, although we are occasionally reminded of the animal side 'even if only in moments of involuntary distraction'.[109] When the animal in us is dominant we give ourselves up to our pleasures, passions and tastes, hardly reflecting at all. In these two states we are nearest to being perfectly happy:

> for as soon as our thoughts lead us to condemn our pleasures, or the violence of our passions leads us to hate reason, we cease to be happy, we lose that unity in our lives in which tranquillity consists, the inner conflict is born again, the two people within us stand in opposition and the two principles make themselves felt in the form of doubts, uneasiness and remorse.[110]

And what is most striking is that the possibility of achieving a harmonious balance between the two states is not for Buffon an ideal to be sought after, but the worst imaginable state. Of complete equilibrium between the two he says, 'That is the lowest point of boredom and of that awful horror of oneself which leaves us with no other wish than to do away with ourselves...'[111] Buffon goes on to describe this predicament as one to which men of middle age are especially subject, when their efforts to harden their souls to the wickedness of men have led to indifference, and when ambition gives way to sloth, and to 'boredom, that gloomy tyrant of all thinking souls, over which wisdom has less sway than madness'.[112]

This rather gloomy description of the human predicament suggests a similar preoccupation rather than an exact parallel with *Jacques le Fataliste*, or indeed any of Diderot's works. But leaving aside its moral application, this passage, as well as reflecting a general conviction about the essential incompatibility of the two aspects of our nature, the impossibility of reconciling action and reflection, shows us a fate which seems to have befallen Jacques' master. He has hardened his soul as a result of the deceptions of his youth, the consequences of which are still with him in the form of Agathe's child, whom he continues to support. Diderot clearly follows the consequences of this state more thoroughly than Buffon, who is only making a passing reflection. Jacques's master is suffering from the total loss of that tension which for Diderot is essential to mental and bodily health; his equilibrium is like that of the subjects who have lost all sense of freedom and whose stillness is one not of supreme wisdom but of abject servitude. It is nevertheless interesting that both Buffon and Diderot, whose ideal pictures of the wise man are so similar, should have also had parallel conceptions of the state which accompanies disillusionment.

If we look for an exact comparison in Diderot's political writings, Jacques' master seems to have reached the penultimate point of personal, or political decay; he is like the French people who abandon themselves blindly to a 'dull, obscurely felt movement which plagues us, torments us and makes us twist and turn until we have found a less uncomfortable position, a movement which troubles a badly governed empire, just as it troubles a sick man!'[113] But he has not quite reached the depths to which Diderot finally decides the French have come: 'But we have even lost this almost unconscious feeling of discomfort. We are no longer aware of ourselves.'[114] He still possesses sensation, but not the will to transform those sensations into active perception. 'He has eyes like you and me; but most of the time one can't tell whether he is looking or not.'[115]

There is no need to reiterate the point that he is the real slave in the relationship and that Jacques is the master; the important point is that the satire reflects back on ourselves, or that part of us which, listening to a story, or living life, neither wishes to be free nor to imagine that the narrator is free, and yet becomes dissatisfied not only when the narrator reveals his freedom but also when he adheres to a truth which does not appeal to us. Diderot gives us an exasperated warning which echoes the exasperation of Jacques with his master:

I understand you; you've had enough, and the best thing in your opinion would be for us to go back to our two travellers. Reader, you're treating me like a mechanical toy, and that's not polite . . . No doubt I need to fit in with your whims sometimes, but sometimes I need to fit in with my own, quite apart from the fact that every listener who lets me begin a story is committed to hearing the end of it.[116]

This plea for the ultimate form of politeness, a willingness to meet the author, and by implication life, half-way, and to see through to the end any course of action to which we have once committed ourselves, might be described as the practical message of *Jacques*. We have for the duration of the novel been given the illusion of freedom – and been shown that we do not always like it, which is another message; we have been allowed to exist in an active relationship with the author, who has sometimes listened to our protestations and sometimes ignored them, allegedly in the interests of truth; we have been saved by the superior perception of the author from those misinterpretations of the evidence to which Jacques and his master so often fall a prey, and we have intervened ourselves to prevent the author exceeding his rights and stepping into the story: 'I can see two men...—You can't see anything; it's nothing to do with you, you weren't there.'[117]

There is a clear parallel here with the relationship between subject and sovereign, not only in respect of the balance which should exist between the two, but also in the fact that our freedom as participating listeners is in effect non-existent, while our impression of this freedom is created by the narrator. From time to time the author gives us a glimpse of his real power, as when he is tempted to prevent Jacques telling the story of his love-life and to introduce a little more excitement into the story: 'but I despise all these tricks, I can just see that given a little imagination and style, nothing is easier than cobbling a novel together'.[118] It seems appropriate here to quote for the third – and last – time from Nicolas Goulas on the right relationship between writer and public. He is talking of the skill of the Grands in masking their ordinary humanity.

Whoever presumes to lift this mask is guilty of a crime, and yet that is what we want the historian and writer to do, and it is that which makes us enjoy and respect what they have to tell. But there are ways of removing the veil: it can be raised gently, without being torn; one can turn down a corner and allow the spectators to glimpse certain imperfections from which the rest can be judged; and certainly one can say that nothing is more acceptable to them than this liberty which proves that one esteems their judgment; so that, being left unsatisfied, they are grateful for the high opinion in which their ability is held.[119]

This is the politeness – also called 'liberty'[120] by Goulas – or the sophisticated complicity between author and public which is one of the finest features of the literature of the *Ancien Régime*, and which is founded on an awareness that such civilized values rest on the most precarious of foundations.

The veil of which Goulas spoke concealed the naked humanity of the *Grands*; that of Diderot, like the web which covers the face of the despot, hides the tyranny of the story-teller which we all want to be:

Have you forgotten that Jacques loved to talk and especially to talk about himself; a general passion amongst people of his condition, and one which raises them out of their abject state, sets them up on the platform, and suddenly transforms them into people of consequence?[121]

The implication is not merely that story-telling gives a sense of power, but that power consists in telling a story, and that the responsibility of power lies both in telling a story which you can vouch for and in allowing the listeners the right to resist if truth seems to be abused. But the final truth is that such a balance resides not in the nature of things but in the 'bon plaisir' of the powerful. And, as we are told in *Jacques le Fataliste*, we all want power over others. Even the poorest of us have our dogs, as Jacques has noticed:

Whence he concluded that every man wished to command over another; and that since, in society, the animal is immediately below the lowest class of citizens governed by all other classes, these citizens would have an animal, so that they too could have someone to command over.[122]

But for those of us who do not need to resort to commanding a dog, the most immediate path to power is through what we say, and the pre-occupation of the age with language, the combined respect and distrust with which it regarded eloquence, the concern of Diderot and his contemporaries to discover a kind of language which would have a fixed relationship with the concepts it was meant to express, all these are surely associated with the conviction that language can bring power, that in speaking and writing we attempt to impose our own version of things on others, and that the most successful are those who tell the most convincing stories.

I think it is clear from what has so far been said that the problems dealt with here arise directly from certain major preoccupations of Diderot's age. Political and artistic order are problematical not because they cannot be conceived of but because they are not, as it were, guaranteed by nature. Now that God was no longer felt to be present within the system nor to underwrite man's inevitable failure to work it, men tended to look for a guarantee of order within nature. But Diderot saw that, in the worlds of politics and art, nature offers no mechanism which might automatically prevent the sovereign or the artist from getting out of hand. Whatever we may say about the people rebelling against a tyrant who exceeds his power, or the public dismissing the artist who goes beyond nature, there is in fact no guarantee that the abuse of power will be checked by its outraged victims, nor even any guarantee that its victims will be outraged.

Diderot's response – response rather than solution – in every case is to think in terms of a controlling mechanism which is of a different order from the rest of the organism, of a central power which lacks all organic involvement with the object of its control. We have seen several examples: the brain which receives neutralized messages from the senses; the ruler who lacks the one thing, possessions, which guarantee the liberty of his subjects; the artist who cuts all the links his sensibility has established with the raw material of his work; the actor who lacks all emotional involvement with the role he plays. In each case the right balance is guaranteed only by the fact that the controlling power voluntarily preserves its difference, that, in fact, thought remains thought and resists the temptation to become extension. This is the ideal relationship implicit in *Jacques le Fataliste* between the several narrators, the stories they tell, and their listeners. The comedy, and the ultimate truth, lie in the fact that narrators and listeners do not always want to play the game, and the facts they relate do not even recognize the rules of it.

Francis Pruner, in his *Unité Secrète de Jacques le Fataliste* (p. 322) claims that this novel is 'a masked book in which, taking advantage of his mask, the author has finally been able to express the whole of his thought, philosophical, social and political'.[123] A brief statement like this cannot supply the key to *Jacques le Fataliste*, any more than it indicates the full interest of this stimulating study of it, but it emphasizes an important feature not merely of the novel's presentation but also of its subject. The concept of the mask is an important one throughout the period, and its common association is with social behaviour: we wear, consciously or unconsciously, a mask with which we attempt to hide our real nature. In fact, as Diderot believed, not just human nature but all nature presents itself to us in disguise; the mask is what stands between us and our perception of reality and is at the same time part of that reality. He says in the *Éléments de Physiologie:*

We must not imagine that the chain of being is broken by the varieties of outward form; form is often nothing but a deceitful mask, and the link which appears to be missing perhaps exists in a being already known to us, to which advances in comparative anatomy have not yet succeeded in assigning its true place.[124]

And Section XLVI of the *Interprétation de la Nature* makes a similar point: 'There are deceitful phenomena which seem at first sight to upset a theory, and which, if they were better understood, would provide its final confirmation'.[125] The process of integrating such new phenomena into an existing system is a long and contentious one.

Then the theory begins to topple; thinkers are divided; some continue to support it; others are persuaded by the experiment which seems to contradict it, and the arguments go on until perspicacity or chance,† which never sleeps, more productive than perspicacity, removes the contradiction and restores to honour ideas which had been almost abandoned.[126]

These two passages are more obviously and immediately applicable to the *Neveu de Rameau* than to *Jacques le Fataliste*. Substitute 'morality' for 'anatomy' in the quotation from the *Éléments de Physiologie*, and Rameau's nephew could easily be the 'being already known to us'—'My acquaintance with this particular one went a long way back' —[127] just as, in our interpretation of human society, he is one of the 'deceitful phenomena' who seems to wreck the system but on closer acquaintance provides a deeper understanding of it, given, that is, that our conception of the system will be somewhat modified by this understanding which the new phenomenon brings. But *Le Neveu de Rameau* presents a single problem: a social system and an apparently anti-social being; in Diderot's scientific writings the assumption is again usually of a single problem; however, the virtue of Diderot's attitude to scientific and philosophical research is that it corresponds exactly to his conception of the way we deal – or rather should deal – with everyday life. We all live by evolving the systems which we think will be best adapted to the daily conduct of life. Some of us have developed a system long ago, like Jacques' master, and have not bothered to keep it up to date; others accept their systems ready-made, on authority; a few, the 'systematical thinkers',[128] create all-embracing systems without due regard for the nature of the world which they are intended to account for; yet others have more than one system, like Jacques's Spinozist, duelling captain. In Jacques we have someone whose fatalistic attitude paradoxically, yet logically, leads him to try to keep his system up to date, to adapt to every new contingency, turning chance into necessity. Inevitably he sometimes fails and sometimes succeeds, and neither failure nor success can always be attributed to his foresight or lack of it. He has no sooner created in his mind an order which seems to cope with his latest experience than there appears another of those 'deceitful phenomena'[129] which call for a new order.

To say that 'life is like this' is simply to express a platitude; to say that we constantly behave as though it is not is more interesting; but to suggest that we cannot help behaving as though it is not is more original and profound, especially when we are led on to its corollary, that we can perhaps understand the nature of life, what is

---

† The permanent and essential role of chance is rarely hinted at by Diderot as clearly as it is in this passage.

involved in being alive, but that this will not only not help us to live it, it is better forgotten if we want to get the most out of it. There is one moment in *Jacques le Fataliste* when the mask is briefly lifted from the relationship between Jacques and his master, and by implication between the story-teller and ourselves, so that we know where we stand. 'Don't you think it might be useful to know once and for all, plainly and clearly, exactly where we stand?'[130] says Jacques as he explains that his master is called the master, but that the real master is Jacques himself. But when they had put their dispute before the innkeeper's wife she declared that the formal relationship between them be briefly observed, after which the original situation must be restored 'and let there remain, between what the one may do and the other must do, the same obscurity as before'.[131] Diderot invites us here to see a parallel with contemporary political events ('a very similar quarrel')[132] arising out of the respective prerogatives of the king and the Parlements. We are obviously concerned here with more than the specific field of politics, but insofar as the passage does allude to political affairs, its stress on the positive value of 'obscurity' recalls a passage which I have already quoted in part from the *Mémoires* of Cardinal de Retz concerning the beginnings of the Fronde.

As they woke, they blindly sought the laws; they could not find them; stricken with panic, they cried out for them; and in all this turmoil, the questions they raised in their efforts to explain, which had once been obscure, and venerable in that obscurity, became a matter for doubt; therefore, for half of those concerned, odious. The people entered the sanctuary: they lifted the veil which must always conceal anything that may be said, anything that may be thought concerning the rights of peoples and those of kings, which are never so much in harmony as when they are shrouded in silence.[133]

The truth expressed in the inn, then, is something which has been a feature of political wisdom for over a hundred years, but it is not the ultimate truth. *Jacques le Fataliste*, like Retz's *Mémoires*, goes on; the characters continue their struggle with life as though it had never been revealed; indeed the moral which Jacques draws – 'Jacques leads his master'[134] – has a hollow ring when Jacques is taken to prison for his master's crime, a crime, moreover, which redresses a wrong done to his master before he ever knew him. Any control over events is suddenly and unjustly torn from Jacques' grasp, and at this point our certainty about his fate yields to hearsay. The stress at the end of the novel is on the unreliability of appearances, the doubtful nature of evidence; any ordered entity which we may have been able to make of the events so far fades into uncertainty at the end. But this surely is another face of the same truth. A neat, clear ending would round off one piece of experience, leaving us free to go on to the next: if this pattern may at times correspond to scientific research, it can never correspond to our experience of life. Since we have little control over what life brings, it is not we who leave an area of experience, it is the experience which leaves us and we cannot immediately be sure exactly where one area ends and another begins. The vision of the chain of being which d'Alembert has in his dream is a vision of life itself.

There is nothing clearly defined in nature... Any given thing is a specific thing only in greater or lesser degree... nothing is of the essence of a particular being... No, presumably because there is no quality which any given being does not share with some other, and it is the greater or less proportion of that quality which makes us attribute it to one being to the exclusion of another...[135]

In the course of our involvement with a given field of experience, then, much may become clear; what was at first a matter of chance is transformed by our active perception into necessity, but there is always a time-lag between the contingency presenting itself and the mind integrating it as a necessary part of a system or else rejecting it as irrelevant. We convert the phenomena which passing time presents to us into an ordered spatial pattern, but as we do so time goes on, producing more events which call for inclusion or rejection. There is always a time-lag, a 'décalage', because perception establishes itself in space while experience is created by time. It is here that we find the essential duality of human experience. Insofar as we become conscious of the area defined by ourselves and our immediate experience, we lose touch with it in time, so that active perception is, however infinitesimally, retrospective. It is this natural and inevitable need to impose order on experience which masks the nature of what is to come, imposing on future events a pattern in which they will have no place. Thus chance, which means the whole area of contingency lying outside the order we have created, is both an evil, in that it disrupts that order, and a source of truth, in that it provides the challenge to reshape our order to fit a new form of reality; 'chance, which never sleeps, more productive than perspicacity'.[136] An active life is therefore a constant struggle to catch up, to give meaning to a world whose meaning must necessarily elude us, but whose presence is the only source of meaning. The real story is told by life itself, not by the king, or the man of influence, or the artist; and life, being its own necessity, has no need to make the story convincing. The obscurity which envelops our relationship with it can only be beneficial.

The positive role of chance

It is characteristic of Diderot that just as he sees in sensibility a force which is not only the greatest source of disorder but also the prime agent of order, so he sees that we must constantly give our affirmation to the world of chance if we are to come to terms with it. Only chance can offer us the means whereby we can control it and it is the recognition of this which no doubt explains Diderot's fascination with those forms of human activity which seem to have the form of chance, such as dreams, fantasies and conversation. His remarks about the nature of conversation in his letter to Sophie Volland offer a striking parallel with what d'Alembert says in the passage just quoted from his dream:

It is as strange a mixture as the dreams of a sick and delirious man. Nevertheless, just as there is nothing unconnected in the mind of a dreamer or madman, so everything hangs together in a conversation... Madness, dreaming and the disorder of conversation consist in going from one subject to another by way of a common attribute.[137]

In these uncontrolled products of our minds he sees the same potential for the revelation of truth as in the chance incidents offered us by experience, and in this he proves to be more perspicacious and more realistic than many of his contemporaries.

The writer of the *Encyclopédie* article, 'Ordre (Metaph.)', alluding to that favourite subject of the age, the distinction between dream and waking experience, claims that the distinction lies in order.

It is order which distinguishes the waking state from sleep; for in the latter state everything occurs without sufficient reason. Everyone knows what strange combinations of things take shape in our dreams. We move from one place to another in an instant. A person appears, disappears, and reappears. We speak to the dead, to strangers, without there being any reason for these happenings. In a word, contradictory events take place in them. Thus the end of a dream often has no connection with the beginning; the result is that, there being no resemblance between the successive events in our dreams, the notion of order is absent from them. But in the waking state, everything has its sufficient reason; the sequence of ideas and movements is unfolded and carried through in conformity with the laws of order established in the universe, and confusion never reaches that point where we should have to acknowledge the co-existence of contradictory events.[138]

This passage is interesting for two reasons. In the first place it gives us an idea of the kind of thinking which Diderot saw as inadequate, the complacent question-begging of which he and Voltaire are the most active opponents. Secondly, many of the 'contradictory events' mentioned in this article are of the kind which occur in *Jacques le Fataliste*. Perhaps the most striking example is the funeral cortege which appears and reappears for no apparent reason, which may or may not indicate that Jacques' captain is dead, and which never acquires a 'sufficient reason'. What Diderot is saying is that things in the waking world as often as not present themselves to us as purely arbitrary, that contradictory things do seem to take place and that the end of a given experience (insofar as we can talk of discrete experiences) can often seem to have no connection with its beginning. It may be that we inhabit a universe which does not admit of 'contradictory events', but so far as the individual is concerned his own world is only a 'possible' one to the extent that his reason, and the world itself, allow him to make it so.

The attraction of fantasies, dreams and conversations is that, as a means of expression, they offer the closest possible parallel with the way we experience reality, and this because of their apparent disorder and their hidden order. Their way of masking the truth is as near as we can get to the appearance of life itself. Moreover, the kind of free association which operates here has more potential for the revelation of truth than step-by-step reasoning. It is possible, too, that Diderot saw, and often found these activities to be productive of the 'chance' of which he speaks in the *Interprétation de la Nature*, which would suddenly reveal the link between an existing set of ideas and a new problem. Characteristic as it is of Diderot's thinking, this process seems very different from the kind of step-by-step pattern suggested by his scientific thought. In this the two key metaphors are those of the points of illumination in the midst of areas of obscurity, and the idea of filling in the 'gaps in the chain'. This is the type of thinking which arises from a spatial representation of things, the picture of a partially unmapped area in which a process of exploration will progressively reduce the areas of obscurity. On this level of enquiry it is conceivable – and was held to be conceivable by Diderot – [139] that total success might eventually be possible, a success which would make irrelevant such distinctions as those made between movement and stability, homogeneity and heterogeneity, necessity and chance. The general laws governing the activity of the universe would thus be revealed, the laws which govern the successive instants which make up our apprehension of reality.

When it comes to the manifestation of these general laws in the particular circumstances of our lives, the other pattern operates – or at least it does if we accept the challenge of time – and the successive systems of order which we create to cope with a given moment are constantly invalidated and reshaped to include the contingencies which the next moment can bring: by facing up to the unexpected we are constantly converting 'surprise' into understanding. Of the three means of comprehending nature mentioned in the *Interprétation de la Nature*[140], observation, reflection and experiment, the third, by which we go back to nature to verify the results of the first two, is inevitably thwarted by the fact that nature has moved on in the meantime. Unless we withdraw into the torpor of Jacques' master, our active lives will be marked by a series of readjustments, of alterations of perspective. But these will be very different from the steady process of enlightenment envisaged in the *Interprétation*. To use the language of Diderot's dramatic theory, the scientist attempts to construct a *tableau*, and this is also what we strive to do in our daily lives; to convert the successive moments of our experience into a scene laid out before us, 'a concrete representation, the final point and resting place of reason'.[141] Our ideal is for life to be like the sort of play proposed by Dorval in which the audience is aware of the whole picture, but in fact we are actors; the play is written for us to act in without having learnt our parts, and we are at the mercy of the next 'coup de théâtre', to which we adjust in only partial knowledge of the surrounding circumstances. The best we can do is to try to be in the position of the audience, and we do well not to remind ourselves that our limitations make this ultimately an impossibility.

Now it is not difficult to find points of comparison between these two kinds of mental process, and in some ways they are parallel, but there is one point on which they reveal a striking opposition, and that is that the order sought by one of them, that which governs the general workings of the universe, is knowable, while its manifestation in the particular events of our individual lives is essentially unknowable and uncontrollable. In thought we are masters, but in action we are victims. It is exactly this distinction which defines the boundary between public and private literature. The public work in its exemplary form, the play, aims to present a world which is totally comprehensible, and Diderot's dramatic theory and practice do attempt to make it as comprehensible as possible, to make us, the audience, approximate as nearly as may be to the position of the spectator in the *Rêve* and the *Paradoxe*, the wise man who observes the fools on the stage. At the other extreme we have the private work, and Diderot's attempt to evolve the perfect example of this is surely *Jacques le Fataliste*, where, conveying an impression of life diametrically opposed to the assumptions of public order, he creates a picture of our personal experience of reality. But although the picture painted in *Jacques* may be negative in comparison with what Diderot offers in his dramatic theory and practice, it nevertheless puts forward a positive point of view, and one typical of Diderot, in suggesting that chance, which on the face of it is inimical to order, does in fact open the way to truth, and this simply because, if we accept its challenge, it enables us to adjust our conception of order to the changing circumstances of our own world. Out of the immeasurable area of contingency which surrounds the circumscribed space of order which we have created, the new phenomenon which is about to present itself is a potential and necessary component of order.

7

CHANCE AND THE MORAL ORDER

Individual happiness and the political order†

It has been possible until now to discuss the question of order with only the briefest of allusions to ethics, yet it could be argued that the major part of Diderot's thinking is directed towards establishing what our relationship ought to be with other people and with the world around us in general, for the kind of 'politeness' Diderot advocates extends not merely to our fellow men but to the totality of our experience, since he claims that we must acknowledge that not merely people but things have an existence in their own right. It is difficult nevertheless to extract from Diderot's writings a clear-cut system of ethics. Much of this can be explained by the general nature of thought in the period. Thinkers in the seventeenth and eighteenth centuries seem to have been less concerned with what we should or should not do, than with the nature of action and our ability to act effectively. This is true from Descartes onwards. The whole emphasis is on man's ability to control his own fate, and the assumption was often made, tacitly or not, that if some kind of balance could be struck between the power of each individual and the powers of other individuals, then all would be well. There is no need to add that the most interesting thinkers had their doubts about this, or at least were aware that much would be lost if such a balance could be achieved, but this preoccupation with power over oneself, power over others, and with the disastrous effects of too much power in one person's hands seems on the whole to have been accompanied by the belief that if only not just the prince, but everyone, has 'his hands tied for wrong-doing',[142] there would be no problem about the good which would ensue.

Such an assumption can only proceed from the belief that the good is there for all to see, and that our perception of what is good is

† This chapter, being in the nature of a summing-up, will contain a number of passages quoted earlier.

only obscured by various misplaced elements in the outside world as we apprehend it, elements which it should be in our power to put back where they belong. Now we know from Diderot's writings – and one could say the same for many of his contemporaries – that the passions are the agents which distort our perception of the truth; and it should be said here that the identity of the good and the true follows automatically from a philosophy which equates happiness with conformity to nature. In Diderot's ideal state, order is ensured by the sovereign silencing his own passions for good and all, so that he can see the right way to govern his people, but there is a further assumption, which is that each citizen will function within certain limits, precisely those within which he cannot do any harm to his fellows. In the *Fragments échappés du Portefeuille d'un Philosophe* of 1772, Diderot distinguishes two aspects of administration: the first concerns general security, defence, the preservation of law, and is 'a simple matter for civil government',[143] but the individual must also be catered for in his individuality, so that the second aspect is a guarantee of property:

everyone has his head [unlike, that is, the many-headed monster in the monastery analogy] and his property, a portion of the general wealth of which he is master, and absolute master, over which he is king, and which he can use and even abuse as he thinks fit. Man in society must be allowed the freedom to be a bad citizen in this matter, because he will not be long in being severely punished by misfortune, and by contempt, which is even more cruel than misfortune.[144]

Another comment stresses the link between property and liberty:

The nature of man and the notion of property combine to emancipate him, and liberty leads the individual and society to the greatest happiness they can desire.[145]

Property seems here to acquire a metaphysical dimension, symbolic of that area of a man's being which is inalienably his own. Here is the space within which a man can be himself without his behaviour encroaching on the rights of others – and the one person not to have such a space is the sovereign.

Diderot probably had something similar in mind when he wrote in the *Observations sur le Nakaz*:

When everything is well ordered in other respects, things find their own level. Make sure that three or four important points are in order and leave the rest to the interest and taste of the private citizens.[146]

As far as it is possible to identify 'the rest', it seems to concern matters of the economy, for example industry,[147] the growth of towns and villages and of population,[148] and there may be a connection too with the two kinds of happiness referred to in the *Mémoires*: one is constant: 'depending on freedom, the safety of property, the nature of taxation, its distribution, its gathering, and which honours the eternal laws';[149] the other is 'accidental, variable and ephemeral ... the continuance of the law would be disastrous: it must be repealed'.[150] Whether the connection is close or not, we have here the same pattern of two aspects of society, one permanent, inflexible, stable, providing a framework for the other which allows for the free play of individuality, significantly expressed in economic terms, for, to the eighteenth-century mind, the growth of industry, the increasing importance of trade and the free flow of money must have been closely associated with change, social mobility and individual freedom, the ferment which theatened to destroy the *Ancien Régime*, but which, in a successful society, could also be the basis of freedom and prosperity.

It is impossible to be clear, from these quotations or indeed from any other part of his writings, exactly how Diderot saw the details of political organization in his ideal society, but the double role of each of its members, as citizens and as 'particuliers', as public and as private beings, is obviously an essential feature of it. This pattern is explained not just by the inevitable fact that members of a society must sacrifice a part of themselves to the general good, but by the conviction that the conditions for individual happiness are essentially anti-social. One might conclude from this that moral good is to be equated with order, public order, and that individual happiness is a potential evil, only prevented from actualization by the limits set upon it by the state, and there is an exact parallel here with the ordered human organism, whose health depends on a balance held between the senses and passions by an efficient organ of perception. But although this may have been the unspoken, even unconscious assumption lying behind much of the period's thinking, it does not represent the whole picture for Diderot. Certainly we find the equation of morality and order in his writings, as for example in the mouth of Dorval: 'I define virtue as a desire for order in moral matters',[151] but this statement assumes a privileged status for moral order which, as Diderot is aware, is not necessarily founded in the nature of things. Order itself is a purely formal, structural matter and has no necessary relationship with ethics.

The status of moral actions

One way in which this problem presents itself is in the question, raised by the nature of genius. This might not seem to have any very obvious connection with ethics were it not for the fact that it is very definitely connected with them in the early part of *Le Neveu de Rameau*. The case of Racine brings up the question of the double standard, not so much the opposition of aesthetic and moral judgments, which comes up later in the dialogue, but whether we should judge men primarily by their immediate impact on their fellows or by the ultimate good they do. The question is really insoluble. To Rameau's judgment: 'The man has only been good to people he didn't know and after his death',[152] *Moi*'s answer is: 'let us ... forget for the moment the point we occupy in time and space; let us cast our eyes over the centuries to come, the most distant lands and nations yet to be born. Let us think of the good of our race.'[153]

The point is that both men are displaying a 'desire for order', one for order in the here and now, the other for an ultimate and timeless order which he clearly sees as having an absolute value. For Rameau, the genius upsets the existing order: 'If I knew anything about history I would show you that evil has always come here below through some man of genius';[154] and Diderot, seeing the genius as a chance phenomenon, out of tune with his times, had given one reason why, in the article 'Encyclopédie':

We must ... have the courage to see ... that it is almost the same with types of literature as it is with the establishment of laws and the original formation of towns; it is always some unusual chance, some strange circumstance, sometimes a flight of genius, which has been responsible for their birth.[155]

He goes on to say that it might almost be better if a people never produced an extraordinary man

under whose influence a newly born art took its first steps too boldly and quickly, and who disturbed its imperceptible natural development. This man's works will inevitably be monstrous compositions, because genius and good taste are two very different qualities. Nature gives us one in an instant; the other takes centuries to produce.[156]

Such monsters, he continues, become models for the future and give a distorted idea of beauty; only nature should be the model for art.

One can understand how the influence of the genius upset Diderot in his role as editor of a work which aimed to give a coherent picture of civilization at a particular point in time. In fact Rameau's ideas are very close to those expressed by Diderot the encyclopedist. Rameau, as a partisan of a style of music which aims at a closer imitation of nature, claims that the new music which corresponds to his ideal will establish itself gradually. 'The reign of nature is quietly coming in, and that of my trinity ... The foreign god unobtrusively takes his place on the altar beside the idol of the country, but little by little he strengthens his position there.'[157] Men of genius on the other hand only upset things:

They change the face of the globe, yet even in the smallest things stupidity is so rife and so powerful that you can't change it without the hell of a fuss. Part of their conception does come about, part remains as it was. Hence two gospels – a Harlequin coat.[158]

'Nature' is seen by Rameau, and by Diderot in his encyclopedic role, as an order in itself; genius as the monster – or one of the monsters – which distorts it. This is the view which sees nature not as the totality of experience, but as that part of experience which follows self-evident laws; it is the attitude of d'Alembert when he divides creation into 'uniformity of nature' and 'lapses of nature'. Rameau, monster though he is, belongs to this world, and in this respect is more 'rational' than *Moi*. *Moi*, by his belief that actions promoting the 'good of our race'[159] may not be appreciated immediately but at some distant point in the future, and moreover that such actions may well appear to upset the existing order of things, is assuming something very like Providence. This is not, of course, a Providence which is actually an external force guiding us in the right direction, like that represented by the angel Jesrad in *Zadig*, but he is necessarily supposing that certain phenomena acquire a privileged status by the effect they have. The pattern is familiar: it is that of an established order being reshaped by the intervention of a chance phenomenon from outside it. But the time-scale is different: we are not concerned with the continual readjustment imposed by constant and inevitable change, the readjustment we need to make in the interests of effective action, but with the impact of certain selected and distinctive phenomena, whose benefit is only perceived from an undefined lapse of time, and in whose perception a value-judgment is involved.

This privileged kind of order, to judge by the examples in the moral sphere given by *Moi* – the rehabilitation of the Calas family, Hoop's restoration of his family to their rightful home,[160] and the various actions which to him are 'infinitely more pleasurable'[161] than sensual pleasures[162] – is based on actions which are carried out in opposition to the competitive laws of nature; they reverse the general tendency of all things to survive at each other's expense, and restore things to those 'rightful' places formerly masked by the workings of 'nature', or self-interest. *Moi*'s description to Rameau of the kind of pleasure such actions give is revealing:

And you are people to be pitied if you can't see that we have risen above our human condition ['sort'], and that it is impossible to be unhappy with two good deeds of this kind to make one secure.[163]

The man who has achieved such actions is lifted out of the general process of cause and effect. It might be better to say that he is lifted into a higher order of cause and effect since in Diderot's determinist philosophy these 'chance' interventions are themselves both effects and causes. The point is that we cannot impose this kind of logical examination on Diderot's thinking; we are concerned with patterns of perception in which, whatever the field in which we perceive an ordered 'fullness', the area beyond its limits is imagined to be more open, giving free play to the activity of the individual, or the workings of chance.

Sensibility as a moral force

Moral actions then, since they reverse the normal order of things, are essentially isolated phenomena, and however much they may contribute to a later order, cannot be regarded as natural in the sense just spoken of. What can be said is that they are connected with the sensibility. This has already been described as the agent which links together what the simple laws of movement tend to separate, from molecules and organs to human beings, and also provides a means of salvation, a translation of divine grace from the hands of God into the nature of matter. Nothing shows more clearly the association in Diderot's mind between sensibility as a physical property of matter and sensibility in its wider, more usual sense as a human and emotional quality, than his discussion of drama as a moral force in the *Discours sur la Poésie Dramatique*; and in these same remarks we can see the distinction between the two concepts of nature, blind nature and good nature.

In the *Discours*, moral actions are anything but austere; on the contrary, they release powerful emotions which themselves draw people together:

It is always virtue and virtuous people that one must have in view when one writes. It is you, my friend [probably Grimm], that I call to mind when I take up my pen; it is you that I have before my eyes when I do anything. It is Sophie that I want to please. If you have smiled at me, if she has shed a tear, if you both love me more for what I have done, I am rewarded. When I heard the peasant scenes in *Le Faux Généreux*, I said: There's something which will please the whole earth, and in all times: there's something which will draw tears from everybody.[164]

Later on in the same section ('De la Comédie Sérieuse'), Diderot is carried away by his enthusiasm into a eulogy of the goodness of nature:

So I repeat: the honest, the honest ... Poet, are you a man of sensibility and delicacy? Play on this string and you will hear it vibrate, or tremble in every soul.

Is human nature good then? Yes, my friend, indeed it is very good. Water, air, earth, fire, all is good in nature; both the hurricane which blows up towards the end of the autumn, shakes the forests, and beating the trees against each other, breaks and separates their dead branches; and the tempest, which beats the waters of the sea and purifies them; and the volcano which pours out from its gaping flanks the floods of glowing matter, raising into the air the vapour which cleanses it.

It is the wretched conventions which pervert man, and not human nature which should be blamed. Indeed, what is there that moves us like the account of a noble action? Where is there a man so wicked that he can listen unmoved to the complaint of a good man?[165]

These passages, partly quoted before, are worth setting out in full here for two reasons. First of all they express an aspect of Diderot and his age which forms a striking, barely credible contrast with so much of his other work, and yet presents an equally real and valid face of his genius and attitudes. A second and more important point here is that we see in these lines the kind of associations which exist in Diderot's mind: First of all the 'honest' and 'sensibility'; secondly the natural goodness of man and the goodness of nature; then the common but rather surprising link between moral good and the violent aspects of nature; and finally the contrast between this violence and the 'wretched conventions'. This is a cathartic interpretation of the disordered aspects of nature, and also one which implies some kind of purpose in nature and even betrays a hint of optimism. It does not have any obvious link with the 'honest'. Diderot's main intention in this particular context is of course to show (as did the partisans of final causes) that even the most striking examples of 'le mal physique', evil in the natural world, are ultimately beneficial, but there is also the implication, in this picture of a violent force restoring a tainted nature to its original purity, of the influence from without, which, as in *Le Père de Famille*, brings about a higher, more authentic order by upsetting a 'false' order, where truth has been obscured. This is a similar picture to that given in the section 'Des Moeurs', where Diderot, having described the true subject-matter of poetry – 'Poetry requires something enormous, barbaric and savage'[166] – describes the moment in the development of societies when true poets flourish: 'It will be after times of disaster and great misfortune, when troubled peoples begin to breathe again. Then men's imaginations, shaken by terrible scenes, will depict things unknown to those who have not witnessed them.'[167] Such genius is always present;

> but the men who carry it within them remain benumbed, unless some extraordinary event heats up the mass and brings them to the surface. Then feelings build up in their breasts and torment them; and those that have a voice, full of the urge to speak, give tongue and are relieved of their burden.[168]

Although the ideas here belong with the general eighteenth-century tradition of going back to some chronological or conceptual original to discover the nature of man, Diderot supposes quite specific conditions for the emergence of natural feeling – and here we are talking about 'good' nature. Just as the forests need to be revived by natural disasters, man can only find the purity of his own nature as a consequence of 'extraordinary events'.[169] Acting in the same way as the heat acts on the embryo in the chicken's egg to release the sensibility in it, or as the colony of free Swiss brings an awareness of freedom to a politically inert people, these events have the effect of a leaven, producing a ferment ('heat up the mass')[170] which releases the latent genius of the poet.

What emerges from this is that there is a good and a bad nature which exactly corresponds to good and bad society. A natural phenomenon, a forest, say, can grow old and disordered, fixed, so to speak, in the past, and needs the hurricane, the violent force from outside, to clear away the dead growth and restore it to its true self. Human society similarly develops a dead growth, the conventions which conceal and deform its original vigour; these conventions themselves form a kind of order which can only be overthrown by the intervention of some powerful external force. But just as the two aspects of nature are equally part of nature, offering two opposing faces of the same natural process, so the effete order of Diderot's own society with its 'people whose morals are petty, mean and mannered'[171] is just as much a part of the human condition as the vigour of the early stages of society; and the tyranny which divides men from each other, leading them into competition with each other like the isolated molecules of nature in disorder, belongs just as much to human experience as the sense of freedom and the sensibility which brings them together. These two faces of experience correspond in the physical universe of Diderot to the downward trend of matter, subject to the simple laws of movement, existing as isolated, hostile particles, and the upward trend of matter awakened to sensibility, forming together into living organisms. It is a vision which reinterprets the concept of the Fall and Redemption in material terms, and yet preserves its structure and its tensions.

In *Jacques le Fataliste* we have seen this pattern applied to everyday experience, where each new event is seen as an external stimulus calling for a reordering of the interpretation made of previous events. In *Le Neveu de Rameau* the problem is presented as the impact of an extraordinary individual on a man who apparently represents a totally unrelated attitude to life. In Rameau we have a perversion of Dorval. Dorval is a character of extreme sensibility and also one for whom order and morality are synonymous. It is certain that, for him, to understand nature is to understand what is good. He is no anarchist; his reforming zeal, as it applies to the theatre, is aimed at making men better by creating an art which conforms to the truth of nature, in the same way as society should. He seems to be a true representative of that aspect of the enlightenment typified by Rousseau, and concerned to discover what nature was like in order to reshape society in conformity with it. Order, the order of nature, thus becomes an objective value, having content as well as form. But there is no need to reiterate at this point that this is not the whole story and if further evidence is needed then Rameau is there to supply it. Perhaps too much emphasis has been laid by commentators on the principle of disorder which runs through the *Neveu de Rameau*, to the extent that the book has tended to be regarded as a picture of the positive existence and validity of disorder in society and in nature. This picture is certainly there, but, as in the *Rêve de d'Alembert*, the disorder is not just something which is manifestly there, it is also something which produces a positive reaction. Out of the *Rêve* there emerges the 'great man'; from this work there comes, not a great man, but something very different, and yet disturbingly similar. And there is similarity not just between some aspects of Rameau and the great man, but also between the nature and assumptions of the society in which Rameau moves and the general conception of human society with which we associate Diderot.

Just as societies, in Diderot's view, are formed by people recognizing their similarities to one another, so Rameau, born a 'nodding

porcelain chinaman'[172] finds himself 'among other nodding porcelain Chinamen',[173] all different, but having in common the fact
that they find one another amusing, 'for fools and madmen amuse
each other, they seek each other out and are mutually attracted'.[174]
Drawn by their similar needs they come together for mutual profit.
The people amongst whom Rameau moves are united by a single
purpose: to acquire money and the pleasure it brings. He makes the
point early on, during the discussion of Racine, that money is only
good for increasing one's enjoyment of life:

And what the devil do you expect people to spend their money on if not to
have a good table, good company, good wines, pretty women, pleasures of
all descriptions, amusements of every kind?[175]

Here is a simple, straightforward standard which cuts right through
the various economic theories of the time. It also provides a firm
basis for the education of his son: 'Money, money. Money is all, and
the rest, without money, is nothing';[176] and this is what he will teach
him 'instead of stuffing his head with fine maxims that he would
have to forget or else beg for bread'.[177] In any case, the contempt
which *Moi* has acquired for wealth is something artificial: 'People
aren't born with that kink. It is acquired, for it isn't natural.'[178] We
all seek our good at the expense of others, he goes on, and this is why
education is necessary, to prevent us from pursuing our natural bent
too far and getting into trouble: 'and what is a good education if not
one that leads to all kinds of enjoyment without danger or difficulty?'[179] As in any well-ordered society, certain limits must be set
upon the free activity of the individual. But these limits do not, for
Rameau, correspond to one's function, as they seem to for Diderot.
'What does it matter whether you have a position or not so long as
you are rich, since you only take up a position to get rich?'[180] This
being so, each profession has developed its 'idioms'[181] which enable
its practitioners to make as much money as possible; and here too
there is a kind of order which prevents this state of affairs from
having too disastrous effects. As Rameau says: 'not many are rascals
when they are not on the job. And everything would work quite well
were it not for a certain number of people of the sort called indus-
trious, punctilious, etc.'[182] Most people pursue these 'idiomatic'
practices within the limits of their professions and are decent
enough people outside them. Those who are a threat to the system
are the ones who carry the method into their ordinary lives, and
thereby do better than their fellows.

There is no guarantee that Rameau's kind of society will function perfectly, then, any more than any other society, but its main advantage over *Moi*'s, as he repeatedly shows, is that it offers an ideal which corresponds to men's actual natures. The virtue which Diderot and Dorval associate with order and the highest aspirations of men is seen by Rameau not just as unattainable for most of us, but as a kind of specialist fad, suited only to a few eccentrics, but which by some quirk of the imagination they want to impose on everyone else.

You think that happiness is the same for all. What a strange illusion! Your own brand presupposes a certain romantic turn of mind that we don't all possess, an unusual type of soul, a peculiar taste. You dignify this oddity with the name of virtue and you call it philosophy. But are virtue and philosophy made for everybody? Some can acquire them, some can keep them.[183]

The manifest advantage of money as a goal is that it is almost universally recognized, and the means of acquiring it and enjoying its benefits can at least be understood, if not attained, by everyone. For Rameau's part his vices are natural to him, to his nation and to his protectors; why then 'mutilate myself into something quite different from what I am. I should give myself a character quite foreign to me.'[184] The virtuous are so often unsociable because 'they have subjected themselves to a discipline that is not in their nature.'[185] Rameau will moreover bring his son up in conformity with this philosophy based on what he sees as the true nature of the world about him, and *Moi* has to admit: 'Certainly with theories of teaching so exactly made to the measure of our society he would go far.'[186] From all this it seems that it is *Moi* who is the 'systematical thinker'; he is the one who has failed to base his philosophy on the nature of things.

To *Moi*'s objection that nature, as opposed to society, should set the standard for our behaviour, *Lui* not only retorts, quite justifiably, that 'she makes strange blunders';[187] he also implies by his comments that the distinction between nature and society is for him a totally unreal one, a distinction only to be perceived by those who can afford the luxury of detaching themselves from the struggle and observing it from the 'epicycle of Mercury'. For him, and implicitly for all those in the 'subservient posture in which you are kept by need'[188] there is only the outside world with its arbitrary sequence of circumstances, and its manifest failure to satisfy our needs and aspirations, whether they be natural, like appetite, or social, like Rameau's desire to be a good musician. But in the face of this chaos, Rameau and his fellows have fashioned their own societies, and the 'maison Bertin' is one of them, 'a school for civilized men, a renewal of the hospitality of older times',[189] full of the failures of the world of art and united against a common enemy, its successes. But this society has its successes too, and *mutatis mutandis*, they resemble those of *Moi*'s world: 'Usually greatness of character comes from a natural balance between several opposing qualities',[190] says Rameau, at which point *Moi* is anxious to change the subject. But once it is admitted that greatness lies in organization, in form – or, one might say, order – rather than in content, there is no reason not to admire the criminal: 'His courage bowls you over. His brutality makes you shudder. What you value in everything is consistency of character.'[191] To the objection that he has not achieved this unity, Rameau gives the same answer as might anyone who was aiming at some ideal: 'I agree, but I have done my best';[192] and he has the modesty to admit that there are others better than him. His world has its hierarchy of heroes like any other, and the top position is occupied by Bouret, a past master in the use of the mask.

Rameau himself cultivates an attitude which is reminiscent of the actor of the *Paradoxe sur le Comédien*. Taking Theophrastus, La Bruyère and Molière as his texts, he constructs models for his own behaviour which benefit from the errors of those he reads about. 'I am myself, and I remain myself, but I act and speak as occasion requires.'[193] He develops a detachment which gives him complete control over the role he decides to play at any given moment: 'my only merit in the matter is that I have done systematically, with an accurate mind and a true aim in view, what most others have done by instinct'.[194] His method surely springs from the same attitude as that of Cardinal de Retz, deciding to 'do wrong by design ... because in this way one avoids the most dangerous source of ridicule to be found in our profession, that of inopportunely mingling sin with devoutness'.[195] Rameau, over a century later, adds another element: 'For the same art which helps me to avoid being ridiculous on certain occasions helps me on others to achieve it in a masterly manner'[196] – but perhaps Retz realized this too. In any case, there is exactly the same awareness in both men that the path to success lies in a self-control which gives one permanent mastery over one's instincts, and this is coupled with the awareness of another fact, that there is one morality for those who pontificate and another – which looks alarmingly like its opposite – for those who are involved in action. As Rameau says: 'When I say vicious, it is by way of speaking your language, for if we came to a clear understanding it might turn out that what you call vice I call virtue, and that what I call vice you call virtue';[197] and as Retz puts it: 'an archbishop's vices may, on innumerable occasions, be the virtues of the leader of a faction'.[198]

The parallel is worth insisting on for two reasons. It suggests firstly that the moral implications of Rameau's character are not merely a brilliant insight of Diderot's but express a particular kind of duality which characterized the whole period, but to which it rarely gave full expression, for reasons indicated in the preceding chapter. The feature in Rameau which so disturbs *Moi* is not so much his immorality as his frankness. 'In all this there was much that we all think and on which we all act, but which we leave unsaid. That, indeed, was the most obvious difference between this man and most of those we meet.'[199] In being frank – and this is the second point – Rameau threatens to undermine the uneasy alliance between ideals and action which, like that between sovereign and subject, is best veiled in obscurity. The implication of Rameau's statements – as of Retz's – is that the values of *Moi*'s world are not merely incompatible, but diametrically opposed, to those of *Lui*'s world, that action necessarily denies the values which thought creates. A similar point is made in *Est-il bon? Est-il méchant?* When Monsieur Hardouin complains that his fate is to do everyone else's bidding and to please no-one, Madame Bertrand replies: 'It's not just a question of helping people, but of helping them in the way they want...',[200] and the whole play illustrates the impossibility of this, of the fact that, as Crocker puts it (*Diderot's Chaotic Order*, p. 167) 'there may be no way of translating ideals into action except by means that contradict them'.

Not only does action contradict the ideal, but the conception of self held by the man of action contradicts that of the *philosophe*. In keeping with his desire to play any role demanded by circumstances and his admiration for Bouret and his mask, *Lui* has no sense of personal unity, of an inalienable core of personality.

Devil take me if I really know what I am. As a rule my mind is as true as a sphere and my character as honest as the day: never false if I have the slightest interest in being true, never true if I have the slightest interest in being false. I say things as they come to me.[201]

This is not entirely true of Rameau, but the point he is making – or perhaps the point Diderot is making over his head – is that consistency in action comes not from an original unity of character, but from the total subordination of the self to self-interest, in other words to the demands of the moment. His one mistake was to imagine 'that I was indispensable'.[202] The Diderot of the *Rêve* would endorse this view, as he would endorse many other things Rameau says, but the attitude of being 'indispensable' is nevertheless implicit in the concept of the reflecting self, observing a world which would be meaningless without it, as Diderot himself maintains in his article 'Encyclopédie'. By the act of perception which creates order in our field of vision we automatically give value to its phenomena, and value to ourselves. This is the 'mistake' which distorts our own role in that world, (and Jacques' in his), and it is Rameau's mistake because he not only sees himself as unique, but attributes value to himself. 'In the middle of this set-to a fell thought came into my head, a thought that made me feel arrogant and filled me with pride and insolence.'[203] Not only this, but he attributes to himself that necessary concomitant of value, freedom. 'I am quite prepared to be abject, but not under compulsion. I am willing to give up my dignity ... but of my own free will and not on somebody else's orders.'[204] Rameau's mistake, then, his tragic flaw, is for once to have claimed the freedom which Diderot insists in *Jacques le Fataliste* that we must claim. This constitutes a basic difference between the two dialogues; they are not contradictory, for they are rooted in the same conception of the human condition, but they present opposing faces of the same reality.

The face presented in the *Neveu*, again basically a matter of politics, is that of the behaviour appropriate in a tyranny. Rameau has suddenly and unaccountably become aware of an inalienable self which has been encroached upon.

Should people be in a position to say 'crawl', and I have to crawl? That is the worm's method and it is mine; we both do the same when we are left alone, but we turn when our tails are trodden on.[205]

But such attitudes are a luxury for Rameau and his like; he is well aware that he lives under a tyranny. His patron spends his life making judgments against which there is no appeal: 'It's His Nibs who decides, always decides, and there is no appeal ... gloomy, inscrutable and uncompromising, like Fate – that's our boss.'[206] Moreover, Rameau seems unaware that there might be any other kind of life. Talking of the 'positions' towards the end of the dialogue, he excludes only the sovereign from this pantomime: 'There is only one man in the whole of a realm who walks, and that is the sovereign. Everybody else takes up positions.'[207] And when *Moi* explains that the sovereign is not exempt either, *Lui*, as so often, fails to get the point: 'That cheers me no end',[208] is his only answer, as he mimes the various positions. For him, there is nothing beyond society and the tyranny of circumstances; and *Moi*'s description of the one being who is 'free to do without pantomime',[209] the philosopher, is received with similar incomprehension.

For the reader of *Jacques le Fataliste*, the answer to the tyranny of life is to behave as though he can do something about it. In the *Neveu* Diderot looks at the problem differently. Here we are offered no figure with whom to identify. *Moi* is a figure of comedy, and this is not just because Rameau seems to have the best arguments. The irony of *Moi* consists in the role which he is offered but is unable to take up. As a thinker, as one who is detached from the hurly-burly of life around him, he should be ideally placed to understand, to perceive the spectacle before him; he is an instrument of perception who has the exceptional privilege of being offered, not reality, but Rameau's consummate miming of it. He sees not the confusing spectacle of actual life, but a representation of it, as the ideas which come up in the conversation are obligingly transformed by Rameau into a 'a concrete representation'. But this representation, far from being 'the final point and resting place of reason',[210] is, if anything, more disturbing to *Moi* than the reality for which it stands, as he alternates between amusement and moral indignation, attraction and revulsion. His ultimate reaction is one of withdrawal: 'we had better not go into it . . . I'm afraid we may only agree on the surface, and if we once begin going into which dangers and difficulties should be avoided we shall cease to agree'.[211] This is the nearest he gets to admitting to Rameau that his conversation has called into question the objective status of the order upon which he bases his life. The comedy of his role lies in the fact that he is an instrument of perception which would rather not perceive.

Moi is equally unnerved by the aesthetic aspect of Rameau's pantomime. 'Every imitative art has its model in nature',[212] he says, mouthing the statements appropriate to his role. But the imitation is not what *Moi* bargained for. Rameau, whose expertise in musical matters makes up for his blindness to ethical values, believes that art should indeed imitate nature, and in this his observations parallel Dorval's views on drama.

It is the animal cry of passion that should dictate the melodic line . . . don't imagine that the technique of stage actors and their declamation can serve as a model. Pooh! we want something more energetic, less stilted, truer to life. The simple language and normal expression of emotion are all the more essential because our language is more monotonous and less highly stressed. The cry of animal instinct or that of a man under stress of emotion will supply them.[213]

But the practical conclusions which Rameau draws from his views are not what *Moi* – or even Dorval – would expect.

Rameau, in fact, points up the logical conclusion of both the *Entretiens sur le Fils Naturel* and the *Paradoxe sur le Comédien*, as well as that of the *Rêve de d'Alembert*. Dorval, 'under the spell', has a vision of the poet under the spell of enthusiasm; as its power increases,

it is no longer a shudder, it is a strong and lasting warmth which sets him on fire, makes him gasp, consumes him, kills him; yet it gives spirit and life to all he touches;[214]

if the force of his enthusiasm grew stronger:

He could only find relief in pouring out a flood of ideas which are pushing, jostling and fighting to get out.[215]

And, at the end of this description, which is so powerfully evocative of Rameau, 'possessed by such a frenzy, an enthusiasm so near to madness that it was uncertain whether he would ever get over it',[216] Dorval emerges from it, like Rameau, 'like a man waking from a deep sleep'.[217] In a note to this passage, Vernière says: 'Diderot will modify this romantic vision thirteen years later in the *Paradoxe sur le Comédien*'.[218] But, as I have suggested, the ultimate message of the *Paradoxe* concerns not art but life; the last few lines are a pointer to this, if any pointer is needed by the time one has reached the end of this dialogue: 'do you think that the actor on the stage is any deeper, any more skilful in feigning joy, sadness, sensibility, admiration, hatred, passion, than an old courtier?'[219] Perhaps it would be more accurate to say that the *Paradoxe* implies that life *is* an art-form, and the *Neveu* contains the further implication that the roles it dictates are purely formal and aesthetic, not moral; that is, they consist in constant readjustments of one's 'position', of one's relationship to surrounding circumstances; it is a question of 'rapports', relationships, not of principles. This is the method which Rameau follows in his life, but not in his pantomimes, in some of which his sensibility is totally absorbed, his personality completely alienated, as though life were a game, and art the only area in which we can afford the luxury of involvement.

Rameau's kind of art pursues realism to its furthest point, that of faithful reproduction of reality, 'never losing sight of tone, proportion, meaning of words and character of music';[220] and it is in his pantomimes that he is most real, that he obtrudes most forcibly on our consciousness. As the notes pour out from his powerful lungs, the chess-players abandon their game, the passers-by stop to look in through the café windows, and *Moi* finds himself 'in the most singular state ... I have ever experienced...'.[221] This scene is in a sense the climax of the dialogue, the point where Rameau, the apostle of reality, of what is, is alienated to the point of becoming that reality. As he unfolds this disordered panorama of human and natural phenomena he is like an elemental force, and his significance lies in his simple presence, in the fact that he and what he represents are monumentally and inescapably *there*. His individuality is absorbed and lost in the total world of which he aspires to be a part, and in this he echoes d'Alembert's dream: 'There is but one great individual, and that is the whole',[222] just as his system of behaviour corresponds to d'Alembert's 'Each form has its own sort of happiness and unhappiness.'[223]

Perhaps the only character in eighteenth-century literature with whom Rameau can be compared, not so much for his sensibility as for his taunting rejection of civilized values, is Goethe's Mephisto ('I am the spirit which always denies').[224] Jean Fabre, in the Introduction to his edition of the *Neveu* (p. lxxxvii, n. 1) quotes John Morley as saying: 'Rameau is the squalid and tattered Satan of the eighteenth century. He is a Mephistopheles out at elbow, a Lucifer in low waters; yet always diabolic, with the bright flash of the pit in his eye...' And surely this is the point: Rameau is evil in that he represents a positive force which, by its simple presence, imposes itself as a reality, and as a more valid reality than the conceptual order, however accurately founded in the nature of things, which it upsets. Diderot is not soliciting our approval for Rameau's philosophy: what he implies is that we cannot help ourselves from giving it a kind of approval: 'That's just what I was saying to you. The enormity of the deed carries you beyond mere contempt'[225] says Rameau. Diderot makes the same point in the *Salon* of 1767, that 'the greatness of his conceptions'[226] can lead us to identify ourselves with a wicked man, adding: 'if we conspire against Venice with the Count de Bedmar, it is virtue in another aspect which wins our assent';[227] and it seems worth recalling that Corneille expressed similar views in connection with *Rodogune*.

Dorval sees his vision of the new poetry marching hand in hand with the new philosophy.

In our own day men of genius have restored the philosophy of the intelligible world to the real world. Will there not also be someone who will do the same for lyric poetry, and bring it down from the enchanted realms to the world we live in?[228]

In the same way, but without drawing any parallel with philosophy, Rameau rejects the 'fairy-tales',[229] the 'insipid mythology',[230] the 'sugary little madrigals which show up the bad taste of the poet as clearly as they do the poverty of the art which uses them',[231] and it is this which leads him to proclaim his trinity, 'truth, which is the father, begets goodness, which is the son, whence proceeds the beautiful, which is the holy ghost'.[232] What is important is not so much to establish precisely what Rameau means by his trinity, as to recognize that he is talking in exactly the same terms as might a *philosophe* and yet that his trinity is erected on a basis totally opposed to moral values, by a man

who discussed a horrible act, an execrable crime, like a connoisseur of painting or poetry examining the beauties of a work of art, or a moralist or historian picking out and illuminating the circumstances of a heroic deed.[233]

The sublime

It is this realization that gives *Moi* some of his most uncomfortable moments; it is the combination of the acceptable with the unacceptable, the linking of two sets of reactions which, his reason tells him, should be kept apart, the revelation that the admirable can be rooted in the despicable, which leaves him in uncertainty 'whether to stay or run away, laugh or be furious'.[234] Now this is a reaction which Diderot also associates with the sublime. Although he rarely commits himself to anything approaching a reasoned definition of the sublime, there are passages in his writings which suggest that *Moi* is, perhaps without realizing it, in the presence of the sublime. In a letter of 1762 to Sophie Volland he says:

Powerful effects always come from a mixture of the voluptuous and the terrible, for instance beautiful half-naked women offering us delicious potions in the bloody skulls of our enemies. That is the model for everything that is sublime. It is subjects like that which make the soul melt with pleasure and shudder with fear. The combination of these feelings plunges it into an extraordinary state and it is the mark of the sublime that it moves us in a quite exceptional way.[235]

The last sentence in particular recalls *Moi*'s awareness of being 'in the most singular state I have ever experienced'[236] as he watches Rameau's musical pantomime.

The extract from Diderot's letter and *Moi*'s reaction to Rameau suggest that the sublime was so much discussed in the eighteenth century – and much more by others than by Diderot – because it constituted a moral problem, not just in the sense that ethics and aesthetics were inextricably linked, but because it involved a positive appreciation of evil, of things inimical to order. It is true that this does not always seem to be the case in Diderot's discussions of it. For example, in the article 'Encyclopédie', speaking of the incompatibility of 'genius' and 'wit' ('bel esprit'), he writes

sound, genuine taste, the sublime in whatever type of art, the moving, the great effects of fear, compassion and terror, noble and elevated feelings and great ideas resist epigrammatical style and contrast in expression.[237]

Here the sublime, the expression of the genius, is seen as the healthy alternative to the over-civilized, intellectualized art which Diderot, like Dorval, and Rameau, despised.

But in the *Salons*, especially in that of 1767, the association of the sublime with fear is much more evident.

Anything which astonishes the mind, anything which inspires a feeling of terror is conducive to the sublime... The night hides the shapes of things, adds horror to their sounds; even that of a leaf in the depths of a forest sets the imagination working, and the imagination troubles the heart, so that everything is magnified.[238]

The sublime as described here is an embodiment of all that makes ordered perception impossible. It produces that 'astonishment'[239] which destroys our judgment, our sense of perspective; it is associated with darkness which upsets our vision and our spatial sense; it makes our emotions dominate over our reason. If such things are to be the subject of art, then it seems that the standards of art must be in direct opposition to those of ordered life, and this is borne out by an earlier passage in the *Salon* of 1767, where Diderot sees the possibility of 'a morality proper to artists, or art',[240] one which 'might well be the opposite of everyday morality';[241] and he goes on: 'I am very much afraid that man may be led straight to disaster along the path which leads the imitator of nature to the sublime.'[242] The exemplars of this sublime morality are doomed to misfortune: 'Heroes, romantic lovers, great patriots, inflexible magistrates, apostles of religion, uncompromising philosophers, all these rare and divine madmen create poetry in the midst of life, and that is the cause of their misfortune.'[243] These are the people who fail to make the compromise necessary for ordered social life; they are the ones who neglect to observe Rameau's 'idioms',[244] or Diderot's division of the citizen into a public and a private person; carried away by a single 'idée fixe', they may well succeed, but at the expense of their own and others' happiness.

Since, as we have seen, not only extremes which shatter order by their enormity, but also action of any kind is contrary to order, it does not seem possible to assume any difference in kind between the sublime and other disruptive phenomena; it is simply a question of what we are used to, a subjective matter dependent on our conception of order at any given time. The importance of the sublime is not simply that it produces a new degree of aesthetic pleasure, but that it puts all activity, all human endeavour into a new perspective, and one which concerns moral behaviour. 'Everyday morality' is a matter of convention, a *modus vivendi* which enables large numbers of disparate individuals – or other forms of life – to live together in a reasonably acceptable way; this everyday morality encompasses not only ordinary people who are content to stick to their own place in society, but people like Rameau, who recognize that some part of one's individuality must be sacrificed if one is to live tolerably. Outside this morality are the extremists, who may make themselves and others unhappy, but who also reveal to us the measure of our own sacrifice and the nature of action in general. The real difference between the ordinary human being and the genius, ordinary activity and 'poetry in the midst of life',[245] the simply beautiful and the sublime, is that the latter break through the limits within which order at any given time operates, and in so doing reveal the arbitrary nature of that order, and the arbitrary ways in which our judgment operates within it. Because it is better for public order and for our peace of mind that we should not know these things, the genius and his appropriate passion, enthusiasm, are seen by the eighteenth century in an ambivalent light.

Diderot's praise of enthusiasm in the article 'Éclectisme' reveals its fascination and its dangers and at the same time brings us back to Rameau:

It is impossible in poetry, painting, eloquence or music to produce anything sublime without enthusiasm. Enthusiasm is a violent movement of the spirit by which we are transported into the midst of the objects which we are to represent; then we see a whole scene take place in our imagination as if it were outside us: and it is, for as long as this illusion lasts, everything present is annihilated, and our ideas take on reality in its place ... if this state is not madness, then it is very close to it.[246]

To have its proper effect in art, enthusiasm must of course be balanced by reason:

Enthusiasm only carries conviction when our minds have been prepared and disciplined by the power of reason ... if enthusiasm predominates in a work, it pervades every part of it with a gigantic, unbelievable, monstrous quality. If such is one's habitual cast of mind, and the acquired or natural bent of one's character, one's speech alternates between the unhinged and the sublime; one commits acts of strange heroism which signal at the same time the greatness, the power and the disorder of one's soul.[247]

This description is almost a portrait of Rameau, with its stress on lack of judgment, instability, and a tendency to become involved to the point of alienation with the products of the imagination.

What it also describes is the process in which imaginary ideas are able to replace the reality around us by the total subjection of the self to the sensibility. Without this preliminary our ideas cannot take on a reality of their own, be experienced, that is, at first hand. This is the initial impulse whose energy must then be neutralized, encompassed by reason and converted into ordered perception. In this way, the artist who creates a representation of reality follows the same process as must the mind which attempts to perceive reality itself. He submits, in other words, to an illusion, and is only then able, by drawing back and reasserting his reason, to create a representation of it. This second stage is what Rameau does not accomplish; he remains within the illusion, and the rationalizing process is left to *Moi*. But *Moi*, ideally placed as he is, does not take up the challenge – or at least he is not seen to take it up – and for the very good reason that Diderot intends it to be taken up by ourselves, the readers. For us, *Moi* plays the same role as does the figure in the picture who is dismayed by the enormity of some natural phenomenon: he experiences the impact; we convert it into truth. It is for us that Rameau, by the challenge of his conversation, his pantomimes and his very existence, 'brings out the truth'.[248]

For this reason, the truth, when it emerges, is not a concrete truth revealed clear-cut in the immobility of order, such as our reason demands, but a truth about that truth. It has often been said that Diderot is primarily concerned with the quest for truth rather than with any end-product of that quest. As Roland Mortier says (*C.A.I.E.F.*, June 1961, p. 296):

the singularity of his work, its irreducible quality, lies more in the path he takes towards the truth than in the nature of the truth attained ... Being, for Diderot, is not being a certain thing, it is changing, experimenting, recreating oneself, denying oneself to rediscover oneself.[249]

We seek order because it is in our nature to do so, but the order we find is not the truth; the truth of the human condition lies in our unending and never satisfied search for order, and Diderot's distinctive achievement is to have established a convincing parallel between that order and the intractable material from which it derives, and to have found the means to express the confrontation of them both, their simultaneous presence as conflicting and equally valid elements in our experience of life.

Le Neveu de Rameau presents this confrontation and achieves the finest expression of the fundamental problem in Diderot's philosophy. The real world out of which Diderot constructs his order is by its nature a world which denies that order. Nowhere more than in this dialogue is it clear that the aspiration towards order is conceived in opposition to the evils of a world which, from a practical point of view, is not a distortion of the truth, or a corrupt version of the genuine article, but something existing in its own right; and because it is its own justification, the standards it imposes relate to itself and are therefore aesthetic, like those of the art which seeks to create a representation of it. In the *Lettre sur les Aveugles* Diderot imagined the kind of world which might present itself to a man deprived of the organ of sight; in the *Neveu* he supposes a man who lacks the ability to detach himself, the moral insight which enables us to see others as having equal validity with ourselves, and to see things from an objective distance. Rameau, knowing of nothing beyond the world of movement, in which 'every living creature ... seeks its own well-being at the expense of whoever is in possession of it',[250] admires only those who achieve success in this. But for most of us, for the 'normally' constituted human being, this aesthetic appreciation is coupled with and often stifled by the tendency to observe the whole scene from outside, from the 'epicycle of Mercury'. This is the attitude which leads us to prize the activities which *Moi* opposes to Rameau's 'wisdom of Solomon': 'fighting for one's country',[251] 'helping one's friends',[252] 'having a position in society and fulfilling its duties',[253] 'seeing to the upbringing of one's children'[254] and to prize above all an action like Voltaire's in restoring the good name of the Calas family. We tend, Diderot implies, to imagine that such moral delights spring from 'the desire for order',[255] but this order has no absolute status, for Rameau's world has its order too. What we do not do, and what we cannot afford to do, is to acknowledge that Rameau's order is as valid as ours, for in so doing we should remove the foundations of our moral world and the possibility of finding mental peace and stability beyond the flux of material reality. But we cannot choose between the two: Rameau makes it clear to *Moi* – or at least to us – that however much he may aspire to be a Diogenes, his humanity, or his animality, makes it an impossibility. Nevertheless, he, and we, will continue to attempt this impossibility because that is the way we are made.

Rameau's artistic credo ends with a brief allusion to Jesuits and Jansenists, with Rameau opting for the Jesuit approach, the 'kind of politics which moves noiselessly ... towards its goal'.[256] Neither Fabre nor Bénac have any comment to make on this fleeting reference in their editions, but it seems significant and inevitable that Rameau should feel unsympathetic towards the Jansenists. Jansen's Augustinian view of the Fall, as freely translated by Sainte-Beuve in his *Port-Royal* (t. 1, p. 615), presents it as a reversal in the relationship between the will and the passions. In Adam the will was dominant, but by his decision to prefer himself to God, he caused the passions to dominate over the will: 'so that, in Adam's sin, it was will which determined desire, and in that of his descendants, it is desire which determines will'.[257] Thus we have a world stood on its head in the sense that the impetus which once came from God now comes from man. There is a parallel to this in the *Éléments de Physiologie* where Diderot rejects the notion that the will is anything but an expression of the passions. But if we do belong to a world in which, as it were, not God, but the devil calls the tune, and if there is nothing beyond that world, how can man, belonging in it, determine his own fate? Rameau – and Cardinal de Retz – have one answer, which is to use it, to adopt its ways and deliberately exploit it, to accept the situation and to make, in the fullest sense of the two words, a virtue of necessity. *Moi*, which means the philosopher in us all, has another: to reverse the situation, to restore in man, or more properly, in the self, the primacy which had belonged to God.

Because the will remains subordinate to the passions, because there is only one world, one substance, this reversal cannot have a direct effect on that world; it is a conceptual possibility, realizable only by the reason in an area beyond the reach of the passions and the sensibility. The moral order and the order of the world can thus never meet, and the two substances, so brilliantly reduced to one in the *Rêve de d'Alembert*, reassert themselves in the Café de la Régence as two faces of the same substance. The self can attain to that simulacrum of divinity to which it aspires, not by destroying the devil, since he is the condition of our existence, but by incorporating him into our conception of the world, by seeing him as a phenomenon which has its own validity, but which we subject to a constant process of invalidation.

Diderot's first achievement is to have identified in the independent world of nature the elements and processes which we can harness to our endeavour to make it our own. Since we can only have a full grasp of a system which is both closed and full, where, that is, there is no freedom either within it or outside it for the contingent elements which defy our processes of reasoning, he has located the highest form of order in the living organism, imagined in a state of suspension in which all its parts are in equilibrium with one another and where there is no influence from outside to upset the balance. Such an organism represents a successful attempt to oppose the laws of movement, to arrest the natural tendency of all things to elude order; and, moreover, the fact that the process is discernible in nature itself provides a natural sanction – the only possible one – for man's own striving to resist the laws of movement.

Diderot's next step is to have appropriated this blind, unconscious process of continuous creation and destruction to the conscious life of man, and it is here that we find the various attempts made by Diderot to create – or perceive – the same processes in the life of man. This really constitutes an attempt to restore to the will the function it has lost in the 'natural' world, for there can be no other word to describe the means by which the 'centre of the network' asserts itself over the sensibility in the great man of the *Rêve*, the sovereign establishes control of the state, the head of a family affirms his authority over its members, the artist arrives at his 'great idea', or the scientist works out his rational system of laws. The important feature of this will – which Diderot never names as such – is that its function is self-limiting, not tyrannical. Its domination over the sensibility is in effect an act of constraint upon itself, a voluntary denial of those links with the passions which, once acknowledged, would destroy it as an independent agent – and here we have a parallel with that 'obscurity' which must be preserved concerning the nature of the link between sovereign and subject, master and servant or artist and public. Because the will is thus confined, because its only act is an act of perception, it can be called reason, but it must be stressed that, just as the seat of reason, or the ideal head of state, or the ideal artist, corresponds exactly to that one of the two substances which Diderot denies, so the reason which they exercise can only be set in motion by a conscious act. One can in fact say that perception is therefore action in the sense that the will, or the reason, creates itself each time it perceives, just as it denies itself whenever we move into action. In this way the order of nature is reversed, the will once more established over the passions, but only to the degree that it is denied the power to act beyond the perceiving self.

211

It might therefore seem that Diderot's prime concern is to arrive at a definition of the world which would correspond with his conception of what that world should be. And so it is; because for Diderot and his age there was no difference in kind between the acts of perception, creation and definition, each being an act carried out both in recognition and defiance of the world they saw before them. It was for Diderot to give the finest expression to this obscurely felt truth: that we establish and preserve our status as separate and autonomous beings by recognizing that we are neither separate nor autonomous, and this is a fitting expression of an age in which men were never more conscious of belonging inescapably to a world which they felt was essentially alien to their aspirations. The dialogue of the *Neveu de Rameau* unfolds in a brief interval in the lives of its protagonists, an interval which prolongs the significant moment when order and disorder clash but are not yet resolved, and during which *Moi* contemplates *Lui* across a gulf which he declines to bridge. The bridging is left to ourselves, with the opportunity to perceive, create and define ourselves by a voluntary act in the face of our opposite.

Moi, in closing his eyes to the truth of Rameau, affirms himself as essentially separate, as one of the two substances of which Rameau represents the other. In this he may be acting misguidedly, but he does reveal a truth. Because the preservation of the self – as opposed to self-preservation – consists in recognizing an order which is in nature, but only visible at arbitrary times and in unforeseeable forms, the self, which is defined by its order and predictability, must be seen as another substance, its order having a conceptual relationship with what we see in nature, but no necessary relationship in fact, just as, to return to the Augustinian and Jansenist parallel, the ways of God have no necessary relationship with the ways of men, so that grace must be regarded as something which cannot be worked for and won, but as a gift within the discretion of God.

Because this attitude is essentially egocentric, not anthropocentric, and the world is felt to be divided not between mankind and nature, but between the self and the field of its perception, it follows that there can be no real distinction between ethics, in the sense of our duties towards our fellow men, and aesthetics or politics or any other field of activity. The relationship between man and his fellows, the sovereign and the state, the artist and his material, the artist and his public, and the scientist and the object of his research is essentially the same, and always involves a moral attitude. The order which they must establish to define their world, and therefore themselves, is structurally the same, whatever their activity. Only when this sense of order is present can they confront the realities of chance, because the real virtue of this order, consisting as it does not in fixed entities but in relationships, not in hierarchy but in balance, is that it can incorporate the new. The intrusive phenomenon from outside is, in its initial appearance, necessarily a force of disorder and therefore a monster, the laws of its being conflicting with those of the order already established. But the more closely our perception of order corresponds to the overall nature of things, the greater possibility we have of incorporating that monster, of 'saving' it and thus restoring order. The more capable we are of achieving this, the closer we are to genius and the closer is the moment of collision between order and disorder – the moment which precedes integration, or elimination – to the sublime.

The process I have just described might be defined as dialectical, and so, to a certain extent, it is. But there is one element lacking which precludes any significant parallel with the concept of the dialectic as it developed in the nineteenth century. The achievement of later thinkers like Hegel, Marx and Darwin was to reconcile the notion of the blind forces of nature and history with the idea of purpose, or at least of direction. They saw how change could be meaningful without a transcendental sanction and were thus able to integrate the concepts of evolution and progress into the structure of the world itself. The thinkers of the preceding century wrote much of biological change, social reform, human perfectibility and so on, but they could not accomplish the final step to evolution and progress as they are now understood because they never lost the idea that the end-point of progress was an absolute, existing outside time and beyond change. Perfection and order could only be achieved in opposition to the blind, irrational forces of nature. They were two different worlds, mutually exclusive, and no eighteenth-century thinker seems to have found a way out of this conceptual impasse.

Perhaps enough has been said already to show how, for Diderot, this antinomy of the two substances, whether envisaged as perfection and change, order and chance, thought and extension or truth and reality, could not be resolved. All the elements were present which might have made Diderot a modern except one, and it is this which stamps him as being irrevocably of his own time. For this reason I have tried to show how he draws together the attitudes of his own age, an age stretching well back into the seventeenth century, and, in pursuing them to their logical conclusion, reveals their potentialities and their contradictions. If he has succeeded in expressing some of the problems of a more modern era, it is only because he has succeeded so well in expressing those of his own.

ORIGINALS OF FRENCH PASSAGES
QUOTED IN THE TEXT

Introduction

1 on a trop expliqué Diderot en se référant à la situation historique ou à un contexte littéraire et philosophique: mieux vaudrait l'expliquer par lui-même.
2 par lui-même

Order and the Ancien Régime

1 maître de moi comme de l'univers.
2 les actions de hommes [...] ne sont [...] composées que d'un certain nombre borné de circonstances et de motifs.
3 qualifier justement leurs actions, connaître dans quelle espèce il faut les ranger (pp. 57–8).
4 Ainsi, savoir l'histoire, c'est connaître les hommes, qui en fournissent la matière; c'est juger de ces hommes sainement: étudier l'histoire, c'est étudier les motifs, les opinions, et les passions des hommes, pour en connaître tous les ressorts, les tours et les détours, enfin toutes les illusions qu'elles savent faire aux esprits, et les surprises qu'elles font aux cœurs (p. 2).
5 il y a une espèce de force de génie et de courage d'esprit à pouvoir envisager, sans s'étonner, la Nature dans la multitude innombrable de ses productions, et à se croire capable de les comprendre et de les comparer (*Œuvres Philosophiques*, p. 7, col. 1).
6 L'étonnement vient souvent de ce qu'on suppose plusieurs prodiges où il n'y en a qu'un; de ce qu'on imagine, dans la nature, autant d'actes particuliers qu'on nombre de phénomènes, tandis qu'elle n'a peut-être jamais produit qu'un seul acte (p. 186).
7 La nature contient le fonds de toutes ces variétés: mais le hasard ou l'art les mettent en œuvre.
8 La nature a ses écarts, et la raison ses abus. Nous avons rapporté les monstres aux écarts de la nature; et c'est à l'abus de la raison qu'il faut rapporter toutes les sciences et tous les arts, qui ne montrent que l'avidité, la méchanceté, la superstition de l'homme et qui le déshonorent (pp. 166–7).
9 Uniformité de la Nature.
10 Écarts de la Nature.

Part I

1 Lorsque j'ai vu la matière inerte passer à l'état sensible, rien ne doit plus m'étonner ... (*Rêve*, p. 303).

2 On en viendra quelque jour à démontrer que la sensibilité ou le toucher est un sens commun à tous les êtres. Il y a déjà des phénomènes qui y conduisent. Alors la matière en général aura cinq ou six propriétés essentielles, la force morte ou vive, la longueur, la largeur, la profondeur, l'impénétrabilité et la sensibilité (*Él. Phys.*, p. 24).

3 L'homme sage n'est qu'un composé de molécules folles (p. 266).

4 *De l'Interprétation de la Nature* (p. 184).

5 pp. 266–7.

6 l'expérience et la raison.

7 chercherait inutilement ces germes dans l'œuf et dans la plupart des animaux avant un certain âge.

8 que la divisibilité de la matière a un terme dans la nature, quoiqu'elle n'en ait aucun dans l'entendement, et qui répugne à concevoir un éléphant tout formé dans un atome et dans cet atome un autre éléphant tout formé, et ainsi de suite à l'infini.

9 l'entendement.

10 deux substances.

11 vous sentirez que, pour ne pas admettre une supposition simple qui explique tout, la sensibilité, propriété générale de la matière, ou produit de l'organisation, vous renoncez au sens commun, et vous précipitez dans un abîme de mystères, de contradictions et d'absurdités (*Rêve*, pp. 276–7).

12 l'utile circonscrit tout (*Int. Nat.*, VI, p. 184).

13 p. 184.

14 expériences.

15 raisonnements.

16 tant que les choses ne sont que dans notre entendement, ce sont nos opinions; ce sont des notions, qui peuvent être vraies ou fausses, accordées ou contredites.

17 utiles.

18 fil.

19 deviendrait le jouet de la moindre agitation qui se ferait dans l'air.

20 p. 185.

21 p. 185.

22 les lois de l'investigation de la vérité sont sévères.

23 Pensée.

24 rentrer en soi et en sortir sans cesse.

25 sortir (de soi).

26 p. 333.

27 donne un volume presque infini à l'individu, ou il le concentre presque dans un point.

28 Qu'est-ce qui circonscrit votre étendue réelle, la vraie sphère de votre sensibilité?

29 existe comme en un point.

30 l'univers est anéanti pour moi, et je suis nulle pour lui.

31 lorsque la vraie limite de votre sensibilité est franchie, soit en vous rap-

prochant, en vous condensant en vous-même, soit en vous étendant au dehors, on ne sait plus ce que cela peut devenir.

32 p. 96.

33 quoique la sensation soit indivisible par elle-même, elle occupe, si on peut se servir de ce terme, un espace étendu, auquel l'aveugle-né a la faculté d'ajouter ou de retrancher par la pensée, en grossissant ou diminuant la partie affectée.

34 il aura même un solide gros comme le globe terrestre, s'il suppose le bout du doigt gros comme le globe, et occupé par la sensation en longueur, largeur et profondeur.

35 c'est au physique comme au moral que nous sommes sujets à nous croire plus grands que nous ne le sommes? (p. 335).

36 p. 336.

37 Il existe au-delà du terme de sa sensibilité.

38 Dans leur état naturel et tranquille, les brins du faisceau ont une certaine tension, un ton, une énergie habituelle qui circonscrit l'étendue réelle ou imaginaire du corps (p. 335).

39 p. 315.

40 p. 316.

41 Par votre identité avec tous les êtres de la nature, vous sauriez tout ce qui se fait; par votre mémoire, vous sauriez tout ce qui s'y est fait (p. 316).

42 p. 316.

43 brins.

44 origine du faisceau.

45 p. 152.

46 p. 156.

47 l'espace circonscrit par le bruit de ses pieds ou le retentissement de sa voix (p. 159).

48 l'œil n'est pas aussi utile à nos besoins ni aussi essentiel à notre bonheur qu'on serait tenté de le croire (p. 153).

49 pp. 136–8.

50 origine du réseau.

51 n'a à son origine aucun sens qui lui soit propre: ne voit point, n'entend point, ne souffre point. Il est produit, nourri; il émane d'une substance molle, insensible, inerte, qui lui sert d'oreiller, et sur laquelle il siège, écoute, juge et prononce (pp. 330–1).

52 Les passions ne sont-elles pas autant de verres colorés placés sur nos yeux qui défigurent les objets? (p. 338).

53 p. 260.

54 succession d'images, de sons, de goûts, de sensations, décousue à l'origine du faisceau ou au sensorium commune.

55 sens interne.

56 pp. 96–7.

57 de sentir ou de se rappeler la sensation des corps, lors même qu'ils sont absents et qu'ils n'agissent plus sur eux.

58 p. 43, n. 48 and p. 49 with n. 91.

59 *A.T.*1, p. 353.

60 *A.T.*1, p. 401.

61 substance molle, insensible, inerte (*Rêve*, pp. 330–1).

62 dealt with especially on pp. 354–5.

63 p. 357.

64 Le grand homme, s'il a malheureusement reçu cette disposition naturelle [a powerful sensibility], s'occupera sans relâche à l'affaiblir, à la
dominer, à se rendre maître de ses mouvements. et à conserver à
l'origine du faisceau tout son empire. Alors il se possédera au milieu
des plus grands dangers, il jugera froidement, mais sainement. Rien de
ce qui peut servir à ses vues, concourir à son but, ne lui échappera; on
l'étonnera difficilement.

65 Il régnera sur lui-même et sur tout ce qui l'environne.

66 affranchi de toutes les tyrannies du monde.

67 maître de lui-même, il l'est des événements; content de son état, il ne
veut être que comme il a toujours été, ne vivre que comme il a toujours
vécu, se suffisant à lui-même, il n'a qu'un faible besoin des autres, il ne
peut leur être à charge; occupé continuellement à exercer les facultés
de son âme, il perfectionne son entendement, il cultive son esprit, il
acquiert de nouvelles connaissances, et se satisfait à tout instant sans
remords, sans dégoût, il jouit de tout l'univers en jouissant de lui-
même (t. 4, p. 330, col. 2).

68 phénomènes généraux.

69 p. 354.

70 à merveille.

71 rapport originel ou contracté par les habitudes de l'origine du faisceau
à ses ramifications.

72 Le principe ou le tronc est-il trop vigoureux relativement aux
branches? De là les poètes, les artistes, les gens à imagination, les
hommes pusillanimes, les enthousiastes, les fous. Trop faible? De là,
ce que nous appelons les brutes, les bêtes féroces. Le système entier
lâche, mou, sans énergie? De là, les imbéciles. Le système entier énergique, bien d'accord, bien ordonné? De là les bons penseurs, les
philosophes, les sages.

73 principe ... tronc ... branches.

74 origine du faisceau.

75 brutes.

76 bêtes féroces.

77 pp. 356–7.

78 Mais qu'est-ce qu'un être sensible? Un être abandonné à la discrétion
du diaphragme. Un mot touchant a-t-il frappé l'oreille, un phénomène
singulier a-t-il frappé l'œil, et voilà tout à coup le tumulte intérieur qui
s'élève, tous les brins du faisceau qui s'agitent, le frisson qui se répand,
l'horreur qui saisit, les larmes qui coulent, les soupirs qui suffoquent,
la voix qui s'interrompt, l'origine du faisceau qui ne sait ce qu'il
devient; plus de sang-froid, plus de raison, plus de jugement...

79 s'occupera sans relâche ... à se rendre maître de ses mouvements et à
conserver à l'origine du faisceau tout son empire.

80 les bons penseurs, les philosophes, les sages.

81 le système entier énergique, bien d'accord, bien ordonné.

82 Les grands poètes, les grands acteurs, et peut-être en général tous les
grands imitateurs de la nature, quels qu'ils soient, doués d'une belle
imagination, d'un grand jugement, d'un tact fin, d'un goût très sûr,

sont les êtres les moins sensibles (p. 310).

83 L'homme sensible est trop abandonné à la merci de son diaphragme pour être un grand roi, un grand politique, un grand magistrat, un homme juste, un profond observateur, conséquemment un sublime imitateur de la nature, à moins qu'il ne puisse s'oublier et se distraire de lui-même, et qu'à l'aide d'une imagination forte il ne sache se créer, et d'une mémoire tenace tenir son attention fixée sur des fantômes qui lui servent de modèles; mais alors ce n'est plus lui qui agit, c'est l'esprit d'un autre qui le domine (p. 362).

84 L'homme sensible obéit aux impulsions de la nature et ne rend précisément que le cri de son cœur; au moment où il tempère ou force ce cri, ce n'est plus lui, c'est un comédien qui joue (p. 335).

85 la sensibilité n'est jamais sans faiblesse d'organisation (*Paradoxe*, p. 311).

86 trop occupés à regarder, à reconnaître et à imiter, pour être vivement affectés au-dedans d'eux-mêmes. Je les vois sans cesse le portefeuille sur les genoux et le crayon à la main (p. 310).

87 ne sera ni un grand roi, ni un grand ministre, ni un grand capitaine, ni un grand avocat, ni un grand médecin.

88 il n'y a que les passions, et les grandes passions, qui puissent élever l'âme aux grandes choses. Sans elles, plus de sublime, soit dans les mœurs, soit dans les ouvrages; les beaux-arts retournent en enfance, et la vertu devient minutieuse (*A.T.* 1, p. 127).

89 Les passions amorties dégradent les hommes extraordinaires. La contrainte anéantit la grandeur et l'énergie de la nature.

90 Ce sont en effet les fortes passions qui, plus éclairées que le bon sens, peuvent seules nous apprendre à distinguer l'extraordinaire de l'impossible, que les gens sensés confondent presque toujours ensemble, parce que n'étant point animés de passions fortes, ces gens sensés ne sont jamais que des hommes médiocres.

91 S'ils ne conçoivent pas plus de tendance au repos qu'au mouvement dans un corps quelconque, c'est qu'apparemment ils regardent la matière comme homogène; c'est qu'ils font abstraction de toutes les qualités qui lui sont essentielles; c'est qu'ils la considèrent comme inaltérable dans l'instant presque indivisible de leur spéculation; c'est qu'ils raisonnent du repos relatif d'un aggrégat à un autre aggrégat (pp. 393–4).

92 La molécule, douée d'une qualité propre à sa nature, par elle-même est une force active. Elle s'exerce sur une autre molécule qui s'exerce sur elle. Tous ces paralogismes-là tiennent à la fausse supposition de la matière homogène (p. 394).

93 Je crois que la forme actuelle sous laquelle la matière existe est nécessaire et déterminée, ainsi que toutes les formes diverses qu'elle prendra successivement à toute éternité. Mais cette vicissitude, ce développement qui est en flux perpétuel est nécessaire. C'est une suite de son essence et de son hétérogénéité. Et je ne vois nulle contradiction à cette supposition.
Si elle est essentiellement hétérogène, elle est essentiellement en vicissitude (p. 127).

94 Tout change, tout passe, il n'y a que le tout qui reste. Le monde

commence et finit sans cesse; il est à chaque instant à son commencement et à sa fin; il n'en a jamais eu d'autre et il n'en aura jamais
d'autre.

Dans cet immense océan de matière, pas une molécule qui ressemble à
une molécule, pas une molécule qui se ressemble à elle-même un
instant: Rerum novus nascitur ordo, voilà son inscription éternelle …
(pp. 299–300).

95 sophisme de l'éphémère.

96 coordination de molécules infiniment actives.

97 enchaînement de petites forces, que tout concourt à séparer (*Él. Phys.*,
p. 8).

98 p. 260 et seq.

99 force morte … force vive.

100 car en mangeant, que faites-vous? Vous levez les obstacles qui s'oppos-
aient à la sensibilité active de l'aliment (p. 261).

101 La sensibilité, c'est une propriété universelle de la matière, propriété
inerte dans les corps bruts, comme le mouvement dans les corps
pesants arrêtés par un obstacle, propriété rendue active dans les
mêmes corps par leur assimilation avec une substance animale vivante
(p. 261).

102 Établissez entre elles une juste harmonie, et n'en appréhendez point de
désordres (IV, p. 11).

103 pp. 48–9.

104 l'animal sain.

105 l'animal tranquille.

106 C'est que, dans le désordre, toutes les forces de la machine sont conspir-
antes, et que dans l'état sain ou tranquille elles agissent isolées: il n'y a
que l'action ou des bras, ou des jambes, ou des cuisses ou des flancs.

107 *Él. Phys.* pp. 49–50.

108 L'on dit que le désir naît de la volonté; c'est le contraire; c'est du désir
que naît la volonté. Le désir est fils de l'organisation (p. 265).

109 pp. 268–9.

110 Rien ne montre tant la conspiration des organes que ce qui arrive dans
la passion, telle que l'amour, ou la colère, ou l'admiration.

111 Dans les accès de passions violentes les parties se rapprochent, se rac-
courcissent, deviennent dures comme la pierre. Pour peu que cet état
ait duré, il est suivi d'une grande lassitude.

112 Il y a deux sortes de maladies. L'une est produite par une cause
étrangère qui apporte le désordre, l'autre par une partie trop vigoureuse qui jette le trouble dans la machine, c'est un citoyen trop
puissant dans la démocratie (pp. 296–7).

113 bon raisonnement, bon jugement suppose l'état de santé, ou la priva-
tion du malaise ou de douleur, d'intérêt et de passion (*Él. Phys.*, p.
234).

114 enchaînement.

115 see in particular *Él. Phys.*, pp. 244–5.

116 les phénomènes ne sont pas enchaînés les uns aux autres (p. 240).

117 p. 316.

118 entre Saturne et vous il n'y a que des corps contigus, au lieu qu'il y
faudrait de la continuïté.

119 n. 2 to p. 316.

120 du moins comme hypothèse logique.

121 Que serait-ce qu'un métier de la manufacture de Lyon si l'ouvrier et la tireuse faisaient un tout sensible avec la trame, la chaîne et le simple? Ce serait un animal semblable à l'araignée qui pense, qui veut, qui se nourrit, se reproduit et ourdit sa toile.

122 Sans la sensibilité et la loi de continuïté dans la contexture animale, sans ces deux qualités l'animal ne peut être un.

123 L'animal est un tout *un*, et c'est peut-être cette unité qui constitue l'âme, le soi, la conscience à l'aide de la mémoire (pp. 22–3).

124 les accès de passions violentes.

125 L'animal tranquille ignore sa force. Mais qu'un accès de fièvre, un transport de passion, un violent intérêt, un mouvement d'amour-propre, la crainte de perdre son honneur, sa vie ou sa fortune, une terreur réelle ou panique, tende ses nerfs, accélère l'impulsion de ses fluides, resserre les canaux qui les renferment, et surtout que la velléité, volonté ou âme ne s'en mêle plus, et vous serez effrayé des effets qu'il produira.
C'est alors qu'il est réduit à un être purement sensible (p. 167).

126 velléité, volonté ou âme.

127 purement sensible.

128 les brutes, les bêtes féroces.

129 p. 354.

130 purement sensible(s).

131 être sensible.

132 Cette qualité si prisée, qui ne conduit à rien de grand (p. 358).

133 p. 359.

134 La caractéristique de l'homme est dans son cerveau, et non dans son organisation (*Él. Phys.* p. 48).

135 sa perfectibilité naît de la faiblesse des autres sens, dont aucun ne prédomine sur l'organe de la raison (*ibid.*, p. 50).

136 Le cerveau n'est qu'un organe comme un autre. Ce n'est même qu'un organe secondaire qui n'entrerait jamais en fonction sans l'entremise des autres organes. Il est sujet à tous les vices des autres organes (*ibid.*, p. 238).

137 Il y a une sympathie très marquée entre le diaphragme et le cerveau (*ibid.*, p. 289).

138 Dans l'état parfait de santé, où il n'y a aucune sensation prédominante qui fasse discerner une partie du corps, état que tout homme a quelquefois éprouvé, l'homme n'existe qu'en un point de cerveau: il est tout au lieu de la pensée (*ibid.*, p. 53).

139 *Rêve*, p. 333.

140 j'existe comme en un point; je cesse presque d'être matière, je ne sens que ma pensée; il n'y a plus ni lieu, ni mouvement, ni corps, ni distance, ni espace pour moi: l'univers est anéanti pour moi, et je suis nulle pour lui.

141 santé parfaite.

142 Si l'on pouvait fixer par la pensée cette situation de pur sentiment, où toutes les facultés du corps et de l'âme sont vivantes sans être agissantes, et attacher à ce quiétisme délicieux l'idée d'immutabilité, on se

formerait la notion du bonheur le plus grand et le plus pur que l'homme puisse imaginer (p. 607).

143 Par exemple, si l'origine du faisceau rappelle toutes les forces à lui, si le système entier se meut pour ainsi dire à rebours, comme je crois qu'il arrive dans l'homme qui médite profondément, dans le fanatique qui voit les cieux ouverts, dans le sauvage qui chante au milieu des flammes, dans l'extase, dans l'aliénation volontaire ou involontaire ... l'animal se rend impassible, il n'existe qu'en un point (pp. 349–50).

144 le principe ou le tronc est ... trop vigoureux relativement aux branches.

145 en un point.

146 Rien n'est plus contraire à la nature que la méditation habituelle, ou l'état de savant. L'homme est né pour agir. Sa santé tient au mouvement. Le mouvement vrai du système n'est pas de se ramener constamment de ses extrémités au centre du faisceau, mais de se porter du centre aux extrémités des filets ... L'homme de la nature est fait pour penser peu, et agir beaucoup. La science au contraire pense beaucoup et se remue peu (*Él. Phys.*, pp. 300–1).

147 qu'elle aurait sans cesse cherchée par une inquiétude automate, comme il arrive aux animaux de s'agiter dans le sommeil ... jusqu'à ce qu'ils aient trouvé la disposition la plus convenable au repos (p. 231).

148 Nature. Qu'est-ce que cet agent? Ce sont les efforts mêmes de l'organe malade, ou de toute la machine ... La nature fait en tout temps dans le malade ce que le malaise de la machine exécute pendant le sommeil; elle se meut spontanément, s'agite jusqu'à ce qu'elle ait trouvé la situation la plus commode ... (p. 300).

149 il n'y a pas sur toute la surface de la terre un seul homme parfaitement constitué, parfaitement sain. L'espèce humaine n'est qu'un amas d'individus plus ou moins contrefaits, plus ou moins malades.

150 Ce que je dis de l'homme, il n'y a pas un seul animal, une seule plante, un seul minéral dont je n'en puisse dire autant ... Si l'on veut en faire le chef-d'œuvre d'un être infiniment sage, et tout-puissant, cela n'a pas le sens commun (*El. Phys.*, p. 307).

151 la main du Créateur ne paraît pas s'être ouverte pour donner l'être à un certain nombre déterminé d'espèces; mais il semble qu'elle ait jeté tout à la fois un monde d'êtres relatifs et non relatifs, une infinité de combinaisons harmoniques et contraires et une perpétuité de destructions et de renouvellements (*H.N.*, I, p. 11).

152 comme en un point.

153 *A.T.*, III, pp. 360–1.

154 l'intervalle qui sépare les phénomènes.

155 Si nous possédions le recueil complet des phénomènes, il n'y aurait plus qu'une cause ou supposition. Alors on saurait peut-être si le mouvement est essentiel à la matière, et si la matière est créée ou incréée; créée ou incréée, si sa diversité ne répugne pas plus à la raison que sa simplicité: car ce n'est peut-être que par notre ignorance que son unité ou homogénéité nous paraît si difficile à concilier avec la variété des phénomènes.

156 L'étonnement vient souvent de ce qu'on suppose plusieurs prodiges où il n'y en a qu'un; de ce qu'on imagine, dans la nature, autant d'actes particuliers qu'on nombre de phénomènes, tandis qu'elle n'a peut-être jamais produit qu'un seul acte (p. 186).

157 étonnement.

158 dans le silence des passions.

159 Lorsque j'ai vu la matière inerte passer à l'état sensible, rien ne doit plus m'étonner ... (p. 303).

160 être sensible.

Part II

1 Un Français qui arrive à Londres trouve les choses bien changées, en philosophie, comme dans tout le reste. Il a laissé le monde plein; il le trouve vide.

2 p. 245.

3 p. 24.

4 j'aurais ajouté l'attraction, si elle n'était peut-être une conséquence du mouvement et de la force.

5 Otez l'obstacle qui s'oppose au transport local du corps immobile, et il sera transféré. Supprimez par une raréfaction subite l'air qui environne cet énorme tronc de chêne, et l'eau qu'il contient, entrant tout à coup en expansion, le dispersera en cent mille éclats. J'en dis autant de votre propre corps (p. 260).

6 p. 395.

7 sensibilité inerte.

8 sensibilité active.

9 p. 394.

10 la molécule, douée d'une qualité propre à sa nature, par elle-même est une force active.

11 elle s'exerce sur une autre molécule qui s'exerce sur elle.

12 *Roth*, I, pp. 213–15.

13 On ne conçoit non plus qu'un être agisse sans motif, qu'un des bras d'une balance sans l'action d'un poids, et le motif nous est toujours extérieur, étranger, attaché ou par une nature ou par une cause quelconque, qui n'est pas nous ... Il n'y a qu'une sorte de causes, à proprement parler; ce sont les causes physiques (pp. 213–14).

14 l'homme, libre ou non, est un être qu'on modifie.

15 Il n'y a point de cause qui n'ait son effet; il n'y a point d'effet qui ne modifie la chose sur laquelle la cause agit. Il n'y a pas un atome dans la nature qui ne soit exposé à l'action d'une infinité de causes diverses (p. 25).

16 tout est en un flux perpétuel ... il n'y a rien de précis en nature (p. 311).

17 Y a-t-il un atome en nature rigoureusement semblable à un autre atome?

18 tout tient en nature.

19 il est impossible qu'il y ait un vide dans la chaîne.

20 il n'y a qu'un seul grand individu, c'est le tout (p. 312).

21 vide dans la chaîne.

22 cette chaîne générale, dont la philosophie suppose la continuïté (*Int.*

Nat., p. 186).

23 entre les phénomènes connus que l'on rapporte à l'une de ces causes, combien y a-t-il de phénomènes intermédiaires à trouver pour former les liaisons, remplir les vides et démontrer l'identité?

24 C'est par ce moyen, et par ce moyen seul, que l'intervalle qui sépare les phénomènes se remplira successivement par des phénomènes intercalés; qu'il en naîtra une chaîne continue, qu'ils s'expliqueront en se touchant, et que la plupart de ceux qui nous présentent des aspects si divers, si'identifieront. (*A.T.*, III, pp. 359–60).

25 *Él. Phys.*, pp. 9 et seq.

26 Contiguïté du règne végétal et du règne animal.

27 la chaîne des êtres n'est pas interrompue par la diversité des formes. La forme n'est souvent qu'un masque qui trompe, et le chaînon qui paraît manquer réside peut-être dans un être connu, à qui les progrès de l'anatomie comparée n'ont pu encore assigner sa véritable place (p. 6).

28 Chaque cause rassemblera autour d'elle un nombreux cortège d'effets; ces systèmes, d'abord isolés, se fondront les uns dans les autres en s'étendant; et de plusieurs causes il n'en restera qu'une plus ou moins lentement réduite à la condition d'effet. Le progrès de la physique consiste à diminuer le nombre des causes par la multiplication des effets.

29 La limite du monde est-elle à la portée de nos télescopes?

30 A ne consulter que les vaines conjectures de la philosophie et la faible lumière de notre raison, on croirait que la chaîne des causes n'a point eu de commencement, et que celle des effets n'aura point de fin (LVI, pp. 234–5).

31 par le préjugé qu'il ne se passe rien au-delà de la portée de nos sens, et que tout cesse où nous ne voyons plus.

32 il conjecture, par ce qui est, ce qui doit être encore; il tire de l'ordre des choses des conclusions abstraites et générales qui ont pour lui toute l'évidence des vérités sensibles et particulières; il s'élève à l'essence même de l'ordre.

33 il voit que la coexistence *pure et simple* [Diderot's italics] d'un être sensible et pensant, avec un enchaînement quelconque de causes et d'effets, ne lui suffit pas pour en porter un jugement absolu; il s'arrête là; s'il faisait un pas de plus, il sortirait de la nature.

34 ces systèmes, d'abord isolés, se fondront les uns dans les autres.

35 Je me représente la vaste enceinte des sciences, comme un grand terrain parsemé de places obscures et de places éclairées. Nos travaux doivent avoir pour but, ou d'étendre les limites des places éclairées, ou de multiplier sur le terrain les centres de lumières (p. 189).

36 on vit en un point qui s'étend jusqu'à une certaine limite, sous laquelle la vie est circonscrite en tous sens; cet espace sous lequel on vit diminue peu à peu; la vie devient moins active sous chaque point de cet espace; il y en a même sous lesquels elle a perdu toute son activité avant la dissolution de la masse, et l'on finit par vivre en une infinité d'atomes isolés (p. 680).

37 Si la matière est infinie et qu'elle existe nécessairement, tous ces déplacements et toutes ces combinaisons, effets naturels du mouvement, deviendront impossibles: la raison en est que chaque partie de matière

existera nécessairement dans la partie de l'espace qu'elle occupe. Ce n'est pas le hasard qui l'aura placé là plutôt qu'ailleurs, ni dans le voisinage de telles parties plutôt que dans le voisinage d'autres: la même raison qui fait qu'elle existe nécessairement, fait aussi qu'elle existe dans un endroit plutôt qu'ailleurs (p. 875).

38 p. 245.

39 ce germe rare.

40 p. 65.

41 éparses.

42 s'accroissant successivement.

43 littérateur, mécanicien, géomètre.

44 c'est qu'ils la considèrent comme inaltérable dans l'instant presque indivisible de leur spéculation; c'est qu'ils raisonnent du repos relatif d'un aggrégat à un autre aggrégat; c'est qu'ils oublient que, tandis qu'ils raisonnent de l'indifférence du corps au mouvement ou au repos, le bloc de marbre tend à sa dissolution (p. 394).

45 modèle idéal.

46 Il y a deux sortes de maladies. L'une est produite par une cause étrangère qui apporte le désordre, l'autre par une partie trop vigoureuse qui jette le trouble dans la machine (*El. Phys.*, p. 296).

47 un être, dont la durée est incompatible avec l'ordre subsistant (p. 209).

48 La thèse de la sociabilité naturelle, qu'il a si souvent et si fortement reprise à son compte, exclut absolument la guerre de tous contre tous (p. 419).

49 Dans le soi-disant état de simple nature, les hommes étaient épars sur la surface de la terre comme une infinité de petits ressorts isolés. Il arrivait de temps en temps à quelques-uns de ces petits ressorts de se rencontrer, de se presser trop fortement et de se briser. Les législateurs, témoins de ces accidents, y ont cherché un remède, et quel est celui qu'ils ont imaginé? De rapprocher les petits ressorts, et d'en composer une belle machine qu'ils ont appelée société (p. 173).

50 épars sur la surface de la terre.

51 Qu'est-ce qu'une académie? Un corps de savants qui se forme de luimême, ainsi que la société des hommes s'est formée, celle-ci pour lutter avec plus d'avantage contre la nature, celui-là par le même instinct ou le même besoin: la supériorité avouée des efforts réunis contre l'ignorance (*Plan d'une Université, A.T.*, iii, p. 519).

52 pp. 767–8.

53 formé et jeté dans cet univers comme par hasard.

54 l'état de guerre commence.

55 et les rendent peut-être plus malheureux étant rassemblés qu'ils ne l'auraient été dispersés.

56 Cet ennemi, c'est la nature, et la lutte de l'homme contre la nature est le premier principe de la société (p. 174).

57 dans la belle machine société, les petits ressorts, animés d'une infinité d'intérêts divers et opposés, ont agi et réagi les uns contre les autres de toutes leurs forces et pour un moment de guerre accidentelle, il en est résulté un véritable état de guerre continue où tous les petits ressorts affaiblis et fatigués n'ont cessé de crier et où il s'en est plus brisé en un an, qu'il ne s'en serait brisé en dix, dans l'état primitif et isolé où le

ressentiment d'un choc était l'unique loi (p. 173).

58 s'ils étaient retenus, c'était moins par une autorité publique que par la crainte du ressentiment particulier.

59 le tumulte règne, et le crime avec le tumulte; et il vaudrait mieux, pour la sûreté des hommes, qu'ils fussent épars, que d'avoir les mains libres et d'être voisins.

60 *A.T.*, I, pp. 466–7.

61 Voilà les hommes arrêtés les uns à côté des autres, plutôt en troupeau qu'en société par l'attrait de leur utilité propre, et par l'analogie de leur conformation.

62 animés tous par des passions violentes, cherchant tous à s'approprier les avantages communs de la réunion, selon les talents, la force, la sagacité, etc., que la nature leur a distribués en mesure inégale, les faibles seront les victimes des plus forts.

63 le commencement de lien que leur utilité propre et leur ressemblance extérieure leur avaient suggéré pour leur conservation réciproque.

64 Qu'il obvie aux temps orageux des régences et des minorités, temps où le ministre est faible et destructeur, où chacun écoute son intérêt aux dépens de la nation; où il importe d'avoir un corps représentatif de la souveraineté, non pour élever, mais pour empêcher la destruction; où nous savons par expérience que, sans une puissance législative qui fasse tête aux dépositaires de la souveraineté, l'édifice de plusieurs siècles se renverse (p. 123).

65 Il y a dans les esprits une nuance de terreur panique: c'est apparemment l'effet d'une longue suite de révolutions et d'un long despotisme. Ils semblent toujours à la veille ou au lendemain d'un tremblement de terre, et ils ont l'air de chercher s'il est bien vrai que la terre se soit raffermie sous leurs pieds ... Je suis sûr que nous avons éprouvé la même chose que les Russes, après la Ligue, après la mort d'Henri III, d'Henri IV, après la Fronde. Et je me souviens très bien qu'à l'aventure de la veille des Rois nous avions tous l'air effarouchés, comme si nous étions au moment de la chute d'une comète sur notre globe (p. 67).

66 vous n'avez pas la première notion de ce qui se passe dans les temps de disette ... C'est alors un conflit tumultueux de crainte, d'avidité, de cupidité; les uns demandent quatre fois plus qu'ils n'en ont besoin pour le moment, parce qu'ils ne savent ce qui sera demain; d'autres enlèvent, achètent à tout prix; d'autres ferment leurs greniers et attendent un prix plus haut (p. 84).

67 les droits sacrés de la propriété qui ne sont malheureusement, s'il faut vous en dire mon avis, que de belles billevesées. Est-ce qu'il y a quelque droit sacré quand il s'agit d'affaire publique, d'utilité générale, réelle ou simulée? On me fait prendre le mousquet, on m'ôte la liberté, on m'enferme sur un soupçon, on coupe mon champ en deux, on renverse ma maison, on me ruine en me déplaçant, on abandonne ma moisson aux animaux, on vide ma bourse par un impôt absurde, on expose ma vie, ma fortune, par une guerre folle. Mettez toutes vos belles idées dans une utopie et cela figurera bien là (p. 85).

68 Qui est-ce qui a des idées exactes de l'utilité publique?

69 c'est une notion si compliquée, dépendante de tant d'expériences et de lumières, que les philosophes même en disputaient entre eux ... L'ig-

norance et l'intérêt, qui obscurcissent tout dans les têtes humaines, montreront l'intérêt général où il n'est pas. Chacun ayant sa vertu, la vie de l'homme se remplira de crimes. Le peuple, ballotté par ses passions et par ses erreurs, n'aura point de mœurs: car il n'y a de mœurs que là où les lois bonnes ou mauvaises sont sacrées; car c'est là seulement que la conduite générale est uniforme (*A.T.* xi, p. 121).

70 l'évidence n'empêche ni le jeu de l'intérêt ni celui des passions; un commerçant déréglé voit évidemment qu'il se ruine, et ne se ruine pas moins. Un souverain sentira qu'il tyrannise ou par lui-même ou par ses ministres, et n'en tyrannisera pas moins. Est-ce l'évidence qui a manqué en France sous le règne passé? (pp. 358–9).

71 Être et paraître devinrent deux choses tout à fait différentes, et de cette distinction sortirent le faste imposant, la ruse trompeuse et tous les vices qui en sont le cortège...

72 l'ambition dévorante, l'ardeur d'élever sa fortune relative... concurrence et rivalité d'une part, de l'autre opposition des intérêts (*Political Writings*, i, pp. 178–9).

73 l'ardeur d'élever sa fortune relative.

74 Au moment où une poignée de concussionnaires publics regorgèrent de richesses, habitèrent des palais, firent parade de leur honteuse opulence, toutes les conditions furent confondues; il s'éleva une émulation funeste, une lutte insensée et cruelle entre tous les ordres de la société. Maudit soit le premier qui rendit les fonctions publiques vénales... maudit soit celui qui engendra ce foyer d'où sortirent cette ostentation épidémique de fortune ...; maudit soit celui qui condamna par contre-coup le mérite à l'obscurité, et qui dévoua la vertu et les moeurs au mépris (*Satire contre le Luxe, Salon de 1767*: *A.T.* xi, p. 91).

75 p. 350.

76 tout ce qui tend à isoler l'homme de l'homme tend aussi à affaiblir la puissance de la lutte contre la nature, et à le rapprocher de la condition primitive de l'homme sauvage; par conséquent doit être regardé comme un mal (p. 175).

77 p. 175.

78 Ce que je dis des grandes sociétés est démontré par l'état des petites, lorsque la division s'y introduit; le lien général se brise, chacun travaille pour soi, et la condition sauvage renaît.

79 veut des individus et point de corps, des nobles et point de noblesse; ... des sujets et point de nation; c'est-à-dire, par la plus absurde des conséquences, une société et des hommes isolés (p. 175).

80 pp. 55–6.

81 ne serait-il pas possible de peupler davantage Pétersbourg, de le rendre plus vivant, plus agissant, plus commerçant en joignant cette multitude de palais isolés par des maisons particulières?

82 ouvriers dans tous les genres, des charrons, des charpentiers, des maçons, des cordiers, etc., comme cela est à Paris.

83 Cette proximité des hommes les lie, leur liaison les adoucit et les civilise; c'est de ces boutiques que sortiront tous les beaux-arts qui seront alors indigènes et durables.

84 Jamais l'Allemagne ne sera civilisée, n'aura des poètes, des statuaires,

des peintres, des hommes éloquents, de grands écrivains, une langue sans laquelle on ne fait rien qui vaille, des mœurs polies, une sorte d'urbanité, etc., jamais, dis-je, que la maison impériale n'ait dévoré les électorats.

85 Serrez vos sujets, et par cette seule opération vous aurez un Empire.

86 surtout presser les provinces les unes contre les autres, les villes les unes contre les autres, les maisons dans la ville les unes contre les autres.

Je n'aime pas les hommes épars, je n'aime pas les palais isolés, je les aime liés par un grand nombre d'autres domiciles particulières (p. 63).

87 liés.

88 Les angles des cailloux qui se touchent, s'émoussent, et les cailloux se polissent.

89 pp. 197–8.

90 sans ordre, sans suite, sans liaison.

91 l'image de la nation sauvage, plus grande, plus noble, n'en subsisterait pas moins.

92 en liant ces maisons par des maisons intermédiaires, l'ensemble me rappellera l'idée d'une ruche.

93 Tant que vos abeilles seront éparses, vous aurez peu de miel. Lorsque vos abeilles seront rassemblées, elles se défendront contre les frelons.

94 Faire des rues.

95 Circonscrire la capitale. Lui donner une enceinte.

96 les abeilles entreront toutes au-dedans de l'enceinte, et peu à peu les alvéoles de la ruche deviendront contiguës.

97 pp. 239–41.

98 p. 63.

99 Quel fut l'effet de cette ceinture sur ses sens, sur son esprit, sur son imagination? De l'accoutumer à se regarder comme chez soi au-dedans de cette ceinture, et comme hors de chez soi au-delà de son enceinte.

100 Ces barricades ou enceintes légèrs auront bientôt leurs effets primitifs: c'est d'accoutumer le paysan à regarder comme sien tout l'espace renfermé entre ces barricades qu'il aura placées lui-même.

101 beau paradoxe.

102 je suis convaincu qu'il ne peut y avoir de vrai bonheur pour l'espèce humaine que dans un état social où il n'y aurait ni roi, ni magistrat, ni prêtre, ni lois, ni tien, ni mien, ni propriété foncière, ni vices, ni vertus.

103 diablement idéal.

104 le droit de propriété est sacré de particulier à particulier, et s'il n'est pas sacré, il faut que la société se dissolve.

105 C'est le contraire de ce droit de particulier relativement à la société. Ce n'est rien, car si c'était quelque chose, il ne se ferait rien de grand, d'utile à la société, la propriété de quelques particuliers croisant sans cesse les vues générales, elle tendrait à sa ruine, parce que le droit de propriété de quelques particuliers croiserait sans cesse les moyens de son opulence, de sa force et de sa sûreté (p. 99).

106 qu'où il n'y a point de propriétés il n'y a point de sujets; qu'où il n'y a point de sujets l'empire est pauvre, et qu'où la puissance souveraine est illimitée, il n'y a point de propriété (p. 123).

107 L'âme d'un esclave est avilie; il se néglige jusqu'à lui-même dont il n'a

pas la propriété. C'est un locataire qui laisse dégrader une maison qui ne lui appartient pas (p. 196).

108 chacun a sa tête et sa propriété, une portion de la richesse générale dont il est maître et maître absolu, sur laquelle il est roi, et dont il peut user ou même abuser à sa discrétion (*A.T.*, vi, p. 449).

109 La nature de l'homme et la notion de la propriété concourent à l'affranchir, et la liberté conduit l'individu et la société au plus grand bonheur qu'ils puissent désirer (p. 450).

110 un bonheur constant qui tient à la liberté, à la sûreté des propriétés, à la nature de l'impôt, à sa répartition, à sa perception, et qui distingue les lois éternelles (*Mém. Cath.*, p. 236).

111 On multiplie beaucoup, et l'on reste où l'on est bien; et l'on est bien où la liberté et la propriété sont sacrées. La liberté et la propriété sont sacrées où tous sont également soumis à la loi et à l'impôt, et où l'impôt est proportionné aux besoins de la société et sa perception aux fortunes; du reste, il ne faut se mêler de rien, tout s'ordonnera de soi-même et est suffisamment protégé (p. 407).

112 sans ordre, sans suite, sans liaison.

113 liés.

114 systématique.

115 Si j'avais à créer une nation à la liberté, que ferais-je? Je planterais au milieu d'elle une colonie d'hommes libres, tels, par exemple, que les Suisses, à qui je conserverais bien strictement ses privilèges et j'abandonnerais le reste au temps et à l'exemple ... Peu à peu, ce levain précieux changerait toute la masse, et son esprit deviendrait l'esprit général (p. 199).

116 Je sais par cœur toutes les objections qu'on peut opposer à ces moyens; elles sont si frivoles que je ne me donne pas la peine d'y répondre (p. 351).

117 Et puis je m'arrête pour considérer un moment par combien de vicissitudes nous avons été conduits au point où nous en sommes, ou plutôt où nous en étions, et par combien de vicissitudes nous aurions eu encore à passer pour arriver à quelque chose de bien, en continuant de nous abandonner aveuglément à ce mouvement obscur et sourd qui nous tiraille, qui nous tourmente et nous fait tourner et retourner, jusqu'à ce que nous ayons trouvé une position moins incommode, mouvement qui agite un empire mal policé, comme il agite un malade! Mais nous avons perdu jusqu'à cette inquiétude automate. Nous ne nous sentons plus.
Il y avait dans le commencement un roi, des seigneurs et des serfs. Il n'y a aujourd'hui qu'un maître et des serfs sous toutes sortes de noms.

118 Tant que cette concession subsiste sans atteinte, l'État prospère. Le peuple se croit libre. L'attaquer est le premier pas du despotisme, l'annuler en est le dernier, et l'époque la plus voisine de la chute d'un empire, surtout si cette innovation se fait sans effusion de sang, car alors il n'y a plus de nerfs, tout est relâché, tout est avili (p. 7).

119 La souveraineté et la liberté ne consistent pas à faire tout ce que l'on veut; la souveraineté et la liberté sont limitées l'une et l'autre par la même barrière: le respect de la propriété de la part du souverain, et son usage de la part du sujet (*Observations*, pp. 367–8).

120 Le terme du malheur ou de l'oppression est limité par la nature. Il est tracé dans le sillon du laboureur. La terre redemande une portion. Celui qui la cultive en doit réserver une seconde pour lui. La troisième appartient au propriétaire. Je défie le despote le plus atroce d'enfreindre cette répartition sans condamner une portion de son peuple à mourir de faim; voilà le moment de la révolte. J'ai pris l'agriculture pour exemple, parce qu'en dernier contrecoup, toute oppression revient sur la terre (*ibid.*, p. 380).

121 Je vends mes domaines, parce que je ne sais ce que c'est que des propriétés particulières à celui qui est censé maître de tout et dont la bourse est dans la poche de ses sujets (*Mém. Cath.*, p. 149).

122 Je ne saurais souffrir qu'un souverain ait des domaines qui lui soient propres (p. 453).

123 Un mauvais roi est celui qui a un intérêt séparé de l'intérêt de son peuple (p. 454).

124 Qu'isolés dans tous les districts ils ne fassent corps qu'en commission; lorsque les représentants sont tous en même temps magistrats, au moindre mécontentement comme représentants, ils déposent leurs robes de magistrats, et le royaume tombe en anarchie.
Occupés et répandus dans différents districts, ils ne seront jamais pauvres; s'ils s'enrichissent, ils deviendront le lien commun des conditions supérieures et des conditions inférieures; une espèce d'amalgame, qui s'unira également bien et avec la noblesse pauvre et avec la riche bourgeoisie (p. 126).

125 Qu'au lieu que notre Parlement enregistrait les volontés du souverain, il faudrait au contraire que ce fût le souverain qui enregistrât les représentations de la commission. Nos magistrats disaient: Nous voulons aussi ce que le roi veut; c'est Votre Majesté et ses successeurs qui diront: Nous acquiesçons aussi à ce que notre nation nous demande par la voie de notre commission; ce qui est fort différent.

126 un être physique, constant, immuable, permanent, éternel ... C'est ce corps rendu permanent que j'opposerais à la ruine à venir de mes lois et de mes institutions (p. 119).

127 Je cimenterais par toutes les voies, pour moi et pour mes successeurs, l'aliénation faite de mes droits à ce corps.
Je ne l'appellerais dans aucune circonstance étrangère à son objet, de peur qu'il ne fût tenté d'empiéter.
Il ne se mêlerait ni de guerre, ni de politique, ni de finances (p. 120).

128 J'emploierais toute cette durée à le mettre en vigueur par un continuel exercice de ses fonctions (p. 121).

129 Son district, et son district entier, se réduirait à la conservation des lois faites et à l'examen des lois soit à faire, soit à abroger, des institutions, etc. (p. 120).

130 Puissent-ils reculer au moins pour quelques siècles, le décret prononcé contre toutes les choses de ce monde; décret qui les a condamnées à avoir leur naissance, leur temps de vigueur, leur décrépitude et leur fin! (*Aux Insurgents d'Amérique*, p. 491).

131 Un peuple libre ne diffère d'un peuple esclave que par l'inamovabilité de certains privilèges appartenant à l'homme comme homme (*Observations*, p. 360).

132 Le droit d'opposition me semble, dans une société d'hommes, un droit naturel, inaliénable et sacré (*Mém. Cath.*, p. 117).

133 quand ce corps ne serait, avec le temps, qu'un grand fantôme de liberté, il n'en influera pas moins sur l'esprit national, car il faut qu'un peuple ou soit libre, ce qui est le mieux, ou qu'il croie l'être; parce que cette opinion a toujours les effets les plus précieux (p. 127).

134 il y avait entre la tête du despote et nos yeux une grande toile d'araignée sur laquelle la multitude adorait une grande image de la liberté. Les clairvoyants avaient regardé depuis longtemps à travers les petits trous de la toile, et savaient bien ce qu'il y avait derrière; on a déchiré la toile, et la tyrannie s'est montrée à face découverte. Quand un peuple n'est pas libre, c'est encore une chose précieuse que l'opinion qu'il a de sa liberté; il avait cette opinion, il fallait la lui laisser; à présent il est esclave, et il le sent et il le voit ... (p. 20).

135 Il faut ou qu'un peuple soit libre, ou qu'il croie l'être. Celui qui détruit ce préjugé national est un scélérat; c'est une grande toile d'araignée sur laquelle l'image de la liberté est peinte. Cette image qui attache tous les yeux du peuple l'élève, le soutient, le réjouit; quelques bons yeux voient à travers les trous de cette toile la tête hideuse du despote. Que fait celui qui déchire la toile? Rien pour le maître dont il est le vil esclave, un mal incroyable à la nation qu'il détrompe, qu'il contriste, qu'il abat, qu'il avilit, en lui montrant tout à coup la tête hideuse. Le corps dépositaire des lois fondamentales d'un État est cette toile d'araignée (p. 358).

136 tout le monde s'éveilla. L'on chercha en s'éveillant, comme à tâtons, les lois: l'on ne les trouva plus; l'on s'effara, l'on cria, l'on se les demanda; et dans cette agitation les questions que leurs explications firent naître, d'obscures qu'elles étaient et vénérables par leur obscurité, devinrent problématiques; et dès là, à l'égard de la moitié du monde, odieuses. Le peuple entra dans le sanctuaire: il leva le voile qui doit toujours couvrir tout ce que l'on peut dire, tout ce que l'on peut croire du droit des peuples et de celui des rois qui ne s'accordent jamais si bien ensemble que dans le silence (p. 74).

137 d'une adroite usurpation firent un droit irrévocable, et, pour le profit de quelques ambitieux, assujettirent désormais tout le genre humain au travail, à la servitude et à la misère (p. 181).

138 Tous les hommes sont hommes, les grands comme les petits, et leurs passions, qu'ils étalent sur le grand théâtre du monde, sont toujours les mêmes. Il est vrai que les grands les couvrent mieux, et ajustent plus proprement le masque qu'ils prennent pour se déguiser. Quiconque entreprend de lever ce masque est criminel, et néanmoins c'est ce qu'on désire que fasse l'historien et l'écrivain, et qui rend les relations plaisantes et estimées. Il y a manière pourtant d'ôter le voile: on le peut lever doucement, sans le déchirer ... (p. 449).

139 Là, on rompt le concert des volontés qui se touchent, en les isolant par la terreur; on établit entre les citoyens une distance morale équivalente pour les effets à une distance physique; et cette distance morale s'établit par un inquisiteur civil qui rôde perpétuellement entre les individus, la hache levée sur le cou de quiconque osera dire ou du bien ou du mal de l'administration (*A.T.*, VI, p. 447).

140 ressorts isolés.

141 Mais dans un monastère tout est à tous, rien n'est individuellement à personne, tous les biens forment une propriété commune; c'est un seul animal à 20, 30, 40, mille, dix mille têtes. Il n'en est pas ainsi d'une société civile ou politique: ici chacun a sa tête et sa propriété, une portion de la richesse générale dont il est maître et maître absolu, sur laquelle il est roi, et dont il peut user ou même abuser à sa discrétion (ibid., p. 449).

142 par l'industrie et par le travail.

143 Faut-il arracher à la nature tout ce qu'on en peut obtenir, ou notre lutte contre elle ne devrait-elle pas se borner à rendre plus aisé le petit nombre de grandes fonctions auxquelles elle nous a destinés, se loger, se vêtir, se nourrir, se reproduire dans son semblable et se reposer en sûreté? Tout le reste ne serait-il pas par hasard l'extravagance de l'espèce, comme tout ce qui excède l'ambition d'une certaine fortune est parmi nous l'extravagance de l'individu? (pp. 45–6).

144 Or, quand les héritages se furent accrus en nombre et en étendue au point de couvrir le sol entier et de se toucher tous, les uns ne purent plus s'agrandir qu'aux dépens des autres; et les surnuméraires que la faiblesse ou l'indolence avaient empêchés d'en acquérir à leur tour, devenus pauvres sans avoir rien perdu, parce que, tout changeant autour d'eux, eux seuls n'avaient point changé, furent obligés de recevoir ou de ravir leur subsistance de la main des riches; et de là commencèrent à naître, selon les divers caractères des uns et des autres, la domination et la servitude, ou la violence et les rapines (p. 179).

145 p. 99.

146 *Mém. Cath.*, p. 177.

147 Les penseurs sont désolés de la durée de la guerre présente (p. 40).

148 un seul animal à ... dix mille têtes.

149 Les penseurs sont désolés de la durée de la guerre présente.

150 l'œil du philosophe et l'œil du souverain voient bien diversement.

151 origine du faisceau.

152 n'a ... aucun sens qui lui soit propre ... il émane d'une substance molle, insensible, inerte, qui lui sert d'oreiller, et sur laquelle il siège, écoute, juge et prononce.

153 l'impression la plus légère suspend son audience (*Rêve*, pp. 330–1).

154 J'avoue qu'un être qui existe quelque part et qui ne correspond à aucun point de l'espace; un être qui est inétendu et qui occupe de l'étendue; qui est tout entier sous chaque partie de cette étendue; qui diffère essentiellement de la matière et qui lui est uni; qui la suit et qui la meut sans se mouvoir; qui agit sur elle et qui en subit toutes les vicissitudes; un être dont je n'ai pas la moindre idée; un être d'une nature aussi contradictoire est difficile à admettre (p. 257).

155 cette sensibilité que vous lui substituez.

156 il n'y a point d'illusion de la réalité; mais d'un côté une illusion qui ne trompe personne, et de l'autre, la réalité.

157 est fondé sur un pacte de mauvaise foi, ou plus exactement, en appelle à un type de foi qui se discrédite dans le moment où elle s'accorde. Chacun ici, auteur ou lecteur, fait semblant.

158 Il n'y a peut-être pas, sur toute la surface de la terre, deux individus qui

232

aient la même mesure de la certitude, et cependant le poète est condamné à faire illusion également à tous! Le poète se joue de la raison et de l'expérience de l'homme instruit, comme une gouvernante se joue de l'imbécillité d'un enfant. Un bon poème est un conte digne d'être fait à des hommes sensés (p. 215).

159 *A.T.*, xi, pp. 11–14.

160 par le retour à l'état de barbarie.

161 la seule condition où les hommes, convaincus de leur ignorance, puissent se résoudre à la lenteur du tâtonnement; les autres restent médiocres, précisément parce qu'ils naissent, pour ainsi dire, savants (p. 14).

162 l'ouvrage d'une cause intellectuelle: le mouvement établit souvent, soit dans un être considéré solitairement, soit entre plusieurs êtres comparés entre eux, une multitude prodigieuse de rapports surprenants … Les rapports sont alors des résultants de combinaisons fortuites, du moins par rapport à nous. La nature imite, en se jouant, dans cent occasions, les productions de l'art; et l'on pourrait demander … combien il faudrait remarquer de rapports dans un être pour avoir une certitude complète qu'il est l'ouvrage d'un artiste; en quelle occasion un seul défaut de symétrie prouverait plus que toute somme donnée de rapports; comment sont entre eux le temps de l'action de la cause fortuite, et les rapports observés dans les effets produits; et si, à l'exception des œuvres du Tout-Puissant, il y a des cas où le nombre des rapports ne puisse jamais être compensé par celui des jets (*Œuvres Esthétiques*, pp. 435–6).

163 cette formule qui détrône toutes les esthétiques jusqu'alors connues.

164 la difficulté de l'événement est plus que suffisamment compensée par la multitude des jets.

165 la matière s'étant mue de toute éternité, … il ne se soit rencontré aucun de ces arrangements admirables dans la multitude infinie de ceux qu'elle a pris successivement (pp. 22–3).

166 Combien de mondes estropiés, manqués, se sont dissipés, se reforment et se dissipent peut-être à chaque instant dans des espaces éloignés … mais où le mouvement continue et continuera de combiner des amas de matière jusqu'à ce qu'ils aient obtenu quelque arrangement dans lequel ils puissent persévérer (p. 123).

167 Qu'est-ce que ce monde … ? Un composé sujet à des révolutions, qui toutes indiquent une tendance continuelle à la destruction; une succession rapide d'êtres qui s'entre-suivent, se poussent et disparaissent; une symétrie passagère; un ordre momentané (p. 123).

168 entretiennent dans le tout et entretiendront à jamais ce passage ou flux perpétuel d'un ordre ou co-ordination, à un autre (p. 205).

169 ses moments sublimes.

170 je pense que s'il est quelqu'un sûr de saisir et de conserver leur sublimité, c'est celui qui les aura pressentis d'imagination et de génie, et qui les rendra de sang-froid.

171 sublimité.

172 un spectacle merveilleux.

173 Mais ce spectacle serait-il à comparer avec celui qui résulterait d'un accord bien entendu, de cette harmonie que l'artiste y introduira

lorsqu'il le transportera du carrefour sur la scène ou sur la toile?

174 D'ailleurs vous me parlez d'une chose réelle, et moi je vous parle d'une imitation; vous me parlez d'un instant fugitif de la nature, et moi je vous parle d'un ouvrage de l'art projeté, suivi, qui a ses progrès et sa durée (pp. 318–19).

175 Il n'y a rien d'imparfait dans la nature, pas même les monstres.

176 Il n'y a d'imperfection que dans l'art parce que l'art a un modèle subsistant dans la nature, auquel on peut comparer les productions (pp. 416–17).

177 La nature ne fait rien d'incorrect. Toute forme, belle ou laide, a sa cause; et de tous les êtres qui existent, il n'y a pas un qui ne soit comme il doit être (p. 655).

178 Si les causes et les effets nous étaient évidents, nous n'aurions rien de mieux à faire que de représenter les êtres tels qu'ils sont. Plus l'imitation serait parfaite et analogue aux causes, plus nous en serions satisfaits.

179 par ce tact fin que nous tenons de l'observation continue des phénomènes, et qui nous ferait sentir une liaison secrète, un enchaînement nécessaire entre ces difformités (p. 666).

180 jugeait des hommes comme les gens de goût jugent des ouvrages d'esprit, par sentiment.

181 instinct de nos grands manouvriers. Ils ont vu si souvent et de si près la nature dans ses opérations, qu'ils devinent avec assez de précision le cours qu'elle pourra suivre … Ainsi le service le plus important qu'ils aient à rendre à ceux qu'ils initient à la philosophie expérimentale, c'est bien moins de les instruire du procédé et du résultat, que de faire passer en eux cet esprit de divination par lequel on *subodore*, pour ainsi dire, des procédés inconnus, des expériences nouvelles, des résultats ignorés (xxx, p. 197)

182 tout se tient.

183 si les principes de la morale étaient une fois bien posés, il sortirait de ce tronc une infinité de petites branches qui y mèneraient et y attacheraient les vertus les plus minutieuses … Si les principes du goût étaient posés, ils embrasseraient tout jusqu'au liseré qui borde l'ajustement d'une petite maîtresse. (*Roth*, IV, p. 196).

184 places éclairées.

185 vaste enceinte des sciences (*Int. Nat.*, p. 189).

186 Le choix du moment où elle expire ne donne pas une Cléopâtre, il ne donne qu'une femme expirante par la morsure d'un serpent. Ce n'est plus l'histoire de la reine d'Alexandrie, c'est un accident de la vie (*A.T.*, x, p. 129).

187 Chaque action a plusieurs instants; … l'artiste n'en a qu'un dont la durée est celle d'un coup d'œil; … il peut … rester, au moment que le peintre a choisi, soit dans les attitudes, soit dans les caractères, soit dans les actions, des traces subsistantes du moment qui a précédé (*Essais sur la Peinture*, pp. 714–15).

188 il n'y a de beautés durables, que celles qui sont fondées sur des rapports avec les êtres de la nature. Si l'on imaginait les êtres dans une vicissitude rapide, toute peinture ne représentant qu'un instant qui fuit, toute imitation serait superflue. Les beautés ont, dans les arts, le

même fondement que les vérités dans la philosophie (p. 160).

189 hommage du mouvement à la stabilité.

190 la vérité dans la philosophie.

191 Qu'est-ce que la vérité? La conformité de nos jugements avec les êtres. Qu'est-ce que la beauté d'imitation? La conformité de l'image avec la chose (p. 160).

192 qu'un homme a conservé son caractère (p. 160).

193 Il me semble qu'il y a bien de l'avantage à rendre les hommes tels qu'ils sont. Ce qu'ils devraient être est une chose trop systématique et trop vague pour servir de base à un art d'imitation. Il n'y a rien de si rare qu'un homme tout à fait méchant, si ce n'est peut-être un homme tout à fait bon.

194 Lorsque Thétis trempa son fils dans le Styx, il en sortit semblable à Thersite par le talon.

195 l'imitation de la nature, et de la nature la plus forte.

196 une absurdité.

197 une fable.

198 La tragédie domestique et bourgeoise à créer. Le genre sérieux à perfectionner. Les conditions de l'homme à substituer aux caractères, peut-être dans tous les genres. La pantomime à lier étroitement avec l'action dramatique. La scène à changer, et les tableaux à substituer aux coups de théâtre, source nouvelle d'invention pour le poète, et d'étude pour le comédien. Car, que sert au poète d'imaginer des tableaux, si le comédien demeure attaché à sa disposition symétrique et à son action compassée? La tragédie réelle à introduire sur le théâtre lyrique. Enfin la danse à réduire sous la forme d'un véritable poème, à écrire et à séparer de tout autre art d'imitation (p. 167).

199 genre sérieux.

200 le burlesque, le genre comique, le genre tragique, le merveilleux (p. 137).

201 C'est l'avantage du genre sérieux, que, placé entre les deux autres, il a des ressources, soit qu'il s'élève, soit qu'il descende (p. 137).

202 et cette poétique serait aussi fort étendue.

203 merveilleux.

204 les grands intérêts, les grandes passions (p. 99).

205 le tableau des malheurs qui nous environnent … une scène réelle, des habits vrais, des discours proportionnés aux actions, des actions simples, des dangers dont il est impossible que vous n'ayez tremblé pour vos parents, vos amis, pour vous-même (p. 149).

206 le mouvement nuit presque toujours à la dignité; ainsi, que votre principal personnage soit rarement le machiniste de votre pièce (p. 139).

207 cris inarticulés (p. 90)

208 La nature-mouvement, telle qu'il la sent, se confond avec la violence des passions.

209 telle qu'il la sent

210 Tout ce qui a trait à la violence et à l'enthousiasme a nom Dorval. Tout ce qui tourne autour de l'idée de l'observation, de rigueur logique, de peinture des conditions, de moralité se rattache au personnage d'Ariste (p. 428).

211 La nature humaine est donc bonne? Oui, mon ami, et très bonne.

L'eau, l'air, la terre, le feu, tout est bon dans la nature, et l'ouragan, qui s'élève sur la fin de l'automne, secoue les forêts, et frappant les arbres les uns contre les autres, en brise et sépare les branches mortes; et la tempête, qui bat les eaux de la mer et les purifie; et le volcan, qui verse de son flanc entr'ouvert des flots de matières embrasées, et porte dans l'air la vapeur qui le nettoie. Ce sont les misérables conventions qui pervertissent l'homme, et non la nature humaine qu'il faut accuser (p. 195).

212 l'honnête.

213 Tout cela naïvement, et d'une seule traite, comme si l'argumentation allait de soi.

214 Un incident imprévu qui se passe en action, et qui change subitement l'état des personnages est un coup de théâtre. Une disposition de ces personnages sur la scène, si naturelle et si vraie, que, rendue fidèlement par un peintre, elle me plairait sur la toile, est un tableau (p. 88).

215 Le poète me ménage, par le secret, un instant de surprise; il m'eût exposé, par la confidence, à une longue inquiétude. Je ne plaindrai qu'un instant celui qui sera frappé et accablé dans un instant. Mais que deviens-je, si le coup se fait attendre, si je vois l'orage se former sur ma tête ou sur celle d'un autre, et y demeurer longtemps suspendu? (p. 227).

216 J'aimerais bien mieux des tableaux sur la scène où il y en a si peu, et où ils produiraient un effet si agréable et si sûr, que ces coups de théâtre qu'on amène d'une manière si forcée, et qui sont fondés sur tant de suppositions singulières, que, pour une de ces combinaisons d'événements qui soit heureuse et naturelle, il y en a mille qui doivent déplaire à un homme de goût (p. 88).

217 Est-il possible qu'on ne sentira point que l'effet du malheur est de rapprocher les hommes; et qu'il est ridicule, surtout dans les moments de tumulte, lorsque les passions sont portées à l'excès, et que l'action est la plus agitée, de se tenir en rond, séparés, à une certaine distance les uns des autres, et dans un ordre symétrique.

218 Il faut que l'action théâtrale soit bien imparfaite encore, puisqu'on ne voit sur la scène presque aucune situation dont on pût faire une composition supportable en peinture (p. 89).

219 pp. 260–1.

220 la poésie veut quelque chose d'énorme, de barbare, et de sauvage.

221 il faut aux arts d'imitation quelque chose de sauvage, de brut, de frappant, et d'énorme (p. 714).

222 *A.T.*, pp. 146–7.

223 sentiment inné, ce goût dominant de l'indépendance.

224 l'un est la prison du luxe, de la mollesse et de l'ennui; l'autre est l'asile de la méditation vagabonde, de la haute contemplation et du sublime enthousiasme. En voyant les eaux captives de Versailles, et les eaux bondissantes de Vaucluse se précipiter à travers les rochers, on dit également, *cela est beau!* Mais on le dit des effets de l'art, et on le sent des jeux de la nature: aussi l'art qui assujettit, fait-il l'impossible pour nous cacher les entraves qu'il lui donne, et dans la nature livrée à elle-même, le peintre et le poète se gardent bien d'imiter les accidents où l'on peut soupçonner quelques traces de servitude. L'excellence de

l'art, dans le moral, comme dans le physique, est de surpasser la nature, de mettre plus d'intelligence dans l'ordonnance de ses tableaux … Voyez combien les accidents les plus terribles de la nature, les tempêtes, les volcans, la foudre, sont plus formidables encore dans les fictions des poètes (p. 634).

225 modèle idéal.

226 pp. 284–7.

227 par un projet … de lui imprimer … un caractère exclusif de toutes les servitudes de notre vie chétive, pauvre, mesquine et misérable (*A.T.*, XI, pp. 12–13).

228 Si le genre sérieux est le plus facile de tous, c'est, en revanche, le moins sujet aux vicissitudes des temps et des lieux. Portez le nu en quelque lieu de la terre qu'il vous plaira; il fixera l'attention, s'il est bien dessiné. Si vous excellez dans le genre sérieux, vous plairez dans tous les temps et chez tous les peuples (p. 138).

229 quelque chose de sauvage, de brut, de frappant et d'énorme.

230 l'excellence de l'art … est … de mettre plus d'intelligence dans l'ordonnance de ses tableaux (p. 634).

231 La principale idée, bien conçue, doit exercer son despotisme sur toutes les autres. C'est la force motrice de la machine qui, semblable à celle qui retient les corps célestes dans leurs orbes et les entraîne, agit en raison inverse de la distance.

232 L'expression exige une imagination forte, une verve brûlante, l'art de susciter des fantômes, de les animer, de les agrandir; l'ordonnance, en poésie ainsi qu'en peinture, suppose un certain tempérament de jugement et de verve, de chaleur et de sagesse, d'ivresse et de sang-froid, dont les exemples sont peu communs en nature. Sans cette balance rigoureuse, selon que l'enthousiasme ou la raison prédomine, l'artiste est extravagant ou froid (*Essais sur la Peinture*, p. 720).

233 Ces gens-ci croient qu'il n'y a qu'à arranger des figures; ils ne savent pas que le premier point, le point important, c'est de trouver une grande idée; qu'il faut se promener, méditer, laisser les pinceaux, et demeurer en repos jusqu'à ce que la grande idée soit trouvée (*A.T.*, X, p. 96).

234 si l'action se complique, si les incidents se multiplient, il s'en rencontrera facilement quelques-uns qui me rappelleront que je suis dans un parterre; que tous ces personnages sont des comédiens, et que ce n'est point un fait qui se passe. Le récit, au contraire, me transportera au-delà de la scène; j'en suivrai toutes les circonstances. Mon imagination les réalisera comme je les ai vues dans la nature (*Entretiens*, p. 150).

235 Une manière de me décider, … c'est de saisir par la pensée les objets, de les transporter de la nature sur la toile, et de les examiner à cette distance, où ils ne sont ni trop près, ni trop loin de moi (p. 195).

236 Il faut que l'action théâtrale soit bien imparfaite encore, puisqu'on ne voit sur la scène presqu'aucune situation dont on pût faire une composition supportable en peinture. Quoi donc! la vérité y est-elle moins essentielle que sur la toile?… Je pense, pour moi, que si un ouvrage dramatique était bien fait et bien représenté, la scène offrirait au spectateur autant de tableaux réels qu'il y aurait dans l'action de moments favorables au peintre (pp. 89–90).

237 Si, quand on fait un tableau, on suppose des spectateurs, tout est perdu. Le peintre sort de sa toile, comme l'auteur qui parle au parterre sort de la scène. (*Roth*, IV, p. 57).

238 Il en est du spectacle comme d'une société bien ordonnée, où chacun sacrifie de ses droits primitifs pour le bien de l'ensemble (p. 320).

239 emploiera cet incident, s'il est donné par l'histoire, mais il ne l'inventera pas. Je jugerai ses moyens plus sévèrement que la conduite des dieux (*Discours*, p. 210).

240 cas rares.

241 Ou il s'empare de ces combinaisons extraordinaires, ou il en imagine de semblables. Mais, au lieu que la liaison des événements nous échappe souvent dans la nature, et que, faute de connaître l'ensemble des choses, nous ne voyons qu'une concomitance fatale dans les faits, le poète veut, lui, qu'il règne dans toute la texture de son ouvrage une liaison apparente et sensible, en sorte qu'il est moins vrai et plus vraisemblable que l'historien.

242 les choses qu'il invente reçoivent de la vraisemblance par celles qui lui sont données (pp. 213–14).

243 Se rappeler une suite nécessaire d'images telles qu'elles se succèdent dans la nature, c'est raisonner d'après les faits. Se rappeler une suite d'images comme elles se succéderaient nécessairement dans la nature, tel ou tel phénomène étant donné, c'est raisonner d'après une hypothèse, ou feindre; c'est être philosophe ou poète, selon le but qu'on se propose (*ibid.*, p. 219).

244 On lit, dans l'histoire, ce qu'un homme du caractère de Henri IV a fait et souffert. Mais combien de circonstances possibles où il eût agi et souffert d'une manière conforme à son caractère, plus merveilleuse, que l'histoire n'offre pas, mais que la poésie imagine (*ibid.*, p. 217).

245 où il ne faut plus peindre la nature.

246 Tous les possibles ne doivent point avoir lieu en bonne peinture non plus qu'en bonne littérature; car il y a tel concours d'événements dont on ne peut nier la possibilité, mais dont la combinaison est telle qu'on voit que peut-être ils n'ont jamais eu lieu, et ne l'auront peut-être jamais. Les possibles qu'on peut employer, ce sont les possibles vraisemblables, et les possibles vraisemblables, ce sont ceux où il y a plus à parier pour que contre, qu'ils ont passé de l'état de possibilité à l'état d'existence dans un certain temps limité par celui de l'action (p. 691).

247 l'on pourrait se demander … combien il faudrait remarquer de rapports dans un être pour avoir une certitude complète qu'il est l'ouvrage d'un artiste; … comment sont entre eux le temps de l'action de la cause fortuite, et les rapports observés dans les effets produits.

248 Je jugerai ses moyens plus sévèrement que la conduite des Dieux.

249 si les causes et les effets nous étaient évidents, nous n'aurions rien de mieux à faire que de représenter les êtres tels qu'ils sont.

250 Au lieu que la liaison des événements nous échappe souvent dans la nature et que, faute de connaître l'ensemble des choses, nous ne voyons qu'une concomitance fatale dans les faits, le poète veut, lui, qu'il règne dans toute la texture de son ouvrage une liaison apparente et sensible; en sorte qu'il est moins vrai et plus vraisemblable que l'historien.

251 p. 150.
252 *A.T.*, xi, pp. 119–20.
253 Je fais deux rôles, je suis double; je suis Le Couvreur et je reste moi. C'est moi Le Couvreur qui frémit et qui souffre, et c'est le moi tout court qui a du plaisir. Fort bien, l'abbé, et voilà la limite de l'imitateur de la nature. Si je m'oublie trop et trop longtemps, la terreur est trop forte; si je ne m'oublie point du tout, si je reste toujours un, elle est trop faible: c'est ce juste tempérament qui fait verser des larmes délicieuses.
254 juste tempérament.
255 pp. 283–7.
256 Il n'y a peut-être pas, dans l'espèce humaine entière, deux individus qui aient quelque ressemblance approchée.
257 Dans un même homme, tout est dans une vicissitude perpétuelle … Ce n'est que par la mémoire que nous sommes un même individu pour les autres et pour nous-mêmes. Il ne me reste peut-être pas, à l'âge que j'ai, une seule molécule du corps que j'apportai en naissant (pp. 283–4).
258 Sont-ce là des choses locales, momentanées et arbitraires, des mots vides de sens? (p. 284).
259 un homme idéal que je me formerai, auquel je présenterai les objets, qui prononcera, et dont je me bornerai à n'être que l'écho fidèle … (p. 284).
260 Mais ce modèle général idéal est impossible à former, à moins que les dieux ne m'accordent leur intelligence et ne me promettent leur éternité … (p. 285).
261 que les peintres et les sculpteurs ont fait de celui qu'ils avaient. Je le modifierai selon les circonstances (p. 286).
262 se sont fait un modèle propre à leur état (p. 285).
263 L'étude courbe l'homme de lettres. L'exercice affermit la démarche, et relève la tête du soldat… Voilà les observations qui, multipliées à l'infini, forment le statuaire, et lui apprennent à altérer, fortifier, affaiblir, défigurer et réduire son modèle idéal de l'état de nature à tel autre état qui lui plaît (p. 286).
264 C'est l'étude des passions, des mœurs, des caractères, des usages, qui apprendra au peintre de l'homme à altérer son modèle, et à le réduire de l'état d'homme à celui d'homme bon ou méchant, tranquille ou colère (p. 286).
265 pp. 266–82.
266 *A.T.*, ix, pp. 239–41.
267 les formes extérieures de la proportion la plus rigoureuse, telles qu'elles se trouvaient au bout du crayon de Raphaël.
268 assommeur des grands chemins.
269 crapuleux, apoplectique.
270 jaloux ou envieux.
271 boiteux ou bossu.
272 pp. 242–9.
273 p. 153.
274 ce ne sont plus, à proprement parler, les caractères qu'il faut mettre sur la scène, mais les conditions.

275 les petites différences qui se remarquent dans les caractères des hommes, ne peuvent être maniées aussi heureusement que les caractères tranchés.

276 Pour peu que le caractère fût chargé, un spectateur pouvait se dire à lui-même, ce n'est pas moi. Mais il ne peut se cacher que l'état qu'on joue devant lui ne soit le sien; il ne peut méconnaître ses devoirs. Il faut absolument qu'il s'applique ce qu'il entend.

277 ces sujets n'appartiennent pas seulement au genre sérieux. Ils deviendront comiques ou tragiques, selon le génie de l'homme qui s'en saisira (p. 154).

278 toutes les relations: le père de famille, l'époux, la sœur, les frères (p. 154).

Part III

1 Leurs besoins sont plus pressants que les miens; et il vaut mieux que je sois gêné qu'eux (*A.T.*, VII, p. 207).

2 J'ai réglé votre sort à venir sur vos talents et vos goûts (p. 221).

3 Moi, j'autoriserais par ma faiblesse honteuse le désordre de la société, la confusion du sang et des rangs, la dégradation des familles? (p. 222).

4 Ses vues ambitieuses, et l'autorité qu'il a prise dans ma maison, me deviennent de jour en jour plus importunes ... Nous vivions dans la paix et dans l'union. L'humeur inquiète et tyrannique de cet homme nous a tous séparés. On se craint, on s'évite, on me laisse; je suis solitaire au sein de ma famille, et je péris ... (pp. 192–3).

5 misérables conventions (p. 223).

6 une infortunée, à qui vous ne pourriez refuser de la commisération si vous la voyiez (p. 241).

7 Ici la pitié succède à l'agitation dans le cœur de Cécile (p. 244).

8 C'est pour la première fois que mon père est d'accord avec cet oncle cruel (p. 233).

9 on établit entre les citoyens une distance morale ... et cette distance morale s'établit par un inquisiteur civil qui rôde perpétuellement entre les individus.

10 M. d'Orbesson, à l'inverse des pères de Molière, a les yeux ouverts et cherche à comprendre.

11 une sorte de drame moral (p. 197).

12 De quoi s'agirait-il en effet? De disposer le poème de manière que les choses y fussent amenées, comme l'abdication de l'empire l'est dans *Cinna*.

13 métaphysique manichéenne et tendancieuse (p. 96).

14 Il faut que les hommes fassent, dans la comédie, le rôle que font les dieux dans la tragédie. La fatalité et la méchanceté, voilà, dans l'un et l'autre genre, les bases de l'intérêt dramatique (p. 214; and quoted by Joly, p. 94).

15 S'il y a quelque chose de touchant, c'est le spectacle d'un homme rendu coupable et malheureux malgré lui.

16 Le désordre, pour un être, n'est jamais que son passage à un ordre nouveau, à une nouvelle façon d'exister, qui entraîne nécessairement

une nouvelle suite d'actions, ou de mouvements différents de ceux dont cet être se trouvait précédemment susceptible (p. 68).

17 C'est ... dans notre esprit seul qu'est le modèle de ce que nous nommons *ordre* ou *désordre* (p. 67).

18 J'ai voulu que le père fût le personnage principal. L'esquisse restait la même, mais tous les épisodes changeaient, si j'avais choisi pour mon héros, ou le fils, ou l'ami, ou l'oncle (*Discours*, p. 210).

19 Si vous faites tomber un torrent des montagnes, et que vous vouliez que j'en sois effrayé, imitez Homère, placez à l'écart un berger dans la montagne, qui en écoute le bruit avec effroi (p. 771).

20 ... si l'on bannit l'homme ou l'être pensant et contemplateur de dessus la surface de la terre; ce spectacle pathétique et sublime de la nature n'est plus qu'une scène triste et muette. L'univers se tait; le silence et la nuit s'en emparent. Tout se change en une vaste solitude où les phénomènes se passent d'une manière obscure et sourde. C'est la présence de l'homme qui rend l'existence des êtres intéressante; ... Pourquoi n'introduirons-nous pas l'homme dans notre ouvrage, comme il est placé dans l'univers? (p. 382).

21 s'est élevé au-dessus du sort.

22 Pour peu que le caractère fût chargé, un spectateur pouvait se dire à lui-même, ce n'est pas moi. Mais il ne peut se cacher que l'état qu'on joue devant lui, ne soit le sien; il ne peut méconnaître ses devoirs. Il faut absolument qu'il s'applique ce qu'il entend (p. 153).

23 La représentation en avait été si vraie, qu'oubliant en plusieurs endroits que j'étais spectateur, et spectateur ignoré, j'avais été sur le point de sortir de ma place, et d'ajouter un personnage réel à la scène. Et puis, comment arranger avec mes idées ce qui venait de se passer? Si cette pièce était une comédie comme une autre, pourquoi n'avaient-ils pu jouer la dernière scène? (p. 78).

24 pp. 314–15.

25 p. 377.

26 Je vous entends, ... vous entraîniez, vous étonniez, vous touchiez, vous produisiez un grand effet. Il est vrai. Mais portez au théâtre votre ton familier, votre expression simple, votre maintien domestique, votre geste naturel, et vous verrez combien vous serez pauvre et faible. ... Croyez-vous que les scènes de Corneille, de Racine, de Voltaire, même de Shakespeare, puissent se débiter avec votre voix de conversation et le ton du coin de votre âtre? Pas plus que l'histoire du coin de votre âtre avec l'emphase et l'ouverture de bouche du théâtre (p. 314).

27 votre âme est épuisée, il ne vous reste ni sensibilité, ni chaleur, ni larmes.

28 Pourquoi l'acteur n'éprouve-t-il pas le même affaissement? C'est qu'il y a bien de la différence de l'intérêt qu'il prend à un conte fait à plaisir et de l'intérêt que vous inspire le malheur de votre voisin. Êtes-vous Cinna? Avez-vous jamais été Cléopâtre, Mérope, Agrippine? Que vous importent ces gens-là? (p. 315).

29 les fantômes imaginaires de la poésie ... des spectres de la façon particulière de tel ou tel poète.

30 ils figureraient mal dans l'histoire: ils feraient éclater de rire dans un cercle ou une autre assemblée de la société (p. 315).

31 récit.

32 l'histoire du coin de votre âtre.

33 en société.

34 s'il s'en tirait bien une fois, il la manquerait mille. Le succès tient alors à si peu de chose! ... Il n'est pas permis, sous peine d'être insipide, maussade, détestable, de descendre d'une ligne au-dessous de la simplicité de Nature (p. 378).

35 Que j'aie un récit un peu pathétique à faire, il s'élève je ne sais quel trouble dans mon coeur, dans ma tête; ma langue s'embarrasse; ma voix s'altère; mes idées se décomposent; mon discours se suspend; je balbutie, je m'en aperçois; les larmes coulent de mes joues, et je me tais (p. 377).

36 ni le système dramatique, ni l'action, ni les discours du poète, ne s'arrangeraient point de ma déclaration étouffée, interrompue, sanglotée. Vous voyez qu'il n'est pas même permis d'imiter la nature, même la belle nature, la vérité de trop près, et qu'il est des limites dans lesquelles il faut se renfermer.

37 le bon sens, qui ne veut pas qu'un talent nuise à un autre talent. Il faut quelquefois que l'acteur se sacrifie au poète (p. 377).

38 une autre sorte de tragédie.

39 Je ne sais pas trop ce que vous y gagneriez; mais je sais très bien ce que vous y perdriez (p. 377).

40 Il faut que je sois bien bon de m'affliger ainsi. Tout ceci n'est qu'une comédie. Dorval en a pris le sujet dans sa tête. Il l'a dialoguée à sa fantaisie, et l'on s'amusait aujourd'hui à la représenter (p. 78).

41 angoisse devant le lecteur ou le spectateur inconnu.

42 Diderot choisit un public à venir, c'est-à-dire qu'il refuse le public réel.

43 Il y a là une attitude dont on ne connaît pas d'exemple au dix-huitième siècle.

44 Pour cette raison, Diderot, auteur de tant d'articles de l'*Encyclopédie*, mesure ses paroles, sachant que cette mesure même assurera leur efficacité.

45 Diderot les considérait comme des délassements ou des confidences réservées à ses intimes. On a remarqué que les idées de Diderot sont beaucoup plus audacieuses dans les œuvres qu'il n'a pas publiées que dans les autres: il ne faut donc pas s'étonner si l'on trouve dans les *romans* toute une part purement intellectuelle, fruit des hypothèses, des paradoxes de l'auteur et se rattachant, de ce fait, plutôt à sa philosophie qu'à son art. Remarquons d'ailleurs qu'à la différence des *Contes* de Voltaire, toute cette philosophie demeure purement spéculative et ne vise pas à l'action.

46 Cette évolution particulière du roman sous l'influence de l'histoire et surtout des mémoires permet de pressentir, grâce à l'aspect intime des œuvres, le changement de sensibilité qui amènera soudain les hommes à préférer le bonheur des individus au bien public.

47 Celui qui, de son autorité privée, enfreint une loi mauvaise, autorise tout autre à enfreindre les bonnes (p. 515).

48 fantôme de liberté.

49 Tout finit par des chansons.

50 *Roth*, ix, pp. 157–8.
51 un désordre poussé fort au-delà du libertinage de la conversation.
52 cette informe et dangereuse production.
53 il est une doctrine spéculative qui n'est ni pour la multitude, ni pour la
    pratique: ... si, sans être faux, on n'écrit pas tout ce que l'on fait, sans
    être inconséquent on ne fait pas tout ce qu'on écrit.
54 Ils soufflent aujourd'hui dans les cœurs des citoyens un double poison,
    la vengeance et l'amour, poison également funeste à la religion et à la
    société ... si on y déplore des maux et des tourments c'est pour exciter
    le désir et non pas le repentir. Libido sentiendi (*Roth*, xii, pp. 15–16).
55 patience dans l'adversité.
56 modération dans la prospérité.
57 reprend l'infamie de l'avarice; l'insensée prodigalité; les traits malins
    de la médisance; la sotte impertinence des petits maîtres, etc.
58 pp. 83–4.
59 Je laisserais là ma morale, et je me garderais bien de rendre importants
    sur la scène des êtres qui sont nuls dans la société (p. 84).
60 pp. 84–5.
61 Et laissez là vos tréteaux; rentrez dans le salon; et convenez que le
    discours de Constance ne vous offensa pas, quand vous l'entendîtes là
    (p. 85).
62 afin que chacun ajoutât à son rôle, en retranchât, et se peignît encore
    plus au vrai.
63 il arriva une chose à laquelle je ne m'attendais guère, et qui est cepen-
    dant bien naturelle. C'est que, plus à leur état présent qu'à leur
    situation passée, ici ils adoucirent l'expression, là ils pallièrent un sen-
    timent (p. 86).
64 Mais quelle différence entre ce que Dorval me disait, et ce que j'écris!
    ... C'est en vain que je cherche en moi l'impression que le spectacle de
    la nature et la présence de Dorval y faisaient. Je ne la retrouve point; je
    ne vois plus Dorval, je ne l'entends plus. Je suis seul, parmi la poussière
    des livres et dans l'ombre d'un cabinet ... et j'écris des lignes faibles,
    tristes et froides (p. 79).
65 p. 89.
66 Le beau tableau, car c'en est un, ce me semble, que le malheureux
    Clairville, renversé sur le sein de son ami, comme dans le seul asile qui
    lui reste ...
67 Vous pensez bien à sa peine, mais vous oubliez la mienne. Que ce
    moment fut cruel pour moi!
68 sous le charme.
69 p. 395.
70 regardons la chose du côté vraiment intéressant; oublions pour un
    moment le point que nous occupons dans l'espace et dans la durée, et
    étendons notre vue sur les siècles à venir, les régions les plus éloignées
    et les peuples à naître. Songeons au bien de notre espèce (p. 404).
71 Pour moi, je ne vois pas de cette hauteur où tout se confond.
72 épicycle de Mercure.
73 c'est votre affaire. Je ne m'en mêle pas. Je suis dans ce monde et j'y
    reste (p. 485).
74 grand branle de la terre.

75 philosophe qui n'a rien et qui ne demande rien (pp. 487–8).

76 Vous êtes des êtres bien à plaindre, si vous n'imaginez pas qu'on s'est élevé au-dessus du sort, et qu'il est impossible d'être malheureux à l'abri de deux belles actions telles que celles-ci (p. 432).

77 Ils m'arrêtent une fois l'an, quand je les rencontre, parce que leur caractère tranche avec celui des autres, et qu'ils rompent cette fastidieuse uniformité que notre éducation, nos conventions de société, nos bienséances d'usage, ont introduite. S'il en paraît un dans une compagnie, c'est un grain de levain qui fermente et qui restitue à chacun une portion de son individualité naturelle. Il secoue, il agite, il fait approuver ou blâmer; il fait sortir la vérité; il fait connaître les gens de bien; il démasque les coquins; c'est alors que l'homme de bon sens écoute, et démêle son monde (p. 397).

78 conteur historique.

79 contes merveilleux.

80 contes plaisants.

81 Celui-ci se propose de vous tromper; il est assis au coin de votre âtre; il a pour objet la vérité rigoureuse; il veut être cru; il veut intéresser, toucher, entraîner, émouvoir, faire frissonner la peau et couler les larmes; effet qu'on n'obtient point sans éloquence et sans poésie. Mais l'éloquence est une sorte de mensonge, et rien de plus contraire à l'illusion que la poésie; l'une et l'autre exagèrent, surfont, amplifient, inspirent la méfiance: comment s'y prendra donc ce conteur-ci pour vous tromper? Le voici. Il parsèmera son récit de petites circonstances si liées à la chose, de traits si simples, si naturels, et toutefois si difficiles à imaginer, que vous serez forcé de vous dire en vous-même: Ma foi, cela est vrai: on n'invente pas ces choses-là.

82 Un peintre exécute sur la toile une tête. Toutes les formes en sont fortes, grandes et régulières; c'est l'ensemble le plus parfait et le plus rare ... J'en cherche le modèle dans la nature, et ne l'y trouve pas; ... c'est une tête idéale; je le sens, je me le dis. Mais que l'artiste me fasse apercevoir au front de cette tête une cicatrice légère, une verrue à l'une de ses tempes, une coupure imperceptible à la lèvre inférieure; et, d'idéale qu'elle était, à l'instant la tête devient un portrait; une marque de petite vérole au coin de l'oeil ou à côté du nez, et ce visage de femme n'est plus celui de Vénus; c'est le portrait de quelqu'une de mes voisines (pp. 791–2).

83 L'étude de *Mystification* et des contes moraux de Diderot montre ... que le secret du conteur n'est pas celui qu'il nous livre dans la postface des *Deux Amis*.

84 Toutes les formes en sont fortes, grandes et régulières; c'est l'ensemble le plus parfait et le plus rare ... c'est une tête idéale.

85 le portrait de quelqu'une de mes voisines ... celui de Vénus.

86 de petites circonstances si liées à la chose.

87 Plus ces cas (he is referring to les cas rares de l'ordre général des choses) seront rares et singuliers, plus il lui faudra d'art, de temps, d'espace et de circonstances communes pour en compenser le merveilleux et fonder l'illusion (pp. 219–20).

88 p. 314.

89 l'histoire du coin de votre âtre.

90 l'emphase et l'ouverture de bouche du théâtre.

91 Enfin considérez que ce n'est ici ni histoire, ni mémoires, ni commentaires, c'est une conversation de deux personnes qui se fient l'un de l'autre, de l'oncle et du neveu qui s'entretiennent l'après-souper. Vous êtes dans le fauteuil, près du lit de repos de la salle de la Mothe, et moi assis sur ce petit lit, appuyé sur un carreau, sans cérémonie, dans la dernière familiarité. Je vous conte ce que j'ai vu et ouï dire, et vous écoutez celui que vous estimez digne de créance (p. 447).

92 Richardson! on prend, malgré qu'on en ait, un rôle dans tes ouvrages, on se mêle à la conversation, on approuve, on blâme, on admire, on s'irrite, on s'indigne (p. 30).

93 Le dialogue, ... a, dans une certain mesure, permis à Diderot de représenter directement les mouvements de ses pensées dans leurs surprenants revirements; Diderot avait besoin, pour traduire ce mouvement, d'un mode d'expression qui admît l'imprévisible et qui surtout permît à l'esprit de se dégager de ses idées et d'établir une certaine distance par rapport à elles (pp. 82–3).

94 Le récit se substitue à la pensée; l'esprit sort d'une situation sans issue par la création artistique (p. 92).

95 en faisant de ses idées des êtres qui agissent dans un récit, Diderot se libère des conflits où tombait sa pensée (p. 94).

96 Lorsqu'on fait un conte, c'est à quelqu'un qui l'écoute, et pour peu que le conte dure, il est rare que le conteur ne soit pas interrompu quelquefois par son auditeur (p. 793).

97 Le droit d'opposition me semble, dans une société d'hommes, un droit naturel, inaliénable et sacré. Un despote, fût-il le meilleur des hommes, en gouvernant selon son bon plaisir, commet un forfait (p. 117).

98 selon son bon plaisir.

99 Tout gouvernement arbitraire est mauvais; je n'en excepte pas le gouvernement arbitraire d'un maître bon, ferme, juste et éclairé.

100 par une chaîne d'expériences dispersées d'espace en espace, entre des raisonnements, comme des poids sur la longueur d'un fil suspendu par ses deux extrémités (p. 184).

101 pp. 504–5.

102 Je ne sais où j'en étais.

103 Maudites soient les clefs et la fantaisie ou la raison qui me les fit emporter! Maudite soit la prudence! etc., etc.

104 p. 520.

105 Jacques s'arrêta tout court, consulta le destin dans sa tête (p. 543).

106 Il a peu d'idées dans la tête; s'il lui arrive de dire quelque chose de sensé, c'est de réminiscence ou d'inspiration (p. 515).

107 il se laisse exister.

108 faculté raisonnable.

109 ne fût-ce que par des distractions involontaires.

110 car pour peu que par des réflexions nous venions à blâmer nos plaisirs, ou que par la violence de nos passions nous cherchions à haïr la raison, nous cessons dès lors d'être heureux, nous perdons l'unité de notre existence en quoi consiste notre tranquillité, la contrariété intérieure se renouvelle, les deux personnes se représentent en opposition, et les deux principes se font sentir et se manifestent par les doutes, les inquié-

tudes et les remords.

111 C'est là le point de l'ennui le plus profond et de cet horrible dégoût de soi-même, qui ne nous laisse d'autre désir que celui de cesser d'être ... (*Œuvres Philosophiques*, p. 338, cols 1–2).

112 l'ennui, ce triste tyran de toutes les âmes qui pensent, contre lequel la sagesse peut moins que la folie (p. 340, col. 1).

113 mouvement obscur et sourd qui nous tiraille, qui nous tourmente et nous fait tourner et retourner, jusqu'à ce que nous ayons trouvé une position moins incommode, mouvement qui agite un empire mal policé, comme il agite un malade!

114 Mais nous avons perdu jusqu'à cette inquiétude automate. Nous ne nous sentons plus (*Mémoires pour Catherine II*, p. 13).

115 Il a des yeux comme vous et moi; mais on ne sait la plupart du temps s'il regarde (p. 515).

116 Je vous entends; vous en avez assez, et votre avis serait que nous allassions rejoindre nos deux voyageurs. Lecteur, vous me traitez comme un automate, cela n'est pas poli; ... Il faut sans doute que j'aille quelquefois à votre fantaisie; mais il faut que j'aille quelquefois à la mienne, sans compter que tout auditeur qui me permet de commencer un récit s'engage d'en entendre la fin (p. 556).

117 Je vois deux hommes ...— Vous ne voyez rien; il ne s'agit pas de vous, vous n'y étiez pas (p. 577).

118 mais je dédaigne toutes ces ressources-là, je vois seulement qu'avec un peu d'imagination et de style, rien n'est plus aisé que de filer un roman (pp. 730–1).

119 Quiconque entreprend de lever ce masque est criminel, et néanmoins c'est ce qu'on désire que fasse l'historien et l'écrivain, et qui rend les relations plaisantes et estimées. Il y a manière pourtant d'ôter le voile: on le peut lever doucement, sans le déchirer; l'on en peut abattre un coin, et laisser entrevoir aux regardants certaines taches qui font juger du reste; et certes l'on peut dire que rien ne leur agrée davantage que cette liberté qui témoigne que l'on a bonne opinion de leur jugement, et leur donnant à désirer, ils savent gré de l'estime qu'on fait de leur suffisance (p. 449).

120 liberté.

121 Avez-vous oublié que Jacques aimait à parler, et surtout à parler de lui; manie générale des gens de son état; manie qui les tire de leur abjection, qui les place dans la tribune, et qui les transforme tout à coup en personnages intéressants? (p. 669).

122 D'où il conclut que tout homme voulait commander à un autre; et que l'animal se trouvant dans la société immédiatement au-dessous de la classe des derniers citoyens commandés par toutes les autres classes, ils prenaient un animal pour commander aussi à quelqu'un (p. 667).

123 un livre masqué, dans lequel, à la faveur de son masque, l'auteur a pu enfin exprimer toute sa pensée, philosophique, sociale et politique.

124 Il ne faut pas croire la chaîne des êtres interrompue par la diversité des formes; la forme n'est souvent qu'un masque qui trompe, et le chaînon qui paraît manquer existe peut-être dans un être connu à qui les progrès de l'anatomie comparée n'ont encore pu assigner sa véritable place (p. 6).

125 Il y a des phénomènes trompeurs qui semblent, au premier coup d'œil, renverser un système, et qui, mieux connus, achèveraient de la confirmer (pp. 221–2).

126 Alors le système chancelle; les philosophes se partagent; les uns lui demeurent attachés; les autres sont entraînés par l'expérience qui paraît le contredire, et l'on dispute jusqu'à ce que la sagacité ou le hasard, qui ne se repose jamais, plus fécond que la sagacité, lève la contradiction et remet en honneur des idées qu'on avait presque abandonnées.

127 être connu — Je connaissais celui-ci de longue main (p. 397).

128 systématiques.

129 phénomènes trompeurs.

130 Croyez-vous qu'il soit inutile de savoir une bonne fois, nettement, clairement, à quoi s'en tenir? (p. 666).

131 et qu'il soit laissé, entre ce que l'un peut et ce que l'autre doit, la même obscurité que ci-devant (p. 663).

132 une querelle toute pareille.

133 L'on chercha en s'éveillant, comme à tâtons, les lois: l'on ne les trouva plus; l'on s'effara, l'on cria, l'on se les demanda; et dans cette agitation les questions que leurs explications firent naître, d'obscures qu'elles étaient et vénérables par leur obscurité, devinrent problématiques; et dès là, à l'égard de la moitié du monde, odieuses. Le peuple entra dans le sanctuaire: il leva le voile qui doit toujours couvrir tout ce que l'on peut dire, tout ce que l'on peut croire du droit des peuples et de celui des rois qui ne s'accordent jamais si bien ensemble que dans le silence (p. 74).

134 Jacques mène son maître.

135 Il n'y a rien de précis en nature ... Toute chose est plus ou moins une chose quelconque ... rien n'est de l'essence d'un être particulier ... Non, sans doute, puisqu'il n'y a aucune qualité dont aucun être ne soit participant ... et que c'est le rapport plus ou moins grand de cette qualité qui nous la fait attribuer à un être exclusivement à un autre ... (pp. 311–12).

136 le hasard, qui ne se repose jamais, plus fécond que la sagacité.

137 les rêves d'un malade en délire ne sont pas plus hétéroclites. Cependant, comme il n'y a rien de décousu ni dans la tête d'un homme qui rêve, ni dans celle d'un fou, tout se tient aussi dans la conversation ... La folie, le rêve, le décousu de la conversation consistent à passer d'un objet à un autre par l'entremise d'une qualité commune (*Roth*, III, pp. 172–3).

138 C'est l'ordre qui distingue la veille du sommeil; c'est que dans celui-ci tout se fait sans raison suffisante. Personne n'ignore les bizarres assemblages qui se forment dans nos songes. Nous changeons de lieu dans un instant. Une personne paraît, disparaît et reparaît. Nous nous entretenons avec des morts, avec des inconnus, sans qu'il y ait aucune raison de toutes ces révolutions. En un mot, les contradictoires y ont lieu. Aussi la fin d'un songe n'a souvent aucun rapport avec le commencement; et il en résulte que la succession de nos idées en songe, n'ayant point de ressemblance, la notion de l'ordre ne s'y trouve pas; mais pendant la veille, chaque chose a sa raison suffisante; la suite des

idées et des mouvements se développe et s'exécute conformément aux lois de l'ordre établi dans l'univers, et la confusion ne s'y trouve jamais au point d'admettre la co-existence des choses contradictoires (p. 944).

139 *Claude et Néron*; A.T. iii, pp. 359–61.

140 p. 189.

141 quelque représentation sensible, le dernier terme et le repos de la raison (*De La Poésie Dramatique*, p. 218).

142 les mains liées pour faire le mal.

143 une pure affaire de police.

144 chacun a sa tête et sa propriété, une portion de la richesse générale dont il est maître et maître absolu, sur laquelle il est roi, et dont il peut user ou même abuser à sa discrétion ... Il faut abandonner à l'homme en sociéte la liberté d'être un mauvais citoyen en ce point, parce qu'il ne tardera pas à en être sévèrement puni par la misère, et par le mépris plus cruel encore que la misère (p. 449).

145 La nature de l'homme et la notion de la propriété concourent à l'affranchir, et la liberté conduit l'individu et la société au plus grand bonheur qu'ils puissent désirer (p. 450).

146 quand tout du reste est bien ordonné, les choses se mettent elles-mêmes de niveau. Ordonnez bien trois ou quatre points importants et abandonnez le reste à l'intérêt et au goût des particuliers (p. 446).

147 p. 410.

148 p. 408.

149 qui tient à la liberté, à la sûreté des propriétés, à la nature de l'impôt, sa répartition, à sa perception, et qui distinguent les lois éternelles.

150 accidentel, variable et momentané ... la durée de la loi deviendrait funeste: il faut la révoquer (pp. 321–2).

151 je définis la vertu, le goût de l'ordre dans les choses morales (p. 128).

152 Cet homme n'a été bon que pour des inconnus et que pour le temps où il n'était plus.

153 oublions pour un moment le point que nous occupons dans l'espace et dans la durée, et étendons notre vue sur les siècles à venir, les régions les plus éloignées et les peuples à naître. Songeons au bien de notre espèce (p. 404).

154 Si je savais l'histoire, je vous montrerais que le mal est toujours venu ici-bas par quelque homme de génie (p. 400).

155 il faut ... oser voir ... qu'il en est presque des genres de littérature, ainsi que de la compilation générale des lois et de la première formation des villes; que c'est à un hasard singulier, à une circonstance bizarre, quelquefois à un essor de génie, qu'ils ont dû leur naissance.

156 sous lequel un art naissant fit ses premiers progrès trop grands et trop rapides, et qui en interrompit le mouvement insensible et naturel. Les ouvrages de cet homme seront nécessairement des composés monstrueux, parce que le génie et le bon goût sont deux qualités très différentes. La nature donne l'un en un moment; l'autre est le produit des siècles (pp. 394–5).

157 L'empire de la nature et de ma trinité ... s'établit tout doucement. Le dieu étranger se place humblement sur l'autel à côté de l'idole du pays; peu à peu il s'y affermit (p. 467).

158 Ce sont eux qui changent la face du globe; et dans les plus petites choses, la sottise est si commune et si puissante qu'on ne la réforme pas sans charivari. Il s'établit partie de ce qu'ils ont imaginé, partie reste comme il était; de là, deux évangiles, un habit d'arlequin (p. 400).

159 bien de notre espèce.

160 p. 432.

161 infiniment plus doux.

162 p. 431.

163 Vous êtes des êtres bien à plaindre, si vous n'imaginez pas qu'on s'est élevé au-dessus du sort, et qu'il est impossible d'être malheureux à l'abri de deux belles actions telles que celle-ci [sic] (p. 432).

164 C'est toujours la vertu et les gens vertueux qu'il faut avoir en vue quand on écrit. C'est vous, mon ami [probably Grimm], que j'évoque, quand je prends la plume; c'est vous que j'ai devant les yeux, quand j'agis. C'est à Sophie que je veux plaire. Si vous m'avez souri, si elle a versé une larme, si vous m'en aimez tous les deux davantage, je suis récompensé. Lorsque j'entendis les scènes du Paysan dans *Le Faux Généreux*, je dis: Voilà qui plaira à toute la terre, et dans tous les temps: voila qui fera fondre en larmes (p. 193).

165 Je répète donc: l'honnête, l'honnête ... Poète, êtes-vous sensible et délicat? Pincez cette corde; et vous l'entendrez résonner, ou frémir dans toutes les âmes.
La nature humaine est donc bonne?
Oui mon ami, et très bonne. L'eau, l'air, la terre, le feu, tout est bon dans la nature; et l'ouragan, qui s'élève sur la fin de l'automne, secoue les forêts, et frappant les arbres les uns contre les autres, en brise et sépare les branches mortes; et la tempête, qui bat les eaux de la mer et les purifie; et le volcan, qui verse de son flanc entr'ouvert les flots de matières embrasées, et porte dans l'air la vapeur qui le nettoie.
Ce sont les misérables conventions qui pervertissent l'homme, et non la nature humaine qu'il faut accuser. En effet, qu'est-ce qui nous affecte comme le récit d'une action généreuse? Où est le malheureux qui puisse écouter froidement la plainte d'un homme de bien? (pp. 195–6).

166 La poésie veut quelque chose d'énorme, de barbare et de sauvage (p. 261).

167 Ce sera après les temps de désastres et de grands malheurs; lorsque les peuples harassés commenceront à respirer. Alors les imaginations, ébranlées par des spectacles terribles, peindront des choses inconnues à ceux qui n'en ont pas été les témoins.

168 mais les hommes qui le portent en eux demeurent engourdis, à moins que des événements extraordinaires n'échauffent la masse, et ne les fassent paraître. Alors les sentiments s'accumulent dans la poitrine, la travaillent; et ceux qui ont un organe, pressés de parler, le déploient et se soulagent (p. 262).

169 événements extraordinaires.

170 échauffent la masse.

171 peuple dont les mœurs sont faibles, petites, et maniérées (p. 262).

172 pagode hétéroclite.

173 à côté d'autres pagodes.

174 car les sots et les fous s'amusent les uns des autres; ils se cherchent, ils s'attirent (p. 480).

175 Et à quoi diable voulez-vous donc qu'on emploie son argent, si ce n'est à avoir bonne table, bonne compagnie, bons vins, belles femmes, plaisirs de toutes les couleurs, amusements de toutes les espèces? (p. 404).

176 De l'or, de l'or. L'or est tout, et le reste, sans or, n'est rien.

177 au lieu de lui farcir la tête de belles maximes, qu'il faudrait qu'il oubliât sous peine de n'être qu'un gueux (p. 475).

178 On ne naît pas avec cette tournure-là. On se la donne, car elle n'est pas dans la nature (p. 478).

179 et qu'est-ce qu'une bonne éducation, sinon celle qui conduit à toutes sortes de jouissances sans péril et sans inconvénient? (p. 479).

180 Qu'importe qu'on ait un état ou non, pourvu qu'on soit riche, puisqu'on ne prend un état que pour le devenir? (p. 429).

181 idiotismes.

182 il y a peu de fripons hors de leur boutique; et tout irait assez bien sans un certain nombre de gens qu'on appelle assidus, exacts, etc. (p. 426).

183 Vous croyez que le même bonheur est fait pour tous. Quelle étrange vision! Le vôtre suppose un certain tour d'esprit romanesque que nous n'avons pas, une âme singulière, un goût particulier. Vous décorez cette bizarrerie du nom de vertu, vous l'appelez philosophie. Mais la vertu, la philosophie, sont-elles faites pour tout le monde? En a qui peut, en conserve qui peut (p. 428).

184 me bistourner et me faire autre que je ne suis, pour me donner un caractère étranger au mien?.

185 ils se sont imposé une tâche qui ne leur est pas naturelle (p. 433).

186 Il est certain que, d'après des idées d'institution aussi strictement calquées sur nos mœurs, il devait aller loin (p. 477).

187 elle fait d'étranges bévues (p. 485).

188 posture contrainte où nous tient le besoin (p. 486).

189 une école d'humanité, le renouvellement de l'antique hospitalité.

190 C'est qu'ordinairement la grandeur de caractère résulte de la balance naturelle de plusieurs qualités opposées (p. 459).

191 Son courage vous étonne, son atrocité vous fait frémir. On prise en tout l'unité de caractère (p. 458).

192 J'en conviens; mais j'y ai fait de mon mieux (p. 458).

193 Je suis moi et je reste ce que je suis, mais j'agis et je parle comme il convient (p. 448).

194 je n'ai d'autre mérite ici que d'avoir fait, par système, par justesse d'esprit, par une vue raisonnable et vraie, ce que la plupart des autres font par instinct.

195 faire le mal par dessein ... parce que l'on évite, par ce moyen, le plus dangereux ridicule qui se puisse rencontrer dans notre profession, qui est celui de mêler à contretemps le péché dans la dévotion (*Mémoires*, p. 46).

196 car le même art qui m'apprend à me sauver du ridicule en certaines occasions, m'apprend aussi dans d'autres à l'attraper supérieurement (p. 448).

197 Quand je dis vicieux, c'est pour parler votre langue, car si nous venions à nous expliquer, il pourrait arriver que vous appelassiez vice ce que j'appelle vertu, et vertu ce que j'appelle vice (p. 449).

198 les vices d'un archevêque peuvent être, dans une infinité de rencontres, les vertus d'un chef de parti (p. 98).

199 Il y avait dans tout cela beaucoup de ces choses qu'on pense, d'après lesquelles on se conduit; mais qu'on ne dit pas. Voilà, en vérité, la différence la plus marquée entre mon homme et la plupart de nos entours (pp. 476–7).

200 C'est qu'il ne s'agit pas de servir, mais de servir chacun à sa manière ... (*A.T.* viii I, p. 231).

201 Que le diable m'emporte si je sais au fond ce que je suis. En général, j'ai l'esprit rond comme une boule, et le caractère franc comme l'osier; jamais faux, pour peu que j'aie intérêt d'être vrai, jamais vrai pour peu que j'aie intérêt d'être faux. Je dis les choses comme elles me viennent (p. 444).

202 que j'étais un homme essentiel (p. 451).

203 Au milieu de cet imbroglio il me passa par la tête une pensée funeste, une pensée qui me donna de la morgue, une pensée qui m'inspira de la fierté et de l'insolence (p. 451).

204 Je veux bien être abject, mais je veux que ce soit sans contrainte. Je veux bien descendre de ma dignité ... mais à ma discrétion et non à l'ordre d'autrui (p. 435).

205 Faut-il qu'on puisse me dire: Rampe, et que je sois obligé de ramper? C'est l'allure du ver, c'est mon allure; nous la suivons l'un et l'autre quand on nous laisse aller, mais nous nous redressons quand on nous marche sur la queue (pp. 435–6).

206 C'est que cela décide, que cela décide toujours et sans appel ... Triste, obscur, et tranché comme le destin, tel est notre patron (p. 436).

207 Il n'y a dans tout un royaume qu'un homme qui marche, c'est le souverain; tout le reste prend des positions.

208 Cela me console (p. 487).

209 dispensé de la pantomime.

210 le dernier terme et le repos de la raison.

211 gardons-nous de nous expliquer ... je crains que nous ne soyons d'accord qu'en apparence, et que, si nous entrions une fois dans la discussion des périls et des inconvénients à éviter, nous ne nous entendions plus (p. 479).

212 Tout art d'imitation a son modèle dans la nature (p. 463).

213 C'est au cri animal de la passion à dicter la ligne qui nous convient ... n'allez pas croire que le jeu des acteurs de théâtre et leur déclamation puissent nous servir de modèle. Fi donc! il nous le faut plus énergique, moins maniéré, plus vrai. Les discours simples, les voix communes de la passion nous sont d'autant plus nécessaires que la langue sera plus monotone, aura moins d'accent. Le cri animal ou de l'homme passionné leur en donne (pp. 470–1).

214 ce n'est plus un frémissement, c'est une chaleur forte et permanente qui l'embrase, qui le fait haleter, qui le consume, qui le tue; mais qui donne l'âme, la vie à tout ce qu'il touche.

215 Il ne connaîtrait de soulagement qu'à verser au dehors un torrent

d'idées qui se pressent, se heurtent et se chassent (p. 98).

216 saisi d'une aliénation d'esprit, d'un enthousiasme si voisin de la folie qu'il est incertain qu'il en revienne (p. 468).

217 comme un homme qui sortirait d'un sommeil profond.

218 Diderot corrigera cette vision romantique, treize ans plus tard, dans le *Paradoxe sur le Comédien* (p. 98, note 1).

219 croit-on que sur la scène l'acteur soit plus profond, soit plus habile à feindre la joie, la tristesse, la sensibilité, l'admiration, la haine, la tendresse, qu'un vieux courtisan? (p. 381).

220 jamais hors de ton, de mesure, du sens des paroles et du caractère de l'air (p. 468).

221 dans la situation la plus singulière que j'aie jamais éprouvée ... (p. 469).

222 Il n'y a qu'un seul grand individu, c'est le tout (p. 312).

223 Chaque forme a le bonheur et le malheur qui lui est propre (p. 313).

224 Ich bin der Geist der stets verneint.

225 voilà ce que je vous disais: l'atrocité de l'action vous porte au delà du mépris (p. 462).

226 la grandeur de ses vues.

227 si nous conjurons contre Venise avec le comte de Bedmar, c'est la vertu qui nous subjugue encore sous une autre face (*A.T.* II, p. 118).

228 Des hommes de génie ont ramené, de nos jours, la philosophie du monde intelligible dans le monde réel. Ne s'en trouvera-t-il point un qui rende le même service à la poésie lyrique, et qui la fasse descendre des régions enchantées sur la terre que nous habitons? (p. 161).

229 féerie.

230 insipide mythologie.

231 petits madrigaux doucereux, qui ne marquent pas moins le mauvais goût du poète que le misère de l'art qui s'en accommode (p. 467).

232 le vrai, qui est le père et qui engendre le bon qui est le fils, d'où procède le beau qui est le saint-esprit.

233 qui discutait une action horrible, un exécrable forfait, comme un connaisseur en peinture ou en poésie examine les beautés d'un ouvrage de goût, ou comme un moraliste ou un historien relève et fait éclater les circonstances d'une action héroïque (p. 462).

234 si je devais rester ou fuir, rire ou m'indigner (p. 462).

235 les grands effets naissent partout des idées voluptueuses entrelacées avec des idées terribles; par exemple de belles femmes à demi nues qui nous présentent un breuvage délicieux dans les crânes sanglants de nos ennemis. Voilà le modèle de toutes les choses sublimes. C'est alors que l'âme s'ouvre au plaisir et frissonne d'horreur. Ces sensations mêlées la tiennent dans une situation tout à fait étrange; c'est le propre du sublime de nous pénétrer d'une manière tout à fait extraordinaire (*Roth*, IV, p. 196).

236 dans la situation la plus singulière que j'aie jamais éprouvée (p. 469).

237 le goût solide et vrai, le sublime en quelque genre que ce soit, le pathétique, les grands effets de la crainte, de la commisération et de la terreur, les sentiments nobles et relevés, les grandes idées rejettent le tour épigrammatique et le contraste des expressions (p. 406).

238 Tout ce qui étonne l'âme, tout ce qui imprime un sentiment de terreur

conduit au sublime … La nuit dérobe les formes, donne de l'horreur aux bruits, ne fût-ce que celui d'une feuille, au fond d'une forêt, il met l'imagination en jeu; l'imagination secoue vivement les entrailles; tout s'exagère (*A.T.* ii, pp. 146–7).

239 étonnement.

240 une morale propre aux artistes, ou à l'art.

241 pourrait bien être au rebours de la morale usuelle.

242 j'ai bien peur que l'homme n'aille droit au malheur par la voie qui conduit l'imitateur de la nature au sublime.

243 Les héros, les amants romanesques, les grands patriotes, les magistrats inflexibles, les apôtres de religion, les philosophes à toute outrance, tous ces rares et divins insensés font de la poésie dans la vie, de là leur malheur (*A.T.* pp. 124–5).

244 idiotismes.

245 la poésie dans la vie.

246 il est impossible en Poésie, en Peinture, en Éloquence, en Musique de rien produire de sublime sans enthousiasme. L'enthousiasme est un mouvement violent de l'âme, par lequel nous sommes transportés au milieu des objets que nous avons à représenter; alors nous voyons une scène entière se passer dans notre imagination, comme si elle était hors de nous: elle y est en effet, car tant que dure cette illusion, tous les êtres présents sont anéantis, et nos idées sont réalisées à leur place … Si cet état n'est pas de la folie, il en est bien voisin.

247 L'enthousiasme n'entraîne que quand les esprits ont été préparés et soumis par la force de la raison … Si l'enthousiasme prédomine dans un ouvrage, il répand dans toutes ses parties je ne sais quoi de gigantesque, d'incroyable et d'énorme. Si c'est la disposition habituelle de l'âme, et la pente acquise ou naturelle du caractère, on tient des discours alternativement insensés et sublimes; on se porte à des actions d'un héroïsme bizarre, qui marquent en même temps la grandeur, la force, et le désordre de l'âme (p. 681).

248 fait sortir la vérité (p. 397).

249 la singularité de son œuvre, ce qu'elle a d'irréductible, réside plutôt dans son cheminement vers la recherche de la vérité que dans le caractère de la vérité atteinte … Être, pour Diderot, ce n'est pas être telle chose, c'est changer, c'est expérimenter, c'est se refaire, se nier pour se découvrir.

250 Tout ce qui vit cherche son bien-être aux dépens de qui il appartiendra (p. 470).

251 défendre sa patrie.

252 servir ses amis.

253 avoir un état dans la société et en remplir les devoirs.

254 veiller à l'éducation de ses enfants (p. 429).

255 le goût de l'ordre.

256 méthode politique qui marche à son but sans bruit (p. 467).

257 de sorte que, dans le péché d'Adam, c'est la volonté qui a déterminé le désir, et que, dans celui de ses descendants, c'est le désir qui détermine la volonté.

BIBLIOGRAPHY

Works by Diderot:

Whenever the work in question appears in one of the Garnier editions, they are the ones to which I have referred:

Œuvres esthétiques: ed. Paul Vernière, Paris, Garnier, 1959.
  Éloge de Richardson
  Entretiens sur le Fils Naturel
  De la Poésie Dramatique (also called *Discours*)
  Paradoxe sur le Comédien
  Recherches Philosophiques sur l'Origine et la Nature du Beau
  Essais sur la Peinture
  Pensées détachées sur la Peinture
Œuvres philosophiques: ed. Paul Vernière, Paris, Garnier, 1956.
  Pensées Philosophiques
  Lettre sur les Aveugles
  De l'Interprétation de la Nature
  Le Rêve de d'Alembert
  Principes Philosophiques sur la Matière et le Mouvement
  Entretien d'un Père avec ses Enfants
  Supplément au Voyage de Bougainville
  Réfutation Suivie de l'Ouvrage d'Helvétius intitulé l'Homme
Œuvres politiques: Paul Vernière, Paris, Garnier, 1963.
  Autorité Politique
  Apologie de l'Abbé Galiani
  Observations sur le Nakaz
  Aux Insurgents d'Amérique
Œuvres romanesques: ed. Henri Bénac, Paris, Garnier, 1962.
  Les Bijoux Indiscrets
  La Religieuse
  Le Neveu de Rameau
  Jacques le Fataliste
  Les Deux Amis de Bourbonne
  Ceci n'est pas un conte
Mémoires pour Catherine II: ed. Paul Vernière, Paris, Garnier, 1966.

Bibliography

For all other works I have used the *Œuvres Complètes*, ed. Assézat and Tourneux (*A.T.*), Paris, Garnier, 1875, except in the following cases:

Correspondance: ed. Georges Roth and Jean Varloot, 16 vols, Paris, Éditions de Minuit, 1955–70.

Éléments de Physiologie: ed. Jean Mayer, Paris, Didier, 1964.

Encyclopédie ou Dictionnaire Raisonné des Sciences, des Arts et des Métiers, 3rd edition, Geneva, 1778.

François Hemsterhuis: *Lettre sur l'homme et ses rapports avec le commentaire inédit de Diderot*; ed. Georges May, New Haven, Conn., Yale U.P., 1964.

Other editions to which I have referred are:

Le Neveu de Rameau: ed. Jean Fabre, Geneva, Droz, 1950.

Quatre Contes: ed. Jacques Proust, Geneva, Droz, 1964.

Writers of the seventeenth and eighteenth centuries referred to:

In the case of well-known works from which no direct quotations are taken, I have not thought it necessary to indicate an edition.

Adanson, Michel: *Familles Naturelles des Plantes*: Paris, Victor Masson, 1847.

　Histoire Naturelle du Sénégal: Paris, 1757.

d'Alembert, Jean le Rond: *Discours Préliminaire de l'Encyclopédie* with the *Système figuré des Connaissances humaines*: Paris, Gonthier, 1965.

Batteux, l'abbé: *Les Beaux-Arts réduits à un même Principe*: Paris, Durand, 1746.

Buffon, Georges Louis Leclerc, comte de: *Œuvres Philosophiques*, ed. Jean Piveteau. Corpus général des Philosophes français, t. xli, 1, Paris, P.U.F., 1954.

For passages not in the above:

Histoire naturelle, générale et particulière, Imprimerie Royale (*H.N.*), Paris 1749–1804.

Condillac, l'abbé de: *Traité des Sensations; Œuvres Philosophiques*, ed. Le Roy. Corpus Général des Philosophes français, t. xxxiii, Paris, P.U.F., 1948–51.

Goethe, Johann Wolfgang von: *Faust*.

Goulas, Nicolas: *Mémoires*, ed. C. Constant, Paris, Renouard, 1879.

Helvétius, Claude Adrien: *Œuvres*, ed. Lefebvre de la Roche, Paris, Servière, 1795.

d'Holbach, Paul Heinrich Dietrich, Baron: *Système de la Nature*; ed. Yvon Belaval, Georg Olms Verlagsbuchhandlung, 1966.

Laclos, Choderlos de: *Les Liaisons dangereuses*.

La Mettrie, Julien Offray de: *L'Homme-Machine*; ed. Paul-Laurent Assoun, Paris, Denoël/Gonthier, 1981.

La Rochefoucauld: *Maximes*.

Bibliography

Le Mercier de la Rivière, Pierre: *L'Ordre naturel et essentiel des Sociétés politiques*, in L.F.E. Daire, *Physiocrates*; Part II, pp. 429–641, Paris, 1846.

Lesage, Alain-René: *Turcaret*.

Maupertuis, Pierre-Louis Moreau de: *Vénus physique, suivie de la Lettre sur le progrès des sciences*; Paris, Aubier Montaigne, 1980.

Pascal, Blaise: *Pensées*.

Pope, Alexander: *Essay on Man*.

Retz, Cardinal de: *Mémoires*; ed. Maurice Allem, Paris, Pléiade, 1956.

Rousseau, Jean-Jacques: *The Political Writings of Jean-Jacques Rousseau*; ed. C. E. Vaughan, Cambridge U.P., 1915.

La Nouvelle Héloïse.

Saint-Réal, l'abbé de: *De l'Usage de l'Histoire*, Ménard et Desenne, Paris, 1821.

Voltaire: *Lettres Philosophiques*.

Secondary sources:

Alexander, Ian W. 'Philosophy of Organism and Philosophy of Consciousness in Diderot's speculative Thought', in *Studies in Romance Philosophy and French Literature presented to John Orr*, pp. 1–21, Manchester University Press, 1953.

Baudiffier, Serge: 'La parole et l'écriture dans *Jacques le Fataliste*'; *Studies on Voltaire and the eighteenth century*, 185, 1980, pp. 283–95.

Becker, Carl: *The Heavenly City of the Eighteenth-Century Philosophers*; New Haven, Conn., Yale U.P., 1932.

Becq, Annie, et al: *Aspects du discours matérialiste en France autour de 1770*; Université de Caen, 1981.

Belaval, Yvon: *L'Esthétique sans Paradoxe de Diderot*; Paris, Gallimard, 1950.

'Sur le Matérialisme de Diderot'; *Europäische Aufklärung. Herbert Dieckmann zum 60. Geburtstag*; ed. Hugo Friedrich and Fritz Schalk, pp. 99–122, München-Allach, Wilhelm Fink Verlag, 1967.

Benot, Yves: *Diderot, de l'athéisme à l'anticolonialisme*; Paris, Maspéro, 1970.

Blum, Carol: *Diderot: The Virtue of a Philosopher*; New York, Viking Press, 1974.

Bryson, Norman: *Word and Image. French painting of the Ancien Régime*; Cambridge University Press, 1982.

Bukdahl, Else Marie: *Diderot critique d'art. I. Théorie et pratique dans les Salons de Diderot*; trans. Jean-Paul Faucher, Copenhagen, Rosenkilde and Bagger, 1980.

Carr, L.: 'Painting and the Paradox of the spectator in Diderot's art criticism'; *Studies on Voltaire and the eighteenth century*, 193, 1980, pp. 1690–8.

Bibliography

Cartwright, M. T.: *Diderot critique d'art et le problème de l'expression; Diderot Studies* XIII, 1969.

Cassirer, Ernst: *Philosophy of the Enlightenment*; trans. Fritz C. A. Koelln and James P. Pettegrove, Princeton, N.J., Princeton University Press, 1951.

Catrysse, Jean: *Diderot et la Mystification*; Paris, Nizet, 1970.

Chouillet, Jacques: *La Formation des Idées Esthétiques de Diderot; 1745–63*; Paris, Colin, 1973.

Cohen, Huguette: *La Figure dialogique dans 'Jacques le Fataliste'; Studies on Voltaire and the eighteenth century*, 162, 1976.

    'Rhetoric versus Truth: Diderot's Writings as an Illustration of Stability and Innovation in Eighteenth-Century Literature'; *Studies on Eighteenth-Century Culture*, 7, 1978, pp. 433–50.

Crocker, Lester: *Two Diderot Studies, Ethics and Esthetics*; Baltimore, Md., Johns Hopkins Press, 1952.

    An Age of Crisis; Man and World in eighteenth century French Thought; Baltimore Md., Johns Hopkins Press, 1959.

    'Jacques le Fataliste, an "expérience morale"'; *Diderot Studies* III, pp. 73–99, 1961.

    '*Le Neveu de Rameau*, une expérience morale'; *Cahiers de l'Association Internationale des Études Françaises*, 13, pp. 133–55, 1961.

    Diderot's Chaotic Order. Approach to Synthesis; Princeton, N.J., Princeton U.P., 1974.

Dieckmann, Herbert: *Cinq Leçons sur Diderot*; Geneva, Droz, 1959.

Doolittle, James: *Rameau's Nephew; A Study of Diderot's 'Second Satire'*; Geneva, Droz, 1960.

Duchet, Michèle: *Anthropologie et Histoire au Siècle des Lumières*; Paris, Maspéro, 1971.

Duchet, Michèle and Launoy, Michel: *Entretiens sur 'Le Neveu de Rameau'*; Paris, Nizet, 1967.

Fabre, Jean: 'Allégorie et Symbolisme dans *Jacques le Fataliste*', in *Europäische Aufklärung. Herbert Dieckmann zum 60. Geburtstag*; ed. Hugo Friedrich and Fritz Schalk, pp. 69–75; München-Allach, Wilhelm Fink Verlag, 1967.

    'Sagesse et Morale dans *Jacques le Fataliste*', in *The Age of the Enlightenment; Studies presented to Theodore Besterman*; ed. W. H. Barber et al., pp. 171–87; Edinburgh, Oliver and Boyd, 1967.

Fargher, Richard: *Life and Letters in France in the Eighteenth Century*; London, Nelson, 1970.

Foucault, Michel: *Les Mots et les Choses: une Archéologie des Sciences Humaines*; Paris, Gallimard, 1966.

France, Peter: *Rhetoric and Truth in France*; Oxford University Press, 1972.

Fried, Michael: *Absorption and Theatricality. Painting and Beholder in the Age of Diderot*; Berkeley, Calif., California University Press, 1980.

Funt, David: *Diderot and the Esthetics of the Enlightenment; Diderot Studies* XI, Geneva, Droz, 1968.

Gillispie, Charles C.: 'The *Encyclopédie* and the Jacobin Philosophy of Science: a study in ideas and consequences' in *Critical Problems in the History of Science*; ed. Marshall Clagett, pp. 255–289; Madison, Wisc., University of Wisconsin Press, 1959.

Gilman, Margaret: 'Imagination and Creation in Diderot'; *Diderot Studies* II, pp. 200–20, 1952.

Goyard-Fabre, Simone: *La Philosophie des Lumières en France*; Paris, Klincksieck, 1972.

Gusdorf, Georges: *Les Principes de la Pensée au Siècle des Lumières*; Paris, Payot, 1971.

Guyot, Charly: 'L'Homme du Dialogue'; *Europe*, 405–6, pp. 153–63, 1963.

Hill, Emita: 'Materialism and Monsters in *Le Rêve de d'Alembert*'; *Diderot Studies* X, pp. 67–93; 1968.

Hill, Emita: 'Human nature and the moral Monster'; *Diderot Studies* XVI, pp. 91–117, 1973.

Joly, Raymond: *Deux Études sur la Préhistoire du Réalisme*; Québec, Presses de l'Université Laval, 1969.

Josephs, Herbert: *Diderot's Dialogue of Language and Gesture*; Columbus, Oh., Ohio State University Press, 1969.

Kempf, Roger: *Diderot et le Roman*; Paris, Seuil, 1964.

Knight, Isabel F.: *The Geometric Spirit. The Abbé de Condillac and the French Enlightenment*; New Haven, Conn., Yale University Press, 1968.

Laufer, Roger: 'La Structure et la Signification de *Jacques le Fataliste*'; *Revue des Sciences Humaines*, No. 112, pp. 517–35; Oct., 1963.

Lefebvre, Henri: *Diderot*; Paris, Éditeurs Réunis, 1949.

Lough, John: *The Encyclopédie*; London, Longman, 1971.

Lovejoy, Arthur O.: *The Great Chain of Being*; Cambridge, Mass., Harvard University Press, 1942.

Loy, Robert: *Diderot's Determined Fatalist*; New York, King's Crown Press, 1950.

Luppol, I. K.: *Diderot*; trans. Y. and V. Feldman, Paris, Éditions Sociales Internationales, 1936.

Mauzi, Robert: *L'Idée du Bonheur au dix-huitième siècle*; Paris, Colin, 1960.

'Diderot et le bonheur'; *Diderot Studies* III, pp. 263–84; 1961.

'La Parodie Romanesque dans *Jacques le Fataliste*'; *Diderot Studies* VI, pp. 118–26, 1969.

May, Georges: 'L'Histoire a-t-elle engendré le Roman?' *Revue d'Histoire littéraire de la France*, pp. 156–76, 1955.

'Le Maître, la Chaîne et le Chien dans *Jacques le Fataliste*'; *Cahiers de l'Association Internationale des Études Françaises*, 13, pp. 269–82, 1961.

Bibliography

'Diderot, Artiste et Philosophe du Décousu'; *Europäische Aufklärung. Herbert Dieckmann zum 60. Geburtstag*; ed. Hugo Friedrich and Fritz Schalk, pp. 165–88. München-Allach, Wilhelm Fink Verlag, 1967.

Mayer, Jean: *Diderot, Homme de Science*; Rennes, Imprimerie Bretonne, 1959.

Mayoux, J. J.: 'Diderot and the Technique of modern Literature'; *Modern Language Review*, pp. 518–31, 1936.

Mølbjerg, Hans: *Aspects de l'Esthétique de Diderot*; Copenhagen, Schultz, 1964.

Moore, W. G.: *La Rochefoucauld*; Oxford, Oxford University Press, 1969.

Mornet, Daniel: *Les Origines Intellectuelles de la Révolution Française*; Paris, Colin, 6th edition, 1967.

Diderot, L'Homme et l'œuvre; Paris, Boivin, 1941.

Mortier, Roland: 'Diderot et le Problème de l'Expressivité; de la pensée au dialogue heuristique'; *Cahiers de l'Association Internationale des Études françaises*, 13, pp. 283–97, 1961.

Mylne, Vivienne: *The Eighteenth-Century French Novel. Techniques of Illusion*; Manchester University Press, 1965; second edition Cambridge, Cambridge University Press, 1981.

Niklaus, Robert: 'Diderot et la Peinture'; *Europe*, Nos. 405–6, 1963, pp. 231–47.

'La Portée des Théories dramatiques de Diderot et ses Réalisations théâtrales'; *Romanic Review*, No. 54, 1963.

O'Gorman, Donal: 'Hypotheses for a New Reading of *Jacques le Fataliste*'; *Diderot Studies*, XIX, 1978, pp. 129–43.

Ozdoba, Joachim: *Heuristik der Fiktion. Künstlerische und philosophische Interpretation der Wirklichkeit in Diderots contes (1748–1772)*; Frankfurt, Lang, 1980.

Paty, M.: 'La position de d'Alembert par rapport au matérialisme'; *Revue Philosophique*, 171, pp. 49–66.

Perkins, Jean A.: *The Concept of Self in the French Enlightenment*; Geneva, Droz, 1969.

Poulet, Georges: *Études sur le Temps Humain*, I; Paris, Plon, 1949.

Proust, Jacques: *Diderot et l'Encyclopédie*; Paris, Colin, 1967.

Pruner, Francis: *L'Unité secrète de Jacques le Fataliste*; Paris, Minard, 1970.

Roger, Jacques: *Les Sciences de la Vie dans la Pensée française du dix-huitième Siècle*; Paris, Colin, second edition, 1971.

Sainte-Beuve: *Port-Royal*; Paris, Hachette, 1878.

Schérer, Jacques: *La Dramaturgie Classique en France*; Paris, Nizet, 1950.

Schwartz, Jerome: *Diderot and Montaigne*; Geneva, Droz, 1966.

Schwartz, Léon: 'L'image de l'araignée dans *Le Rêve de d'Alembert* de Diderot'; *Romance Notes*, 1973, pp. 264–7.

Seguin, Pierre: *Diderot, le discours et les choses. Essai de description du style d'un philosophe en 1770*; Paris, Klincksieck, 1978.

Bibliography

Sherman, Carol: *Diderot and the Art and Dialogue*: (Histoire des Idées et Critique Littéraire, 156), Geneva, Droz, 1976.

Siegel, J. S.: 'Grandeur–Intimacy: the Dramatist's Dilemma'; *Diderot Studies* IV, pp. 247–60, 1963.

Smiétanski, Jacques: *Le Réalisme dans 'Jacques le Fataliste'*; Paris, Nizet, 1965.

Starobinski, Jean: *Rousseau. La Transparence et l'Obstacle*; Paris, Gallimard, 1971.

Strenski, Ellen: *Diderot's Political Thought*; Unpublished Thesis, Reading University, 1967.

Strugnell, Anthony: *Diderot's Politics. A Study of the Evolution of Diderot's political Thought after the Encyclopédie*; The Hague, Nijhoff, 1973.

Sumi, Yoichi: *'Le Neveu de Rameau'. Caprices et logiques du jeu*; Tokyo, France Tosho, 1975.

Thomas, Jean: *L'Humanisme de Diderot*; Paris, Études Françaises, 1932.

Trousson, Raymond: *Voyages aux pays de nulle part: histoire littéraire de la pensée utopique*; Éditions de l'Université de Bruxelles, 1975.

'Rapport de synthèse' (Utopias and Utopians); *Studies on Voltaire and the eighteenth century*, 191, pp. 613–36.

Vartanian, Aram: *Diderot and Descartes*; Princeton, N.J., Princeton University Press, 1953.

'The *Rêve de d'Alembert*, a bio-political view'; *Diderot Studies* XVII, pp. 41–6, 1973.

'Necessity or Freedom? The Politics of an Eighteenth-Century Metaphysical Debate'; *Studies on Eighteenth-Century Culture*, 7, 1978, pp. 153–74.

Vianu, Hélène: 'Nature et Révolte dans la Morale de Diderot'; *Europe*, 405–6, pp. 65–77, 1963.

Vyverberg, Henry: *Historical Pessimism in the French Enlightenment*; Cambridge, Mass., Harvard University Press, 1958.

Weinstein, Arnold: *Fictions of the Self. 1550–1800*; Princeton, N.J., Princeton University Press, 1981.

Werner, Stephen: *Diderot's Great Scroll: Narrative Art in 'Jacques le Fataliste'*; *Studies on Voltaire and the eighteenth century*, 128.

Willey, Basil: *The Eighteenth-Century Background*; London, Chatto and Windus, 1940.

Wilson, Arthur: *Diderot*; Oxford, Oxford University Press, 1972.

Winter, Ursula: *Der Materialismus bei Diderot*; Paris, Minard, 1972.

INDEX